First World War
and Army of Occupation
War Diary
France, Belgium and Germany

20 DIVISION
Divisional Troops
Royal Army Medical Corps
61 Field Ambulance
1 November 1915 - 9 June 1919

WO95/2109/2

The Naval & Military Press Ltd
www.nmarchive.com
Published in association with The National Archives

Published by

The Naval & Military Press Ltd

Unit 10 Ridgewood Industrial Park,

Uckfield, East Sussex,

TN22 5QE England

Tel: +44 (0) 1825 749494

www.naval-military-press.com

www.nmarchive.com

This diary has been reprinted in facsimile from the original. Any imperfections are inevitably reproduced and the quality may fall short of modern type and cartographic standards.

© **Crown Copyright**
Images reproduced by permission of The National Archives, London, England, 2015.

Contents

Document type	Place/Title	Date From	Date To
Miscellaneous	2109/2		
Heading	20th Division 61st Field Ambulance Nov 1915-1919 Jun		
Miscellaneous	61st Field Ambulance, 1914-1919		
Heading	20th Division 61st F.A. Vol: 2 Nov 15		
War Diary	Estaires	01/11/1915	30/11/1915
Heading	20th Div 61st FA. Vol: 3 December 1915		
War Diary	Estaires	01/12/1915	31/12/1915
Heading	20th Div 61st F.A. Vol: 4 Jan 1916		
War Diary	Estaires	01/01/1916	20/01/1916
War Diary	Steen Becque	21/01/1916	21/01/1916
War Diary	Eeke	22/01/1916	31/01/1916
Heading	61st F.A. 20th Div Vol 5 Feb 1916		
War Diary	Eeke	01/02/1916	04/02/1916
War Diary	Watou	05/02/1916	29/02/1916
Heading	20th Div 61 F. Amb. March 1916 April 1916		
Heading	61 F Amb Vol 6		
War Diary	A 23a.5.3	01/03/1916	31/03/1916
War Diary	Sheet 28 A.23.a.5.3	01/04/1916	14/04/1916
War Diary	A.23.a.5.3	14/04/1916	17/04/1916
War Diary	Watou	18/04/1916	23/04/1916
War Diary	Watou K.4.b.66	24/04/1916	26/04/1916
War Diary	Calais	27/04/1916	30/04/1916
Heading	20th Div No. 61 F. Amb. May 1916		
War Diary	Calais	01/05/1916	06/05/1916
War Diary	Zutkerque	06/05/1916	07/05/1916
War Diary	Volkerinchove	08/05/1916	08/05/1916
War Diary	Wormhoudt	08/05/1916	20/05/1916
War Diary	Lebbe Farm	21/05/1916	24/05/1916
War Diary	Lebbe Farm F.30.c.2.2	25/05/1916	31/05/1916
Heading	War Diary of Lt Col W.G.S Harvey R.A.M.C. Officer Commanding 61st Field Ambulance 20th (Light) Division July 1916		
War Diary	Lebbe Farm	01/07/1916	17/07/1916
War Diary	Wormhoudt	17/07/1916	20/07/1916
War Diary	Bailleul	21/07/1916	23/07/1916
War Diary	Mont Noir	23/07/1916	26/07/1916
War Diary	Frevent	26/07/1916	26/07/1916
War Diary	Bouquemaison	26/07/1916	26/07/1916
War Diary	Vauchelles	26/07/1916	28/07/1916
War Diary	Bois De Warnimont	29/07/1916	30/07/1916
Heading	War Diary 61st Field Ambulance R.A.M.C. August 1916		
War Diary	Bois De Warnimont	01/08/1916	16/08/1916
War Diary	Orville	16/08/1916	18/08/1916
War Diary	Gorges	19/08/1916	20/08/1916
War Diary	Ville-Sous-Corbie	21/08/1916	21/08/1916
War Diary	Meaulte	21/08/1916	21/08/1916
War Diary	Dive Copse	21/08/1916	30/08/1916

Heading	20th Div War Diary 61st Field Ambulance R.A.M.C. September 1916		
War Diary	Dive Copse	30/08/1916	08/09/1916
War Diary	Bronfay Farm	09/09/1916	30/09/1916
Heading	20th Div War Diary 61st Field Ambulance R.A.M.C. Oct. 1916		
War Diary	Bronfay Farm	30/09/1916	03/10/1916
War Diary	Carnoy	03/10/1916	23/10/1916
War Diary	Daours	24/10/1916	24/10/1916
War Diary	Vaux	24/10/1916	30/10/1916
Heading	20th Div War Diary 61st Field Ambulance R.A.M.C. November 1916 Vol 14		
War Diary	Vaux	31/10/1916	01/11/1916
War Diary	Soues	02/11/1916	03/11/1916
War Diary	Hangest	04/11/1916	16/11/1916
War Diary	Corbie	16/11/1916	30/11/1916
Heading	20th Div. War Diary 61st Field Ambulance R.A.M.C. December 1916 Vol 15		
War Diary	Corbie	01/12/1916	09/12/1916
War Diary	Meaulte	09/12/1916	10/12/1916
War Diary	Carnoy	11/12/1916	24/12/1916
War Diary	Treux	25/12/1916	30/12/1916
Heading	20th Div. War Diary 61st Field Ambulance R.A.M.C. January 1917 Vol 16		
War Diary	Treux	31/12/1916	03/01/1917
War Diary	Guillemont	03/01/1917	27/01/1917
War Diary	Meaulte	27/01/1917	30/01/1917
Heading	20th Div. War Diary 61st Field Ambulance R.A.M.C. February, 1917 Vol 17		
War Diary	Meaulte	01/02/1917	07/02/1917
War Diary	A.2.a.5.5 (Carnoy)	08/02/1917	10/02/1917
War Diary	Carnoy	11/02/1917	28/02/1917
Heading	20th Div War Diary 61st Field Ambulance R.A.M.C. March 1917 Vol 18		
War Diary	Carnoy	28/02/1917	06/03/1917
War Diary	Guillemont	06/03/1917	26/03/1917
War Diary	Combles	26/03/1917	30/03/1917
Heading	War Diary 61st Field Ambulance-20th Div R.A.M.C. April 1917 Vol 19		
War Diary	Combles	31/03/1917	01/04/1917
War Diary	Bus	02/04/1917	29/04/1917
Heading	War Diary of 61st Field Ambulance-20th Div. May 1917 Vol 20		
War Diary	Bus	01/05/1917	05/05/1917
War Diary	Ruyaulcourt	05/05/1917	19/05/1917
War Diary	Bus	19/05/1917	20/05/1917
War Diary	Beaulencourt	21/05/1917	21/05/1917
War Diary	H.12.b.3.3	22/05/1917	24/05/1917
War Diary	H.16.a.9.2	24/05/1917	30/05/1917
Heading	War Diary of 61st Field Ambulance R.A.M.C. June 1917 Vol 21		
War Diary	Beugnatre	01/06/1917	28/06/1917
War Diary	Achiet-Le-Grand	29/06/1917	29/06/1917
Map	Appendix I Sheet 57c 1/40,000		
Diagram etc	Appendix II Plan of Adv. Dressing Station		
Heading	War Diary of 61st Field Ambulance July 1917 Vol 22		

Miscellaneous	Summary of Medical War Diaries For 61st F.A. 20th Divn. 14th Corps, 5th Army. From 21.7.17		
Miscellaneous	61st F.A 20th Divn. 14th Corps 5th Army O.C. Lt. Col V.S. Harvey. Western Front Phase "D" 1. Passchendaele Operations July-Nov 1917 (a) Operations commencing 1/7/17.		
War Diary	Achiet-Le-Grand	30/06/1917	30/06/1917
War Diary	Canaples	01/07/1917	22/07/1917
War Diary	Proven	23/07/1917	30/07/1917
Heading	War Diary of 61st Field Ambulance August 1917 Vol 23		
Miscellaneous	Summary of Medical War Diaries For 61st F.A. 20th Divn. 14th Corps, 5th Army. From 21.7.17		
Miscellaneous	To B.2.1.a.3.1.		
War Diary	Casualties R.A.M.C.	12/08/1917	12/08/1917
War Diary	Operations	16/08/1917	16/08/1917
War Diary	Assistance	16/08/1917	16/08/1917
War Diary	Casualties R.A.M.C.	16/08/1917	16/08/1917
War Diary	Military Situation Medical Arrangements	17/08/1917	17/08/1917
War Diary	Casualties R.A.M.C.	19/08/1917	19/08/1917
War Diary	Moves	19/08/1917	19/08/1917
War Diary	Decorations	30/08/1917	30/08/1917
Miscellaneous	To B.2.1.a.3.1.		
War Diary	Casualties R.A.M.C.	12/08/1917	12/08/1917
War Diary	Operations	16/08/1917	16/08/1917
War Diary	Assistance	16/08/1917	16/08/1917
War Diary	Casualties R.A.M.C.	16/08/1917	16/08/1917
War Diary	Military Situation Medical Arrangements	17/08/1917	17/08/1917
War Diary	Casualties R.A.M.C.	19/08/1917	19/08/1917
War Diary	Moves	19/08/1917	19/08/1917
War Diary	Decorations	30/08/1917	30/08/1917
War Diary	Proven	31/08/1917	05/09/1917
War Diary	Pellissier Farm.	05/09/1917	21/09/1917
War Diary	Singapore Camp.	22/09/1917	30/09/1917
Heading	War Diary of 61st Field Ambulance September 1917 Vol 24		
War Diary	Moves	09/09/1917	09/09/1917
War Diary	Moves Medical Arrangements	10/09/1917	10/09/1917
War Diary	Casualties U.S.M.C.	11/09/1917	11/09/1917
War Diary	Casualties R.A.M.C.	20/09/1917	20/09/1917
War Diary	Casualties R.A.M.C.	21/09/1917	21/09/1917
War Diary	Casualties R.A.M.C.	22/09/1917	22/09/1917
War Diary	Casualties R.A.M.C.	23/09/1917	23/09/1917
War Diary	Casualties R.A.M.C.	28/09/1917	28/09/1917
War Diary	Moves	09/08/1917	09/08/1917
War Diary	Moves Medical Arrangements	10/09/1917	10/09/1917
War Diary	Casualties U.S.M.C.	11/09/1917	11/09/1917
War Diary	Casualties R.A.M.C.	20/09/1917	20/09/1917
War Diary	Casualties R.A.M.C.	21/09/1917	21/09/1917
War Diary	Casualties R.A.M.C.	22/09/1917	22/09/1917
War Diary	Casualties R.A.M.C.	23/09/1917	23/09/1917
War Diary	Casualties R.A.M.C.	28/09/1917	28/09/1917
War Diary	Singapore Camp	31/07/1917	09/08/1917
War Diary	Nutza Farm	09/08/1917	09/08/1917
War Diary	Canada Farm.	10/08/1917	28/08/1917
Diagram etc	Appendix I		

Heading	War Diary 61st Field Ambulance October 1917 Vol 25		
Miscellaneous	Summary of Medical War Diaries For 61st F.A., 20th Divn. 14th Corps, 5th Army.		
War Diary	Headquarters	02/10/1917	02/10/1917
War Diary	Moves And Transfer	02/10/1917	02/10/1917
Miscellaneous	Summary of Medical War Diaries For 61st F.A., 20th Divn. 14th Corps, 5th Army.	02/10/1917	02/10/1917
War Diary	Headquarters	02/10/1917	02/10/1917
War Diary	Moves And Transfer	02/10/1917	02/10/1917
War Diary	Canada Farm.	29/09/1917	29/09/1917
War Diary	Singapore Camp.	29/09/1917	02/10/1917
War Diary	Barastre	03/10/1917	04/10/1917
War Diary	Fins	05/10/1917	30/10/1917
Heading	War Diary of 61st Field Ambulance Nov 1917 Vol 26		
War Diary	Fins	03/11/1917	30/11/1917
Heading	War Diary of 61st Field Ambulance Month Of December 1917 Vol 27		
War Diary	Fins.	01/12/1917	05/12/1917
War Diary	Acheux	06/12/1917	06/12/1917
War Diary	Maresquel	07/12/1917	07/12/1917
War Diary	Sehen	08/12/1917	13/12/1917
War Diary	Ebblinghem	14/12/1917	31/12/1917
Heading	War Diary of 61st Field Ambulance January 1918 Vol 28		
War Diary	Ebblinghem	31/12/1917	05/01/1918
War Diary	Westoutre	06/01/1918	29/01/1918
Heading	War Diary For 61st Field Ambulance For February 1918 Vol 29		
War Diary	Westoutre	31/01/1918	10/02/1918
War Diary	Reninghelst	10/02/1918	16/02/1918
War Diary	Bandringhem	17/02/1918	21/02/1918
War Diary	Rouy-Le-Petit	22/02/1918	24/02/1918
War Diary	Esmery Hallon	24/02/1918	27/02/1918
Heading	War Diary 61st Field Ambulance March 1918 Vol 30		
War Diary	Esmery Hallon	28/02/1918	19/03/1918
War Diary	St. Sulpice	22/03/1918	22/03/1918
War Diary	Omencourt	25/03/1918	25/03/1918
War Diary	Le Quesnel	26/03/1918	26/03/1918
War Diary	Sains	28/03/1918	29/03/1918
War Diary	Esmery Hallon	20/03/1918	21/03/1918
War Diary	Aubigny	21/03/1918	22/03/1918
War Diary	St. Sulpice	22/03/1918	22/03/1918
War Diary	Esmery Hallon	23/03/1918	23/03/1918
War Diary	Omencourt	23/03/1918	25/03/1918
War Diary	Roiglise	25/03/1918	25/03/1918
War Diary	Bouchoir	26/03/1918	26/03/1918
War Diary	Le Quesnel	26/03/1918	26/03/1918
War Diary	Le Quesnel Mezieres	26/03/1918	27/03/1918
War Diary	Near Morisel	27/03/1918	28/03/1918
War Diary	Domart	28/03/1918	28/03/1918
War Diary	Boves	28/03/1918	28/03/1918
War Diary	Sains	29/03/1918	31/03/1918
Heading	War Diary of 61st Field Ambulance For April 1918 Vol 31		
War Diary	Sains	01/04/1918	01/04/1918
War Diary	Namps	02/04/1918	07/04/1918

War Diary	Campsart	07/04/1918	10/04/1918
War Diary	Boencourt Harcelaines	11/04/1918	16/04/1918
War Diary	Harcelaines	17/04/1918	17/04/1918
War Diary	Eu	18/04/1918	18/04/1918
War Diary	Estree Cauchie	19/04/1918	29/04/1918
Heading	War Diary of 61st Field Ambulance May 1918 Vol 32		
War Diary	Estree Cauchie	01/05/1918	01/05/1918
War Diary	Ablain St. Nazaire	02/05/1918	30/05/1918
Heading	War Diary of 61st Field Ambulance June 1918 Vol 33		
War Diary	Ablain St. Nazaire	30/05/1918	30/06/1918
Heading	War Diary 61st Field Ambulance July 1918 Vol 34		
War Diary	Ablain St. Nazaire	01/07/1918	31/07/1918
Heading	War Diary of 61 Field Ambulance August, 1918 Vol 35		
War Diary	Ablain St. Nazaire	01/08/1918	31/08/1918
Heading	War Diary 61st Field Ambulance September 1918 Vol 36		
War Diary	Ablain St. Nazaire	01/09/1918	30/09/1918
Heading	War Diary 61st Field Ambulance October 1918 Vol 37		
War Diary	Ablain St. Nazaire	29/09/1918	07/10/1918
War Diary	Houvelin	07/10/1918	30/10/1918
Heading	War Diary of 61st Field Ambulance November, 1918 Vol 38		
War Diary	Houvelin	31/10/1918	31/10/1918
War Diary	Cambrai	01/11/1918	03/11/1918
War Diary	Rieux	04/11/1918	04/11/1918
War Diary	Vendegies Sur-Ecaillon (Q.14.d. Sheet 51 1/40,000)	05/11/1918	06/11/1918
War Diary	Sepmeries	07/11/1918	07/11/1918
War Diary	Jenlain	08/11/1918	08/11/1918
War Diary	St. Waast	09/11/1918	09/11/1918
War Diary	Feignies	10/11/1918	23/11/1918
War Diary	La Flamengrie	24/11/1918	24/11/1918
War Diary	Preux Au Sart	25/11/1918	25/11/1918
War Diary	Vendegies	26/11/1918	27/11/1918
War Diary	Cagnoncles	28/11/1918	29/11/1918
Heading	War Diary 61st Field Ambulance December 1918 Vol 39		
War Diary	Cagnoncles	30/11/1918	30/11/1918
War Diary	Cambrai	01/12/1918	02/12/1918
War Diary	Marieux	03/12/1918	31/12/1918
Heading	20 Div War Diary 61st Field Ambulance January, 1919 Vol 40		
War Diary	Marieux	25/12/1918	10/01/1919
War Diary	Marieux (Somme)	28/12/1918	31/01/1919
War Diary Miscellaneous	Marieux	11/01/1919	31/01/1919
Heading	War Diary of 61st Field Ambulance February, 1919 Vol 41		
War Diary	Marieux (Somme)	01/02/1919	28/02/1919
Heading	War Diary of 61st Field Ambulance March 1919 Vol 42		
War Diary	Marieux. (Somme).	22/12/1918	31/03/1919
Heading	War Diary of 61st Field Ambulance For April, 1919 Vol 44		
War Diary	Marieux (Somme)	05/04/1919	30/04/1919
Heading	War Diary For The Month of May, 1919 61st Field Ambulance Vol 44		
War Diary	Marieux	01/05/1919	31/05/1919

Heading   61st F.A. June 1919
War Diary   Marieux   01/06/1919   09/06/1919

biopsie

20TH DIVISION

61ST FIELD AMBULANCE

NOV 1915 - ~~DEC 1918~~
1919 JUN

61st FIELD AMBULANCE, 1914--1919

The Unit was formed at Twesledown Camp in the early days of October 1914 It was composed at that time of men for the most part entirely new to the Army and Army life, but a few old soldiers were to be found even in those days in its ranks. Our first S.M. was S.M.Gregg himself a time expired soldier. He was a first class Instructor and a good type of the British Regular Army and the Unit was indeed fortunate in possessing a man of such capabilities to direct its early progress. He spared neither himself nor his N.C.O's in the march towards proficiency. The whole nine months we spent here were filled with strict training, cal.- culated to fit us both physically and intellectually for our duties in the War Zone. perhaps one of the most memorable days was the one when the whole of the Aldershot Command was drawn up for inspection by the the late Lord Kitchener. The weather during the whole day was atrocious the inspection having to be abandoned owing to the terrible snow storm which was raging. At this time the Unit was commanded by Lieutn afterwards Capt. Grandy but in May 1915 Major W.J.S.Harvey a Regular Officer was given the command. Shortly after this the Ambulance was ordered to proceed to Salisbury Plain where the 20th Division was at that time being mobilised . The Unit suffered its first loss here in the transfer of the S.M. he having been given a Commission as Quarter Master. The few weeks spent here were busy with Divisional training and the training drawing of Field Ambulance Equipment. Just before leaving for France the Division were inspected by His Majesty the King who expressed great pleasure at the smart and soldierly appearance of the whole parade. The Unit left for France at mid-night on July 21st 1915 being split up at Southampton into two parties, one party and the Transport leaving by the S.S.City of Chester and the other by the S.S.Connaught . The two parties joined together again at Hallines from which place the Unit made preparations for a three days trek. A great misfortune befell the Ambulance here in the death of Private Curwen who was accidentall y drowned whilst bathing. He was buried with full Military Honours in the Church Yard of this Village. As we were about to leave the Village we were joined by the Mechanical Transport Detachment . The march towards the line gave us our first expereince of active service conditions, the

Billets on this move consisting chiefly of the open fields and the usual French barns. The difficulties of the march were greatly increased by the fact that all the men were wearing new boots, and the condition of the roads and the heat of the day made marching anything but a pleasure. A temporary camp was formed at Bailleul during which time two of the Sections were attached to the 82nd Field Ambulance for training in actual line work. Towards the middle of August the Division was given its first responsibility, being ordered to hold the Sector in front of Estaires. The Field Ambulance Head Quarters were situated in this town whilst the A.D.S. was opened up at La Flingue Preparations were immediately set on foot for our part in the battle of Loos, Dug-outs being constructed at convenient spots for the collection and treatment of wounded. It was during this engagement that Lt Maling won his V.C.. Although the numbers of wounded in this engagement were small in comparison to those of later battles the fact that all the wounded were cleared before the day was out, speaks highly both of the arrangements made and the efficiency in which they were carried out. The operations were repeated on October 13th when a Dummy attack was made to draw German Troops from the south. There is nothing of special interest to note on this Sector until the Division made a Gas attack and the Ambulance Bearers were put in the front line Trenches for the purpose of dealing with any casualties which were fortunately few in number. A period of rest and re-organisation took place before the Unit was put in on the left of the Ypres Sector, Head Quarters being this time at Elverdinge, while the A.D.S. was on the world famous Canal Bank. The ingoing troops had an uncommonly warm reception and the bravery and endurance of the Stretcher Bearers engaged won for them unstinted praise from Major General Davies the Divisional Commander. It was whilst the Unit was in this area that the Canteen was opened for the first time. The men were billeted in small sand bagged shelters and made anything but a pleasurable acquaintance with the celebrated Flanders mud and rats. It was here also that we had personal experience of the Huns disregard for the Geneva Convention, the Hospital on many occasions having narrow escapes from some local heavy shelling. The rest period was spent in Watou, Calais, and Wormhoudt. Perhaps the most outstanding feature was the success which attended the Football Match which took place at Calais between the Unit and the Belgian Flying Corps. The Ambulance found the line again on the right of the Ypres Sector, the A.D.S. being actually in the ruined city itself. The Head Quarters were situated behind Poperinghe and the Ambulance was also responsible for a D.R.S. in Wormhoudt. This time the work of the Field Ambulance was inspected by H.R.H. Prince of Wales who seemed genuinly interested in and pleased with its work. Whilst on this front the Ambulance was able to render signal assistance to the Canadian Forces when they were attacked on the first of June 1916. The Division shortly after this were transferred to the Somme area, and after a pleasant rest were moved into the fighting zone. With their appearance on the Somme the Unit opened up fresh pages in their experience. The Medical Units of the Division were more or less pooled and the Bearers of this Unit were detached and placed under the Command of Lieut:Col:Osborne . Our own Head Quarters and Nursing Sections remained with Lieut:Col: Harvey who was in charge of the C.M.D.S. . It says much for the organisation of the latter place when it is realised that as many as 2000 lying cases could be treated and evacuated in 24 hrs. During the time Lieut: Col: Harvey was in charge its site was moved twice without any difference in its ability to cope with the numbers of wounded; no mean task when one considers the congestion of traffic and the state of the roads. In these operations he received invaluable assistance from S.M. Iddon, now unfortunately dead. The bearers themselves experienced all those heart breaking diffimulties so very ofetn described in accounts of this period. Perhaps it would not be amiss to explain the disposition of the stretcher bearers during these engagements. The Regimental M.O's always had at their disposal at least two squads for the evacuation of wounded and this allotment could be augmented if the nature of the fighting demanded it. These squads carried down to a re-lay and by means of such stages the casualties were eventually collected at a loading post which owing to the lack of good roads could only on most occasions be served by horsed ambulances. The frightful conditions under which everybody was working could not be better exemplified than to remember that it took as many as 10 heavy draught horses to pull these vehicles. The demand for bearers was so great in these days that very often squads had to be reduced to 3 and even 2 men . A story is told of three of our small bearers who were carrying a heavy Guards Officer. The third man was engaged the whole time in lifting out of the mud , the legs of the bearer who was carrying the head and shoulders. It was during this part of the Units history that we had the misfortune to have two killed in action. The first was the Bearer Officer Capt: Leahy, the news of whose death was received everywhere with the greatest regret. It is impossible to say how high he stood in the affection of the men, ready at all times with help and having a cheery smile for everybody all men would have essayed the impossible to carry out his orders, he met his death whilst working in a trench with men of his detachment. The second death was that of J.Clarke who had been with us only about three months. He was attached to a R.A.P. and was sniped through the head just as his squad was being relieved. It was at this time also that we got our first real taste of gas warfare and owing to the gallant conduct of an N.C.O. and man of the Bearer Sub-Section the Ambulance was able to record its first honours, Military Medals being awarded to Staff Sergt Tesseyman and Private Thorpe. One of our parties at this time had a very regrettable duty to perform, it was the preparation for burial of the body of Lieut: Raymond Asquith, son of the ex-premier, and it was with great sorrow that we saw the body, of so brilliant a scholar, lowered into a soldiers grave. The end of October saw the re-union of the Unit at Vaux. The Unti however was soon moved to Hangest and it was here that the first Units Sports took place. The whole time here was filled with sport of one sort and another, many Football Matches being played. Perhaps the most exciting match was a Rugby Match in which the Officers and N.C.O's managed to beat the men by the narrow margin of 3 points, the match was refreed by the Commanding Officer Lieut: Col: Harvey. Too much could not be said at this point in appreciation of the value of Lieut: Col: Harvey's interest in and encouragement of sport. The remainder of the rest and training period was spent in Corbie ; a very pleasant change from the rural solitude of Hangest. It was whilst we were here that the Ambulance Cars which joined us in France were withdrawn and the present Wolsley's issued. Our next experience of line work was on that particular sector over which our attacks had pressed during the previous Autumn . The whole time was dreary and monoton- ous, little being done even in the short intervals of rest to amuse the troops beyond an occasional football match. Christmas was spent at Treux and the rations of the day were the occasion for an incident which will always be remembered by the Ambulance. Our rations were more or less entirely composed of Bully Beef and Biscuits. After drawing breakfast from the Cookhouse the men passed a party of German Prisoners working on the roads. Imagine the surprise of our men when one of the prisoners augmented their store by the gift of a whole loaf of bread! It was on this front that news came through of the award of a D.S.O. to Lieut: Col: Harvey. S.M.Eddon left us here to take up a Commission in the R.F.A. and his successor S.M.Desmond joined us shortly afterwards. It was here also that the death of S.M.Murdy A.S.C. took place. Perhaps the most interesting time and certainly the happiest from a bearers point of view was the period when we were engaged in following up the Bosche as he retured in March 1917 the only straffe in which we took part was the attack on Metz when a large stretcher bearer party was sent out to help 60th Field Ambulance. We had an exciting hour or two also when after relieving an Australian Division we were forced to move our quarters owing to the persistent attention paid to our Camp by a battery of German "High velocities" . The horsed ambulances were again used here and Driver Shoebottom for a very steady and level headed bit of driving fully merited the strong recommendation for some official recognition of the act, but which unfortunately met with no success. The first American Officers to be attached to the Unit joined us at this time. If however these six months on the Somme battlfield were the most dreary and monotonous we have spent in France, the rest period immediately following them was certainly the most enjoyable . The Unit was stationed in Canaples and everybody talks to-day with happy recollections of the three weeks spent there. The weather was good and so were the facilities for sport of every sort. That the men should enjoy themselves here was only a natural sequence of the fact that they had spent six months out of the reach of civilians . The records of the Canteen would show a very interesting item at this time did they show the sales of certain useful French products. July found the Unit ready for the battle of Pilkem Ridge and for this stunt the bearers of the Division were ubder the Command of the 61st. Our casualties were rather heavy and the Unit received several awards of Military Medals in recognition of its work. Heavy though the casualty list was on this first engagement it was unfortunately exceeded on the second one when the bearers were under the command of the 60th F.A. . At zero hour this Unit had 24 complete squads of stretcher bearers but by the time the Ambulance was relieved there was not one squad complete and two or three of them were completely wiped out. One of the biggest losses the Unit sustained at this time was the wounding and subsequent death of Harold Thorpe a monument for good, he was respected by Officers, N.C.O's and men. A man of superlative fearlessness his influence on the moral of the Unit was immeasureable. He lies buried near Proven with a plain wooden cross marking his last resting place, just as he would have wished without show and with all simplicity. Between the two stunts the Unit had an opportunity of demonstrating to the remainder of the Brigade the high standard of sport maintained. In a Brigade sports the Unit or representatives of the Unit, entered nine events, out of which we obtained 6 firsts and 1 second the latter strangely enough being the Stretcher Bearer Competition. It was with very great relief that the Ambulance left this area and took up quiter positions at Fins which however rapidly changed their aspects as the attack on Cambrai developed and the counter attack was met. There is one incident which took place here without which no history, however brief, would be complete, it took place on the occasion of the counter attack. The night of November 29th found a bearer party of ours in Masnieres at a forward A.D.S. . The morning of the 30th found the enemy in possession of the village, the display of a red flag secured immunity from bombing, but the post was examined for Infantry by a German Officer and Sentries were posted at the entrances . At this juncture a Staff Officer - since awarded the V.C., - broke away from his guard organised a small Infantry party of about a score, and contested the possession of the village. The wounded from this encounter were collected often at great risk and dressed. Not only did the bearers collect all the wounded but when circumstances permitted, collected and delivered ammunition to the small party who were engaged in the defence of the village, this continued through the second day as well. During the second night however when the defenders had been reduced to two or three, the whole party moved off, taking with them some ten stretcher cases, and making some slightly wounded Germans act as stretcher bearers. The whole party passed through the lines and safely disposed of their wounded. The Ambulance was in charge of the C.M.D.S. and in recognition of the admirable organisation the O.C. Major Rogerson was awarded the Military Cross whilst at the same time the bearer Officer Capt Jones was awarded a similar decoration. Until early in the New Year the Ambulance enjoyed a well earned rest at Ebblingham and in spite of great material and atmospheric difficulties succeeded in making a passable Christmas. The N.Y.D's the Concert Party of the Unit gave their first performance here under the most depressing conditions. The six weeks spent on the Ypres Sector after this are almost devoid of interest; the Ambulance Bearers being attached to the 62nd F.A. and the ordinary routine work being the order of the day. One thing happened however which must be mentioned, this was the transference of Lieut: Col: Harvey to a C.C.S. . He had been in command of the Unit all the time in France and it was with sincere regret that we heard of his departure. His consideration for all ranks; his desire for the comfort of everybody and his lively interest in the sport of the Unit had won for him a high place in the regard of all Officers, N.C.O's and men, not only throughout the Ambulance but throughout the Division. On our transference to the 5th Army front we had ample proof of the spirit he had instilled into the Unit. His place was taken by Lieut: COL:McLennan. On the 21st of March we received a sudden but not unexpected call into action, and we moved forward with little expectation of having to retrace our steps within 24hrs . But such was the case, we rested the night in Aubigny near Ham and sent out the usual squads to Infantry Units. It was during this night that we had three men captured, on the 22nd the Head Quarters and M.D.S. were brought back to Ham which in less than 24 hrs had changed from a lively little Market Centre to a deserted village.. This history would not be complete without reference to the eggs, commandeered, for the purpose of feeding patients. Evening saw us again moving backwards and by this time we had become involved in the retreat "proper" . Although at this time intercommunications between ourselves Infantry Units and A.D.M.S. were in an extremely precarious condition we were to all intents and purposes practically never out of touch with our Battalions and the cool, shrewd, levelheadedness of the C.O. contributed in no small degree to this performance he received invaluable assistance in this matter by the untiring, unflagging energy of the Mechanical Transport under Sergt BRomby who unfortunately was wounded and had to be evacuated. The Bosche at the time had shelled out the M.D.S. and it was here owing to the speed with which we had to evacuate that we lost one of the two pieces of equipment ,a set of flag poles- we lost during the retreat. The other- a Medical Comforts Pannier - was abandoned by this A.D.S. party in oder to evacuate some stretcher cases for which transport could not be obtained. The days following this were more or less of a similar nature, A.D.S. falling back on the M.D.S. until that in turn had to fall back on a new M.D.S. . When the situation was extremely grave and the congestion on the roads had to be lessened we were ordered to remain with the Division and deal with whatever cases came our way. The work of the F.A. at this time (March 28 to April 1 st) deserve special mention, but especially that done by the Tent Sub under Major Rogerson and Sergt Thornhill. Although this party was expecting to receive the wounded of the Division they were very quickly engaged in and successfully coping with the wounded and sick of the whole Corps , numerous Army troops, a Cavalry formation and French troops who could be numbered in hundreds. For two full days it appeared that this Unit was the only one in action, beyond a small detachment from the Cavalry F.A's and it deserves unstinted praise for in addition to every patient being fed and dressed he was correctly ticketed and diagnosed no small item in itself in a stunt. This exploit was a fitting climax to the work performed during the whole of the retreat. Fortunately at this time the situation was eased to such an extent as to allow of the Division being withdrawn and an enjoyable rest took place near Gamarshes. May however found us holding the line again in front of Vimy Ridge and although a Bosche attack was daily expected we were allowed to settle down to the quiet monotony of line work. Towards the end of our stay here however we were persistently disturbed by nocturnal visits from the enemies aircraft, and by heavy shelling from a high velocity gun, whose sole redeeming feature was its inaccuracy. This shelling probably caused the death of Bob Williams, a stretcher bearer well known to the Regiments A friend of Harold Thorpe and of a similar fearlessness in danger, he was killed exactly one year after him. At the time he was Regimental Tailor, and for two or three days before his death had predelections of some unforseen accident. With our departure from this Sector we practically ended our experience of line work for we only managed to get in touch with the enemy again for 24 hrs before the signing of the Armistace. But one or two changes took place which are worth while mentioning. The first was the appointment of Q.M.S.Mitchell to the rank of S.M. and the subsequent evacuation of S.M. Desmond who possessed the longest service as S.M. of the Unit. The appointment of S.M.Mitchell to the vacancy gave general satisfaction, as he had been with the Unit since its formation The second was the transfer of Lieut: Col: McLennan to the post of A.D.M.S. 3rd Division and he was quickly followed by Sergt Rawlins, who for two years had performed the arduous duties of Orderly Room Sergt: in a highly efficient manner. About this time also a Tent Sub Section, under Major Quinn was detailed for the task of opening up and organising a Hospital in Douai for the reception of sick and wounded civilians. With that our war service may be said to have ended for although detachments were organised for the purpose of receiving feeding and transporting repatriated prisoners, they were only of short duration just before the Unit got into action for the last 24 hrs, Lieut : Col: White. M.C. took over command. Such then is the brief, and incomplete history of the 61 st Field Ambulance' a Unit which has shown itself thoroughly efficient in all its duties. And the greatest proof of its efficiency can be found, not in its list of decorations and awards, but from the praise which has been bestowed upon it from the lips of the men of the 20th DIVISION in whose service it has been its honour and privilege to serve.

61272a.
Vol: 2

121/7635

30th Division

Nov 15

Nov 1915

Army Form C. 2118

WAR DIARY
or
INTELLIGENCE SUMMARY
(Erase heading not required.)

Instructions regarding War Diaries and Intelligence Summaries are contained in F. S. Regs., Part II. and the Staff Manual respectively. Title Pages will be prepared in manuscript.

Place	Date	Hour	Summary of Events and Information	Remarks and references to Appendices
ESTAIRES	1/11/15		No remarks	
	2		"	
	3		No 387 Orderly Cpl Rowley J. appointed Act. Cpl wire Fay this date - Authy DDMS 2nd Army Corp	
	4		No remarks	
	5		"	
	6		Pte O.H. Plumbell Resive resid. to C.C.S. sick this day	
	7		No remarks	
	8		"	
	9		"	
	10		"	
	11		"	
	12		"	
	13		"	
	14		Route of orders No 14 this date received – Arranged to hand over A.D.S. Le FLINQUE to Guards Div. For Tomorrow the temporarily. Arrang. for A.D.S. at FLEURBAIX also Advanced Aid Posts.	
	15		No remarks	
	16		"	
	17		"	
	18		"	
	19		Receipt of 20th Div. Of. Order No 2 s this date ordering transfer to BAC St MAUR to take over Billets & Special Hospital of 2 Gd. 9 Amb. To take place on 26.11.15	

J. B. Gurney Maj. R.A.M.C.
O.C. 6. F. Amb.

1875 Wt. W593/826 1,000,000 4/15 I.R.C. & A. A.D.S.S./Forms/C. 2113.

Army Form C. 2118

WAR DIARY
or
INTELLIGENCE SUMMARY
(Erase heading not required.)

Instructions regarding War Diaries and Intelligence Summaries are contained in F.S. Regs., Part II. and the Staff Manual respectively. Title Pages will be prepared in manuscript.

Place	Date	Hour	Summary of Events and Information	Remarks and references to Appendices
ESTAIRES	20/9/15	-	Arrangements made with 36ᵗʰ F.Amb to take over.	
	21		No movements	
	22		20ᵗʰ Bn of order No 25 cancelled by D.Div 21/1/25/3/15 of 9midan – Unit to remain at present. We are prepared to move to 36⁴ F.A. relieve at shortest notice.	
			Receipt of R.O.W.C. G.O. no 15 – Instruction to open established an A.D.S. near FLEURBAIX – XXᵗʰ Div.	
			1/4000 map no 36 PORT à CLOUS from H.Q.I.Q.I.G. – on 24ᵗʰ inst –	
	23		Receipt of R.O.W.C. G.O. No 15 Continued with further minor details. XXᵗʰ Div	
	24		O-D etc formed as directed	
			Personnel – 2 Officers	
			1 Nissen hut D.	
			3/4 Tent Sub D	
			Ref. Aid Posts – Ref 1/4000 map of 20.36 – H. 36 a. 2.7.	
				H. 35 c. 9. 6.
				H. 27 b. 2.2
				H. 21. c. FLEURBAIX
			Line of evacuation of wounded from these trenches good – entirely by good roads – 3 lines of trams	

J.E.Davern
Maj Rowe
O.C. 6/F.Amb

Army Form C. 2118

WAR DIARY
INTELLIGENCE SUMMARY
(Erase heading not required.)

Instructions regarding War Diaries and Intelligence Summaries are contained in F. S. Regs., Part II. and the Staff Manual respectively. Title Pages will be prepared in manuscript.

3

Place	Date	Hour	Summary of Events and Information	Remarks and references to Appendices
ESTAIRES	25/11/15		Killed, wounded & evacuation generally of sick & wounded working reasonably well.	
	26		No remarks.	
	27		Lt. Guy Rouge transferred to R.K.O. 113th R.B. in exchange with Lt. Malin. V.C. Rouge joining his unit. 2nd Lieut. No. 713.02419 & Lt. Beattie D. joined on Probation as warrant off. & idean.	
	28		No Remarks	
	29			
	30			

Ellowayrequie
Major Swile
O.C. 61st

61 ef Fa.
Pd. 19
pd. 3

131/7936

F16/11

December 1915

Army Form C. 2118

WAR DIARY
or
INTELLIGENCE SUMMARY
(Erase heading not required.)

Instructions regarding War Diaries and Intelligence Summaries are contained in F. S. Regs., Part II. and the Staff Manual respectively. Title Pages will be prepared in manuscript.

Place	Date	Hour	Summary of Events and Information	Remarks and references to Appendices
ESTAIRES	1/12/15		60 (Light) Inf. Bde. O.S.O. 51 received.	Album ing
"	2/12/15		No. 29472 S.S. Rowe all Transferred to No. 2 Co. Office. No. 35295 I.T. Wellington H. transferred to 62nd F.A. mb.	p.t.o
"	3/12/15		No remarks	p.t.o
"	4/12/15		60 (Light) Inf. Bde O.O. 52 dd - 4/12/15 received.	p.t.o
"	5/12/15		No remarks	p.t.o
"	6/12/15		"	p.t.o
"	7/12/15		No. 73/021129 Sergt. BEATTIE Detachment to 161 Coy. A.S.C	p.t.o
"			No. 73/02160 A/Sergt. HILL A.T. (ASC) joins unit.	p.t.o
"	8/12/15		60 (Light) Inf. Bde O.O. 53 dd - 8/12/15 received.	p.t.o
"	9/12/15		No remarks	p.t.o
"	10/12/15		60 (Light) Inf. Bde OO 54 dd - 10/12/15 received	p.t.o
"	11/12/15		Rams O.O. No. 47 dd - 11/12/15 and 20th Div. O.O. 1 gd - 10/12/15 received	p.t.o
"	12/12/15		60 (Light) Inf. Bde O.O. 55 dd - 12/12/15 received.	p.t.o
"	13/12/15		S.A. 310 Bde Defence scheme received	p.t.o
"	14/12/15		Billet at PORT a CLOUS Farm (H 21 a.1.9 - 1/40000 Sht. 36) handed over. to 62? Amb. New A Dr. Stn. formed at SAILLY G 22 T. 4. 6 - 1/40000 Sht. 36	p.t.o

WAR DIARY
or
INTELLIGENCE SUMMARY

(Erase heading not required.)

Army Form C. 2118

Place	Date	Hour	Summary of Events and Information	Remarks and references to Appendices
ESTAIRES	15/12/15		No remarks	JWO
"	16/12/15		"	JWO
"	17/12/15		60th (Right) Inf Bde O.O. 56 d/- 15/12/15 received	JWO
"	18/12/15		60th (Right) Inf. Bde O.O. 57 d/- 17/12/15 received	JWO
"	19/12/15		No remarks.	JWO
"	20/12/15		60th (Right) Inf Bde O.O. 58 d/- 20/12/15 received	JWO
"	21/12/15		Amendments to 60th (Right) Inf Bde O.O. S.E. d/- 21/12/15 received	JWO
"	22/12/15		No. 33231 Pte Dunn WH, No. 62130 Pte Roberts MP. } Transferred to A.D.M.S. XI Corps. No. 30630 - Murphy W, No. 53905 - Thaddowe a No. 34951 - Oxton B, No. 33283 - Yielden LV	JWO
"	23/12/15		60th Inf Bde O.O. No 60 d/- 23/12/15 received. Reserve O.O. 18 d/- 23/12/15 received 60th Inf Bde O.O. No 61 d/- 23/12/15 received XX Div	JWO
"	24/12/15		Buses at SAILLY (G.22.b.4.6. Sht 36) handed over to 60 F. Amb. New advanced Dressing Station formed at Farm taken over from 60 F. Amb. at H.25.d.8.7 (Ref. Sq. Hat. 1/40000 Sht 36) S.26.20 Div O.O. 32 received.	JWO
"	25/12/15		Amendment to 60 Bde O.O. 61 received.	JWO
"	26/12/15		Xmas supplement to 60 Bde O.O. 61 received	JWO
"	27/12/15		Xmas supplement to 60 (Rock Bde) No 61 received	JWO
"	28/12/15		No 60 d/- 27/12/15 received	JWO

WAR DIARY

INTELLIGENCE SUMMARY

(Erase heading not required.)

Army Form C. 2118

Place	Date	Hour	Summary of Events and Information	Remarks and references to Appendices
OSTAIRES	28/12/15		S.G. 379 a/- 28/12/15 received	J.W.D
	6/15		LIEUT R.S. MILLER R.A.M.C (T.L) reported for duty and is taken on the strength.	J.W.D
	"		LIEUT E.P. LEAHY R.A.M.C. (T.L.) of this unit temporarily attached to 6th Oxo Bucks as MO i/c the Bn.	J.W.O
	29/12/15		S.G. 379/389 a/- 29/12/15 received.	
	30/12/15		S.G. 394/396 a/- 30/12/15 received G.S. 393/13 a/- 30/12/15 1 Bn Army. G 973 d-22/12/15 received	J.W.O
	31/12/15		No 31234 Cpl. H.G. Beckham No. 37694 Cont. R. Worpole rame No 41872 L.C. E.H.P. Rawlins rankNo. 367 a/Cpl & Bailey rame appointed acting-sergeants with pay from 30/12/15 (Authority 82nd 3rd Corps. no A/11/15 a/- 30/12/15	J.W.O

J. Dowen
Maj.
O.C. 617 Amb

61st F.a.
Bot: 4

20

28th Div
F/16/2

Jan 1916

Army Form C. 2118

WAR DIARY
or
INTELLIGENCE SUMMARY

(Erase heading not required.)

Instructions regarding War Diaries and Intelligence Summaries are contained in F.S. Regs., Part II. and the Staff Manual respectively. Title Pages will be prepared in manuscript.

Place	Date	Hour	Summary of Events and Information	Remarks and references to Appendices
ESTAIRES	1-1-16	—	S 28 d/. 31½. (a/20/99⅝) received.	
"	1-1-16		No. 319952 Pte. Collins E. and No. 31417 Pte. March J. appointed Lance Corporals with pay.	
			SR/641 Sgt Sniper J. Transferred to 160 Coy A.S.C.	
			T3/024632 Sgt Purves (A.S.C.) Transferred from 160 Coy A.S.C.	
			No. M2/101987 Pte. Wright A.S.C. (M.T.) Transferred to 62 F.Amb.	
"	2.1.16		2nd Div. O.O. 247 a/. 2/- received	
"	3.1.16		O.O. 19 R.A.M.C. 2nd Div. received	
"	4.1.16		S 33/ 80. 19 a/. 2/- received	
			60 Inf. Bde O.O. 61 dated 4.1.16 received	
			No. 34481 L.C. Tudesdale Ram appointed acting Corporal with pay (Authority 2nd 3rd Corps No A/1.1.16 d/- 4/76)	
			No. 347762 Pte. Evans S.L. appointed Lance Corporal with pay from 4/76	
"	5.1.16		C.L. 421 received. S 3rd /0019 d/- 5/76 received.	
			2nd Div A.D.M.T. S 27/ d/- 5.1.16 received	
"	6.1.16		No. M2/050126 Pte. Pickering E. A.C.M.T. No. M2/085605 Pte A.E.J. Cozens transferred from 2oth. Div. Supply Column.	
"	7.1.16		Pte M2/104739, Pte. Rancid R.P.V. And No. M2/103283 Pte. Bonneville transferred to 20th Div. Supply Column.	
			A.J.H.S. 20th Div. S 27 O.O. 19 dated 7.1.16 received	
"	8.1.16		60 Infy Bde. O.O. 66 dated 7.1.16 received. Admd. 20th Div. S 38 a/. 67d, Admd. to 20 a/- 4/76	
			S 39 d 40, 60 Inf Bde. 4th Supplement S. O.O. 61, Z.O.117 (60 Inf Bde) d/-6.1.16, Admd. 20th. Div. S 39 a m 3/-	
			S. 2nd. Div a/20/991/2.1, 60 Infantry Bde. O.O. 65 d/- 8/76, Admd 20th. Div. S 390 m 3/- dated 6/76 received	

Army Form C. 2118

WAR DIARY
or
INTELLIGENCE SUMMARY
(Erase heading not required.)

Place	Date	Hour	Summary of Events and Information	Remarks and references to Appendices
ESTAIRES	9.1.16		No remarks	
	10.1.16		ditto	
	11.1.16		ditto	
	12.1.16		ditto	
	13.1.16		'B' Section leave ESTAIRES	
	14.1.16		B Section arrive STEENBECQUE	
	15.1.16		No remarks	
	16.1.16		ditto	
	17.1.16		ditto	
	18.1.16		ditto	
	19.1.16		ditto	
	20.1.16		ditto	
STEENBECQUE	21.1.16		A & C Sections join 'B' Section at STEENBECQUE	
EECKE	22.1.16		Leave STEENBECQUE arrive in Billets at EECKE	
"	23.1.16		No remarks	
"	24.1.16		ditto.	
"	25.1.16		ditto.	
"	26.1.16		ditto.	
"	27.1.16		ditto.	
"	28.1.16		ditto.	
"	29.1.16		ditto	

Army Form C. 2118

WAR DIARY
or
INTELLIGENCE SUMMARY
(Erase heading not required.)

Instructions regarding War Diaries and Intelligence Summaries are contained in F.S. Regs., Part II. and the Staff Manual respectively. Title Pages will be prepared in manuscript.

Place	Date	Hour	Summary of Events and Information	Remarks and references to Appendices
EEKE	30/7/16		Coch. Inf. Bde. O.O. No 70 (supplement) received	
"	31/7/16		No remarks	

J Elbourn
Lt. Col.
O.C. 61 F. Amb.

61ˣʳ F.A.
20ᵗᵉ Div.
Vol 5.

61 F-A

S/ Februar

WAR DIARY
or
INTELLIGENCE SUMMARY

Army Form C. 2118

Instructions regarding War Diaries and Intelligence Summaries are contained in F.S. Regs., Part II. and the Staff Manual respectively. Title Pages will be prepared in manuscript.

(Erase heading not required.)

Place	Date	Hour	Summary of Events and Information	Remarks and references to Appendices
EECKE	1-2-16		No remarks	
	2-2-16		do	
	3-2-16		do	
	4-2-16		do	
WATOU	5-2-16		Arrive WATOU.	
	6-2-16		No remarks	
	7-2-16		do	
	8-2-16		do	
	9-2-16		do	
	10-2-16		2nd Div. S. 57/2. d/- 7% S 57/2 d/- 10% and M 160 d/- 10% received. No.M2/104972 Afothn. Reach A case 1917, Reinforcement note of Pioneer Bywater ats 8C.	
	11-2-16		No remarks	
	12-2-16	9:30am	Move out of WATOU. Arrive at new billets No. 25 tons A 23. a. s. 3. 12 noon	
	13-2-16		M 208 d/- 13% and S. 61 - 2 dates 11% received 93 women passed through ant from 12 noon 12-2-16 to 12 noon 13-2-16	
	14-2-16		No remarks	
	15-2-16		do	
	16-2-16		A.O. M.S. xx Div. S-62 d/-16⅔% received	
	17-2-16		A.D.M. xx Div. S-63-2 d/- 16⅔% received	
	18-2-16		No remarks	
	19-2-16		A.D.M.S. xx Div. M 211 received. A.D.M.S. xx Div. R-3 d/ 197½ received	

Army Form C. 2118

WAR DIARY
or
INTELLIGENCE SUMMARY

(Erase heading not required.)

Instructions regarding War Diaries and Intelligence Summaries are contained in F. S. Regs., Part II. and the Staff Manual respectively. Title Pages will be prepared in manuscript.

2/1

Place	Date	Hour	Summary of Events and Information	Remarks and references to Appendices
	20.2.16		A.&M.S. Div. S.O. 22 dt. 20/2/16 received	filed
	21.2.16		60 Inf. Bde. O.O. 74 dated 21/2/16 received	filed
			R.O.M.S. xx Div. S. 65 dt. 21/2/16 received	filed
	22.2.16		60 Inf. Bde. O.O. 75 dated 22/2/16 received	filed
	23.2.16		No. 31825 Pte HINDS K (ambulance wounded, and struck off the strength.	filed
	24.2.16		A.&M.S. xx Div. S-69 dt. 24/2/16 received	filed
	25.2.16		No remarks	filed
	26.2.16		do	filed
	27.2.16		do	filed
	28.2.16		do	filed
	29.2.16		do	filed

J. Hargrave Rowe
Lieut. R.A.M.C.
O.C. 617 Amb.

S
March 1916.
April 1916.

No. 61 F. Amb.

20th Div

COMMITTEE FOR THE
MEDICAL HISTORY OF THE WAR
Date 9 - JUN. 1915

61 F. Arnold
vol 6

Army Form C. 2118

WAR DIARY
or
INTELLIGENCE SUMMARY

(Erase heading not required.)

Instructions regarding War Diaries and Intelligence Summaries are contained in F.S. Regs., Part II. and the Staff Manual respectively. Title Pages will be prepared in manuscript.

Place	Date	Hour	Summary of Events and Information	Remarks and references to Appendices
Abbassia	1-3-16		10th Inf. Bde. O.O. No. 4/8 received	Appendix 3(a)(c)(?)
	2.3.16		No remarks	(see)
	3.3.16		ditto	(see)
	4.3.16		G.T. 229 dated 9/3/16	(see)
			20th Div.	
	5.3.16		No remarks.	
	6.3.16		Same O.O. 24 dated 4/3/16 and G.S. 151/50 dated 4/3/16 received	(see)
	7.3.16		20th Div. 20 Div.	
	8.3.16		A.D.M.S. S-4th dated 8/3/16 received	(see)
	9.3.16		A.D.M.S. 20th Div. S-4/5/6 receive. Lieut H.M. MILLS R.A.M.C. joins unit.	(see)
			60th Lt. Bde. O.O. 49 dated 9/3/16 received	(see)
			60 Lt. Bde. relieves top 59th Inf. Bde. night of 10th 11th.	(see)
	10.3.16			
	11.3.16		Same O.25 dated 11/3/16 received.	(see)
			20 Div.	
	12.3.16		A.D.M.S. 20th Div. S-44 dated 12/3/16 received	(see)
			60th Inf. Bde. O.O. No. 51 rules 12/3/16 received.	(see)
	13.3.16		No remarks.	(see)
	14.3.16		A.D.M.S. 20th Div. S-75 & S-79 dated 14-3-16 received	(see)
			Relieve 2nd. 2 and night of 14/15	

Army Form C. 2118

WAR DIARY
or
INTELLIGENCE SUMMARY
(Erase heading not required.)

Place	Date	Hour	Summary of Events and Information	Remarks and references to Appendices
A 23 a 5.3	15.3.16		No remarks	Alloway Sgt
	16.3.16		ditto	fwd
	17.3.16		20 th. Inf. Bde. O.O. 82 dated 17-3-16 received	fwd
	18.3.16		No remarks	fwd
	19.3.16		R.A.M.C. O.O. 26 dated 19.3.16 received	fwd
			20th Div	
	20.3.16		60 th. Inf. Bde. O.O. 83 dated 20.3.16 received	fwd
	21.3.16		A.D.M.S. 20th Div. S-90 received	fwd
	22.3.16		No remarks	fwd
	23.3.16		Relieved by 62nd. F. Amb. night of 22/23.	fwd
	24.3.16		ditto	fwd
	25.3.16		ditto	fwd
	26.3.16		R.A.M.C. O.O. 27 dated 26.3.16 received	fwd
	27.3.16		No remarks	fwd
	28.3.16		A.D.M.S. 20th Div. S. 9.314th received	fwd
			60 Inf Bde. O.O. 85 S/- 2.4.16 received	
	29.3.16		No remarks	fwd
	30.3.16		ditto	fwd
	31.3.16		Relieved 62nd. F. Amb. night of 30/31.	fwd

J. E. Bayne
O.C. 61st FIELD AMBULANCE.

Army Form C. 2118

WAR DIARY
or
INTELLIGENCE SUMMARY
(Erase heading not required.)

61 J ccroll Vol 7

Instructions regarding War Diaries and Intelligence Summaries are contained in F.S. Regs., Part II. and the Staff Manual respectively. Title Pages will be prepared in manuscript.

Place	Date	Hour	Summary of Events and Information	Remarks and references to Appendices
Sheet 2B A 27. a. 5.3.	1.4.16		No remarks.	Albain D.Col.
"	2.4.16		Both Inf. Bde. R.O. No. 86 dated 2nd April 1916 received. A.D.M.S. 20th Div. S-99 dated 27th received.	JWD
"	3.4.16		Lieut H. W. WARD R.A.M.C. having proceeded to ENGLAND on the termination of his engagement on the 3rd inst. is struck off the strength from that date.	JWD
"	4.4.16		A.D.M.S. 20th Div S.101 dated 4th received. Lieut H.M. MILLS takes over Medical Charge of 12th R.B.	JWD
"	5.4.16		A.D.M.S. 20th Div. S.102 dated 5th received.	JWD
"	6.4.16		No remarks.	JWD
"	7.4.16		Both H. And. took over from us Adv. Dress'g Sta. on the R. Sector Aid Posts at LA BRIQUE, LA BELLE ALLIANCE manned by them	JWD
"	8.4.16		No remarks.	JWD
"	9.4.16		No. 40589 Pte. Wagstaff H. Reme. evacuated sick and struck off the strength	JWD

Army Form C. 2118

WAR DIARY
or
INTELLIGENCE SUMMARY
(Erase heading not required.)

Instructions regarding War Diaries and Intelligence Summaries are contained in F. S. Regs., Part II. and the Staff Manual respectively. Title Pages will be prepared in manuscript.

Place	Date	Hour	Summary of Events and Information	Remarks and references to Appendices
Sect 28 A.23.a. S.3.	10.4.16		A.D.M.S. S-105 dated 10/4/16 received	JEW
			60th Infy Bde B.O. No. 88 dated 9/4/16 received	JEW
"	11.4.16		A.D.M.S. S-109 dated 11/4/16 received	JEW
			Lieut. W.G.G. COULTER R.A.M.C. reports his arrival and is attached temporarily for instruction.	
			Adv. Dressing Stn. on L/Sector taken over from 62 Fld Amb on the night of 11/12th, also R/Aid Posts manned by us.	
"	12.4.16		No. 30853 Pte READER F. R.A.M.C. evacuated wounded (Gun Contn'd Fracture L Tibia).	JEW
			Lieut. J.P. JONES R.A.M.C. reports his arrival and is taken on the strength.	
			No. 72/S.R./0138/ Sgt T. HART A.S.C. attached acting staff-sergeant-major with pay from 25-3-16	
"	13.4.16		A.D.M.S. S-101 dated 10/4/16 received	JEW
			20 Div.	JEW
			60th Inf Bde O.O. No. 89 dated 13/4/16 received	
"	14.4.16		Lieut. & Qr.Mr. W.J. TITE R.A.M.C. Reserve having this day reported his arrival is taken on the strength accordingly.	
			A.D.M.S. S-111 & S-94 dated 14/4/16 and M-402 dt. 14/4/16 received.	JEW

WAR DIARY or INTELLIGENCE SUMMARY

Army Form C. 2118

(Erase heading not required.)

Place	Date	Hour	Summary of Events and Information	Remarks and references to Appendices
A 23. a. 5. 3.	14.4.16		60th. Inf. Bde. O.O. No. 90 dated 14/4 received	JRW
	15.4.16		60th. Inf. Bde. O.O. No. 91 dated 14/4 received	JRW
	16.4.16		Instructions to 60th. Inf. Bde. O.O. No. 89 & No. 91 dated 15/4 received	JRW
	17.4.16	2pm	B.O.C. Section leave billets & move off to WATOU	JRW
WATOU	18.4.16	12 noon	Hd. Qrs arrive at new billets at WATOU SW 27 K 4.6.6.6.	JRW
	19.4.16		No remarks	JRW
	20.4.16		A.D.M.S. 20th Div. S.119 received	JRW
	21.4.16		A.D.M.S. 20th Div. S.120 & S.121 dated 20/4 & S.117 dated 16/4 received	JRW
			60 Inf Bde O.O. No. 93 dated 20/4 received	
			A.D.M.S 20th Div. S.123 & S.124 dated 21/4 received	
			60th. Inf. Bde O.O. No. 94 dated 21/4 received	
			20 Div. Q/20/2030/23 dated 22/4 received	
			20 Div. Q/20/3030/23 dated 22/4 received	
	22.4.16		20 Div. SG 828/G.21 dated 22/4 received	JRW
			60th. Inf. Bde. 246. O.O. 92 (89829) dates 22/4 received	
			93 (89832)	
			94 (89830)	
	23.4.16		No. 35913 Sgt. F.G.L. REED R.A.M.C. evacuated sick. Second Supplement to 60th Inf. Bde. O.O. 93 and O.O. 94 received.	JRW

Army Form C. 2118

WAR DIARY
or
INTELLIGENCE SUMMARY

(Erase heading not required.)

Instructions regarding War Diaries and Intelligence Summaries are contained in F. S. Regs., Part II. and the Staff Manual respectively. Title Pages will be prepared in manuscript.

IV

Place	Date	Hour	Summary of Events and Information	Remarks and references to Appendices
WATOU K.4.b.66	24.4.16		No remarks.	
	25.4.16		Admt 2nd Div. S.126 dated 24/4/16 received. Amendment to batt. Inf. Bde No. 94 dated 25th April 1916 received.	G.1.O.
CALAIS	26.4.16		Capt. E.A. Maling V.C. R.A.M.C. having departed to England on duty on the staff, not to struck off the strength accordingly. No. 84919 Pte. Booker evacuated sick and struck off the strength. Arrived at BEAUMARAIS CAMP CALAIS.	G.1.O.
CALAIS	27.4.16		Amendment to A.B. Ind. S. 111 d/- 27/4/16 received	G.1.O.
	28.4.16		No remarks	G.1.O.
	29.4.16		do.	G.1.O.
	30.4.16			G.1.O.

J. Bowen
Lieut Colonel
O.C. 81st FIELD AMBULANCE.

May 1915.

No. 61 F. Amb.

COMMITTEE FOR THE
MEDICAL HISTORY OF THE WAR
Date 26 JUN 1915

WAR DIARY or INTELLIGENCE SUMMARY

61 Fd Amb Army Form C. 2118
Vol 8

Place	Date	Hour	Summary of Events and Information	Remarks and references to Appendices
CALAIS	1/5/16	—	No. MS/1896 Col. GREEN W. A.S.C. (M.T.) joins unit from Base	
	2/5/16		No remarks	
	3/5/16		Lieut & Coulter W.G.B. R.A.M.C. evacuated to Base – Sick	
	4/5/16		A.S.M.T. 20th Div. S/181 & S/182 received	
	5/5/16		T/S.Sgt. Ret. S/SM. Hay J. R.C. (A.T.) evacuated to Base sick	
			81381 L/C. Chambers J.H. R.A.M.C "	
			515-81 Pte. Ricardo J. "	
			62257 " Smith A. "	
			84688 " Arthur J. "	
			63255 " Goodwin W. "	
			39618 "	
			50435 " Aire A.Z. "	
			and struck off strength accordingly	
			10th Inf. Bde. No A/4414/4436 at 4th recvn	
			10th Inf. Bde. OP. No. 95 received	
	6/5/16 4 am		Unit leaves CALAIS.	
ZUTKERQUE		11 am	Unit arrives ZUTKERQUE, billets taken for night	
			A.M.T. 2nd Div. S/133 S/134 received	
			A.R.S. Hires at WORMHOUDT	
			3rd Supp't to 10th Inf. Bde. OP. 95 a/- 696 received	
	7/5/16 4am		Unit leaves ZUTKERQUE	
		12 noon	Unit arrives VOLKERINCKHOVE, billets taken over for night	

Army Form C. 2118

WAR DIARY
or
INTELLIGENCE SUMMARY

(Erase heading not required.)

Instructions regarding War Diaries and Intelligence Summaries are contained in F.S. Regs., Part II and the Staff Manual respectively. Title Pages will be prepared in manuscript.

Place	Date	Hour	Summary of Events and Information	Remarks and references to Appendices
VOLKERINCKHOVE	8/9/16	4am	Unit leaves VOLKERINCKHOVE.	No
WORMHOUDT		9:30am	Unit arrives WORMHOUDT. Div. Rest. Station opened at WORMHOUDT. "B" Section proceeds to HERZEELE and opens F. Amb. A.D.M.S. S-186 d/- 8/9/16 received. LT. J.S. CRAWFORD RAMC (TC) reports his arrival and is taken on strength accordingly. Book. Intn. 80280. 96 d/- 7/9/16 received. A.D.S. Books terminating 31-12-15 despatched to ADI's Office at the Base. A.A. & Q.M.G.	No
	9/9/16		No remarks.	No
	10/9/16		No. 44618 Cpl. Branson W RAMC. No. 47776 Pte. Beaver H RAMC. 81718 Pte. " " 61458 " " " 81127 " Charlton E. 61619 " Cunnington V.C. 816 sgt. Swann J. reinforcements from No. 5 Gen. Base Depot are taken on the strength.	No
	11/9/16			
	12/9/16		A.D.M.S. 20th Div. S-140 received.	No
	13/9/16		Cook. Srgt. Adler. E.C. 60. 97 received wounded sick and struck off strength. No. 76996 Pte. Watkins E.G.	No
	14/9/16		No remarks.	No
	15/9/16		"B" Section hand over duties at HERZEELE to 60 Fd. Amb. and arrive WORMHOUDT 11:00 pm. A.D.M.S. 20th Div. S-141 d/- 13/9/16 received. LT. COL. WALKER RAMC (TC) reports his arrival and is taken on strength accordingly.	No

Army Form C. 2118

WAR DIARY
or
INTELLIGENCE SUMMARY
(Erase heading not required.)

Instructions regarding War Diaries and Intelligence Summaries are contained in F.S. Regs., Part II. and the Staff Manual respectively. Title Pages will be prepared in manuscript.

Place	Date	Hour	Summary of Events and Information	Remarks and references to Appendices
WORMHOUDT	15/5/16		Same o/o. 36 d/- 15% received. xx Div.	g/o
	16/5/16		A.s.m.j. S.141 received. Supply to Co en Inf. Bde o/o. 97 d/- 16% received. G.S. 143 dj. 15% received. Second Supt. to Co Inf Bde o/o. 97 at 16% received.	g/o
	17/5/16		No remarks.	g/o
	18/5/16		A.s.m.j. 20th Div. S.146 received.	g/o
	19/5/16		A.s.m.j. 20th Div. S.149 and S.16 received. Advance party leave for the front. Increased establishment offrs/ots strength No.76/20/116 G. Strength F.S. Reg. Sig FPS. dj- 19% received. Est. Sity. Bde Sig FPS.	g/o
	20/5/16			g/o
LEBBE FARM	21/5/16 8am		Unit leaves WORMHOUDT for LEBBE FARM.	g/o
	10am		Arrives LEBBE FARM Sheet 27 Trones F.30.C.2.2.	
	23/5/16		No remarks.	g/o
	28/5/16		Same o/o 32 d/- 28% and G.I. 17 received. xx Div	g/o
	24/5/16		Co Ch. Ent. Bde o/o. 98 d/- 24% received.	g/ll

Army Form C. 2118

WAR DIARY
or
INTELLIGENCE SUMMARY

(Erase heading not required.)

Instructions regarding War Diaries and Intelligence Summaries are contained in F.S. Regs., Part II. and the Staff Manual respectively. Title Pages will be prepared in manuscript.

Place	Date	Hour	Summary of Events and Information	Remarks and references to Appendices
LEBBE FARM F.30. c. 2. 2	25/5/16		No remarks	—
"	26/5/16		No. 74873 Pte. Sincott A. No. 48030 Pte. Cayzer C.J. No. 75024 Pte. Coyle J.R. No. 96609 Pte. Cleale J. Rejoin unit from Base, and are taken on the strength accordingly.	—
"	27/5/16		No remarks	—
"	28/5/16		Took W.f. Bec. to No. 99 Feervies	—
"	29/5/16		No remarks.	—
"	30/5/16		No. 73/025/84 Dr. Strand F.J. returned to duty from Hospital No. 73/027675 Dr. Cople H. abs. No. 74/143695 Dr. Grey E. abs and No. 72/016280 Dr. Whitakin H.H. all joined unit & are taken on the strength accordingly.	—
"	31/5/16			

J. Lennon
Lieut. Col.
O.C. 61st FIELD AMBULANCE

Confidential

War Diary

of

Lt Col W.J.S Harvey R.A.M.C

Officer Commanding

61st

Field Ambulance

20th (Light) Division

July 1916

Army Form C. 2118

Sheet I.

WAR DIARY
or
INTELLIGENCE SUMMARY
(Erase heading not required.)

Place	Date	Hour	Summary of Events and Information	Remarks and references to Appendices
LEBBE FARM	1/7/16	—	60 Inf. Bde. O.O. N° 109 dated 30-6-16 received.	Signature — C. Col. J.E.D.
	2/7/16		A.D.M.S. / 2o Div. N° S.183 dated 2-7-16 received.	
			A.D.M.S. / 2o Div. O.O. N° 40 dated 2-7-16 received.	
			N° 37583 Pte Radley J.W. bafs boy moved to 4th Bn. @ 6 p. diem from 18/5/16.	
			60 Inf. Bde. N° S.G. 1028/1107 dated 2-7-16 received.	
			A.D.M.S. / 2o Div. N° S.185 dated 2.7.16 received.	
	3/7/16		A.D.M.S. / 2o Div. N° S.186 dated 3.7.16 received.	J.E.D.
			60 Inf. Bde. N° S.G. 1028/1116 dated 3.7.16 received.	
			60 Inf. Bde. N° 424 Daily Report N° 40 received.	
	4/7/16	—	60 Inf. Bde. S.G. 1028/1120 dated 4.7.16 received.	J.E.D.

Army Form C. 2118

Sheet II.

WAR DIARY
or
INTELLIGENCE SUMMARY
(Erase heading not required.)

Instructions regarding War Diaries and Intelligence Summaries are contained in F. S. Regs., Part II. and the Staff Manual respectively. Title Pages will be prepared in manuscript.

Place	Date	Hour	Summary of Events and Information	Remarks and references to Appendices
LEBBE FARM	4/7/16	-	60 Inf. Bde. No M1432 received.	JLO
	5/7/16	-	A.D.M.S. 20 Div. D.R.O. No 41 dated 5.7.16 received.	JLO
	6/7/16	-	A.D.M.S. 20 Div. D.R.O. No 42 dated 7.7.16 received.	JLO
			60 Inf. Bde. O.O. No 110 dated 7.7.16 received.	
			No 37948 Pte Queen C. evacuated wounded on 7.7.16 and struck off the strength.	
			60 Inf. Bde. Amendment to O.O. No 110 dated 7.7.16 received.	
			A.D.M.S. 20 Div. Amendment to O.O. No 42 dated 7.7.16 received.	
			No 26554 Pte Nolan P. transferred from No 22 M.A.C. on 7.7.16 and taken on the strength.	
	8/7/16	-	No 78030 Pte Garrad C.J. transferred to No 5 M.A.C. on 8.7.16 and struck off the strength	JLO

Army Form C. 2118

Sheet III.

WAR DIARY
or
INTELLIGENCE SUMMARY
(Erase heading not required.)

Instructions regarding War Diaries and Intelligence Summaries are contained in F.S. Regs., Part II. and the Staff Manual respectively. Title Pages will be prepared in manuscript.

Place	Date	Hour	Summary of Events and Information	Remarks and references to Appendices
LE BIZE FARM	8/7/16		A.D.M.S. 20 Div. — N° S.1301 dated 7.7.16 received & passed to 62 2.Amer.	yes
			A.D.M.S. 20 Div. — G.M. 15 dated 8.7.16 received.	
			A.D.M.S. 20 Div. — G.M. 18 dated 8.7.16 received.	
	9/7/16		A.D.M.S. 20 Div. — N° S.188 received.	yes
			A.D.M.S. 20 Div. — O.O. N° III dated 9.7.16 received.	
	10/7/16		A.D.M.S. 20 Div. — N° S.188 dated 10.7.16 received.	
			60 Inf. Bde. N° S.G. 885/1165 Ryfs Bryan Defence Scheme received.	
			A.D.M.S. 20 Div. — O.O. N° 43 dated 10.7.16 received. also S.191 dated 10.7.16.	yes
			N° 73/0342241 Pur. Parcman A.V.S. attached to 17,4,5,6 on 21/6/16 for dental Treatment, about to transport to England struck off the strength.	

Army Form C. 2118

Instructions regarding War Diaries and Intelligence Summaries are contained in F. S. Regs., Part II. and the Staff Manual respectively. Title Pages will be prepared in manuscript.

WAR DIARY
or
INTELLIGENCE SUMMARY
(Erase heading not required.)

Sheet IV.

Place	Date	Hour	Summary of Events and Information	Remarks and references to Appendices
LEGGE FARM	11.7.16		No. 29785 Pte Hedger L.A. transferred from 62 J.Amb. and taken on the strength.	JW
			60 Inf Bde. O.O. No. 112 dated 10.7.16 received.	
			A.D.M.S. No. S.192 & S.193 dated 11.7.16 received. 20 Div.	
			A.D.M.S. No. S.194 dated 11.7.16 received. 20 Div.	
			A.D.M.S. No. S.195 dated 11.7.16 received. 20 Div.	
			60 Inf. Bde. No. S.G. 1120 dated 10.7.16 received.	
	12.7.16		Advanced Dressing Station at the Prison, YPRES, advanced Aid Post and Aid Post at MENIN ROAD, Aid Post at POTIJZE handed over to 62nd Field Ambulance. Officers and 6 men at the Aid Post at the Convent POPERINGHE and the orderly at 20 th Div. Ad.Qrs. POPERINGHE relieved by 62nd Field Ambulance.	JW
			A.D.M.S. O.D. No. 112 dated 12.7.16 received. 20 Div.	

Army Form C. 2118

Sheet V.

WAR DIARY
or
INTELLIGENCE SUMMARY
(Erase heading not required.)

Instructions regarding War Diaries and Intelligence Summaries are contained in F.S. Regs., Part II. and the Staff Manual respectively. Title Pages will be prepared in manuscript.

Place	Date	Hour	Summary of Events and Information	Remarks and references to Appendices
LEBBE FARM	12/7/16		A.D.M.S. 20 Div. N° S199 dated 10.7.16 received.	JW
	13/7/16		60 Inf. Bde. O.O. N° 113 dated 12.7.16 received.	JW
			A.D.M.S. 20 Div. N° S 200 and M 868 dated 13.7.16 received	JW
	14/7/16		A.D.M.S. 20 Div. 60 Inf. Bde. O.O. N° 114 dated 14.7.16 received.	
			A.D.M.S. 20 Div. N° S 203 dated 13.7.16 received.	
			A.D.M.S. 30 Div. N° S 202 dated 14.7.16 received.	
	15/7/16		A.D.M.S. 20 Div. N° S 203 and D.O. N° 44 dated 15.7.16 received.	JW
			A.D.M.S. 20 Div. N° M 882 dated 15.7.16 received.	
			A.D.M.S. 20 Div. N° S 205 dated 15.7.16 received.	

Army Form C. 2118

Sheet VI.

WAR DIARY
or
INTELLIGENCE SUMMARY

(Erase heading not required.)

Instructions regarding War Diaries and Intelligence Summaries are contained in F. S. Regs., Part II. and the Staff Manual respectively. Title Pages will be prepared in manuscript.

Place	Date	Hour	Summary of Events and Information	Remarks and references to Appendices
LEBBE FARM.	16/7/16		No Remarks.	JWD
	17/7/16	11 am	Billets and Hospital at LEBBE FARM near POPERINGHE handed over to O.C. 17th Field Ambulance. Field Ambulance marched via WATOU, HOUTKERQUE, HERZEELE to new Billets at WORMHOUDT.	JWD
WORMHOUDT.		5 pm	Field Ambulance arrived at WORMHOUDT. A.D.M.S. 20 Div. M 893 and S 206 dated 17.7.16 received.	
	18/7/16		A.D.M.S. 20 Div. No. S 207 and S 208 and M 883 dated 18.7.16 received.	JWD
			A.D.M.S. 20 Div. No. 208 and No. 883 dated 18.7.16 received.	
			A.D.M.S. 20 Div. No. M 885 dated 18.7.16 received.	
	19/7/16		Lieut. J. Macey R.A.M.C. reported his arrival and taken on the strength.	JWD

Army Form C. 2118

Sheet VII

WAR DIARY
or
INTELLIGENCE SUMMARY
(Erase heading not required.)

Instructions regarding War Diaries and Intelligence Summaries are contained in F. S. Regs., Part II. and the Staff Manual respectively. Title Pages will be prepared in manuscript.

Place	Date	Hour	Summary of Events and Information	Remarks and references to Appendices
WORMHOUDT	19/7/16	3.30 a.m.	Capt. QUINN R.A.M.C. and 36 Other Ranks and 4 Motor Ambulances leave WORMHOUDT to report to A.D.M.S. NEW ZEALAND Division at ARMENTIÈRES, for duty.	
		9 a.m.	Telegram received from CAPT. QUINN reporting arrival at ARMENTIÈRES at 7.53 a.m.	
			A.D.M.S. 2o Div. Nº 889 dated 18.7.16 received.	
			A.D.M.S. 2o Div Nº 892 dated 19.7.16 received	
			A.D.M.S. 2o Div. Nº 894 dated 19.7.16 received.	
			today A.D.M.S. 2o Div. O.O. Nº 45 dated 19.7.16 received.	
		5.15 p.m.	Advance Party of 1 Officer and 6 Other Ranks leave WORMHOUDT for BAILLEUL.	

1875 Wt. W593/826 1,000,000 4/15 J.B.C. & A. A.D.S.S./Forms/C. 2118.

Army Form C. 2118

WAR DIARY
or
INTELLIGENCE SUMMARY

(Erase heading not required.)

Army VIII

Place	Date	Hour	Summary of Events and Information	Remarks and references to Appendices
WORMHOUDT	19/7/16	8 p.m.	Advance Party report arrival at BAILLEUL at 6.55 p.m.	JW
	20/7/16		A.D.M.S. No. S. 211 dated 20.7.16 received	JW
		4.15 p.m.	Unit leaves WORMHOUDT and preceeds by Motor Buses to BAILLEUL arriving 6.15 p.m. Hospital taken over from 7th Field Ambulance. Small party left behind at Divisional Rest Station at WORMHOUDT.	
			No. 2083 Lieut. Pearce W.S. evacuated sick and struck off the strength.	
BAILLEUL	21/7/16		A.D.M.S. No. S. 214 + S. 215 dated 21.7.16 received.	JW
			CAPT QUINN and Party returned to unit from Duty with A.D.M.S. NEW ZEALAND Division at 4.30 p.m.	

Army Form C. 2118

WAR DIARY
or
INTELLIGENCE SUMMARY

(Erase heading not required.)

Sheet IX.

Instructions regarding War Diaries and Intelligence Summaries are contained in F. S. Regs., Part II. and the Staff Manual respectively. Title Pages will be prepared in manuscript.

Place	Date	Hour	Summary of Events and Information	Remarks and references to Appendices
BAILLEUL	21/7/16	-	A.D.M.S. 20 Div. No. O.D. 46 dated 21.7.16 received.	JMO OMO
	22/7/16	.	A.D.M.S. 20 Div. No. M 926 dated 22.7.16 received.	
			60 Inf. Bde. O.O. No. 120 dated 22.7.16 received.	
			60 Inf. Bde. O.O. No. 121 dated 22.7.16 received.	
			A.D.M.S. 20 Div. No. S 217 dated 22.7.16 received.	
			Divisional Rest Station at WORMHOUDT handed over to Lunarcis Division F.Amb. and party left behind on 20/7/16 rejoin unit.	
	23/7/16	-	A.D.M.S. 20 Div. No. O.O. 47 dated 22.7.16 received.	JMO

Army Form C. 2118

Sheet X.

WAR DIARY
or
INTELLIGENCE SUMMARY
(Erase heading not required.)

Instructions regarding War Diaries and Intelligence Summaries are contained in F. S. Regs., Part II. and the Staff Manual respectively. Title Pages will be prepared in manuscript.

Place	Date	Hour	Summary of Events and Information	Remarks and references to Appendices
BAILLEUL	23/7/16		60 Inf. Bde. O.O. No 122 dated 23.7.16 received.	JWO
	24/7/16	4.15 p.m.	Unit transferred at BAILLEUL handed over to 110th. 3 Army. Unit marched to MONT NOIR arriving 6.15 p.m.	JWO
MONT NOIR	23/7/16		A.D.M.S. No S 220 dated 23.7.16 received. 20 Div.	JWO
	24/7/16		60 Inf. Bde. O.O. 123 dated 24.7.16 received.	JWO
	25/7/16	8 p.m.	Unit leaves MONT NOIR & marches via WESTOUTRE to HOPOUTRE siding near POPERINGHE. No. 35710 Pte. Thompson W.E. R.A.M.C. and 7/S/1291 Pte. Thompson L. A.S.C. attached 61 2 Amb. evacuated sick and struck off the strength.	JWO
	26/7/16	1.15 a.m.	Unit entrains at HOPOUTRE siding for Reserve Army area.	JWO
		7.15 a.m.	Unit detrains at FRÉVENT.	

Army Form C. 2118

WAR DIARY
or
INTELLIGENCE SUMMARY
(Erase heading not required.)

Sheet No. VI.

Place	Date	Hour	Summary of Events and Information	Remarks and references to Appendices
FRÉVENT	26/7/16	8.30 a.m	Unit leaves FRÉVENT and marches via BOUQUEMAISON, LUCHEUX, HALLOY, ORVILLE, SARTON, MARIEUX, to VAUCHELLES, arriving 8.30 p.m.	JW
			60 Inf. Bde. O.O. 124 dated 26-7-16 received.	
			60 Inf. Bde. O.O. 125 dated 26-7-16 received.	
BOUQUE MAISON			A.D.M.S. No. S 221 dated 26-7-16 received. 20 Div.	
VAUCHELLES	27/7/16		A.D.M.S. No. S 223 dated 27-7-16 received and passes to 62 F.Amb. 20 Div.	JW
			A.D.M.S. No. S 224 dated 27-7-16 received. 20 Div.	
			60 Inf. Bde. O.O. 126 received and 27-7-16	
			No. 81718 The hours D. Rome evacuated sick & struck off the strength.	

Army Form C. 2118

WAR DIARY
or
INTELLIGENCE SUMMARY
(Erase heading not required.)

Sheet XII

Place	Date	Hour	Summary of Events and Information	Remarks and references to Appendices
VAUCHELLES	28/7/16	10.30 a.m.	Unit leaves VAUCHELLES in motors and AUTHIE to bivouac in BOIS de WARNIMONT arriving 11.45 a.m. Before Dressing Station at AUTHIE taken over by 1/1st F.Amb. Advanced Dressing Stations at BOLIMCAMPS and EUSTON (K.33.c.2 & K.31.59d) taken over: also advanced post at Red Cottage (K.28.a.3.3.) to assist Left B.H. Aid Post at Observation Wood (K.28.a.3.3.) Right Bearer Aid post in Louvville U. (K.34.b.5.5.) Left B.H. Aid Post at Red Cottage, H O.R. at Right Bear. Aid Post. Disposition of Personnel. 6 O.R. at Red Cottage, 4 O.R. at Bearer Aid Post. 1 Officer 17 O.R. at Bolincamps. 1 Officer 30 O.R. at AUTHIE 1 Officer 9 O.R. at EUSTON. Remainder at Headquarters.	(Sd) (Sd)
BOIS de WARNIMONT	29/7/16		A.D.M.S. 20 Div. S.225 & 226 dated 28.7.16 received. No remarks.	(Sd)
	30/7/16		R.A.M.C. S.227 dated 29.7.16 and S.228 dated 30.7.16 received.	(Sd)

J.Brown
Lieut. Col.
O.C. 61 F.Amb.

War Diary.

61st Field Ambulance R.A.M.C.

August 1916.

COMMITTEE FOR THE
MEDICAL HISTORY OF THE WAR
Date -5 OCT. 1915

Army Form C. 2118

WAR DIARY
or
INTELLIGENCE SUMMARY
(Erase heading not required.)

Sheet 1.

Place	Date	Hour	Summary of Events and Information	Remarks and references to Appendices
BOIS du MARNIMONT	1/8/16		A.D.M.S. / 20 Div. No. S 239 - S 231 dated 31-7-16 received & passed to 62 J. Am.	Allan Lieut.
			A.D.M.S. / 20 Div. No. S 232 dated 31-7-16 received & passed to 62 J.Am.	
			No. 37942 Sgt. NOAKES T.S. transferred to No. 11 Stationary hospital ROUEN and struck off the strength.	
	2/8/16		A.D.M.S. / 20 Div. No. S 234 & S 235 dated 2.8.16 received.	JCW
			No. T2/SR/01339 Acy. Sgt. Major MURDY W.T. transferred from 160 Coy. A.S.C. 20th Div t train, on probation as Warrant Officer Class I.	
	3/8/16		60 Inf. Bde. O.O. 127 dated 3-8-16 received.	JCW
	4/8/16		A.D.M.S. / 20 Div. O.O. 49 & O.O. 50 dated 4.8.16 received	JCW
			A.D.M.S. / 20 Div. S 239 & M 8/32 dated 4.8.16 received.	JCW

Army Form C. 2118

WAR DIARY
or
INTELLIGENCE SUMMARY

(Erase heading not required.)

Sheet 2.

Instructions regarding War Diaries and Intelligence Summaries are contained in F. S. Regs., Part II. and the Staff Manual respectively. Title Pages will be prepared in manuscript.

Place	Date	Hour	Summary of Events and Information	Remarks and references to Appendices
BOIS de HARTMONT	1/10		60 Inf/Bde Supplement to O.O. 127 dated 1.8.16 received	g/40
	2/10		60 Inf Bde O.O. 128 dated 5.8.16 received	g/41
	3/10		No movement.	g/42
	7/10		A.D.M.S. 20 Div. M 2/58 dated 7.8.16 received	g/43
	8/10		47212 Sergt TESSEYMAN W.F. transferred from No 11 Stationary Hospital on 8.8.16 not taken on the strength.	g/44
	9/10		60 Inf Bde G 190 dated 8.8.16 received.	g/45
	10/10		A.D.M.S. 20 Div. No 8 2 W1 and S 2 W1 dated 10.8.16 received.	g/46
	11/10		A.D.M.S. 20 Div. O.O. 61 and S 2w2/1 dated 10.8.16 received 60 Inf Bde O.O 129 dated 11.8.16 received.	g/47

Army Form C. 2118

WAR DIARY
or
INTELLIGENCE SUMMARY
(Erase heading not required.)

No. 3.

Instructions regarding War Diaries and Intelligence Summaries are contained in F.S. Regs., Part II. and the Staff Manual respectively. Title Pages will be prepared in manuscript.

Place	Date	Hour	Summary of Events and Information	Remarks and references to Appendices
BOIS de WARNIMONT	12/8/16		A.D.M.S. 20 Div. No. S 245 dated 12-8-16 received.	JW
			A.D.M.S. 20 Div. No. S 246 dated 12-8-16 received.	JW
	13/8/16		60 Inf. Bde. No. 190/299 dated 12-8-16 received.	
			30990 Pte HETHERINGTON E. Rank 61 F.Amb. wounded. Gun-shot wound right side neck. Returned to Duty 15.9.16.	
			A.D.M.S. 20 Div. No. M8/95 dated 13.8.16 received.	
	14/8/16		60 Inf. Bde. Amendments to O.O. 129 and 190/335 dated 13-8-16 received.	JW
			Advanced Dressing Stations at EUSTON & COLINCAMPS, & manned post at RED COTTAGE handed over to 62 F.Amb. Bearers at Right. Regt. Aid Post at SACKVILLE ST. relieved by 62 F.Amb. All 61 F.Amb. personnel return to Headquarters.	

WAR DIARY
or
INTELLIGENCE SUMMARY

Army Form C. 2118

Place	Date	Hour	Summary of Events and Information	Remarks and references to Appendices
BOIS de WARNIMONT	14/8/16		34472 L/Sgt. Rainbow E. evacuated sick on 14.8.16 and struck off the strength.	JW
			A.D.M.S. 20 Div. O.O. 52 dated 14.8.16 received.	
			A.D.M.S. 20 Div. O.O. 53 dated 14.8.16 received.	
	15/8		60 Inf. Bde. O.O. 130 dated 15.8.16 received.	JW
			The undermentioned have joined the Unit from the Base as re-inforcements & were taken on the strength.	
			1768 Pte Eaton J. 357 Pte Clarke E.W. 48471 Pte Williams J.R.
			74345 " Bootley J. 75290 " Stone J.	
	16/8		Camp Hospital at BOIS de WARNIMONT handed over to No. 3 F.Amb. Unit marches via AUTHIE and THIEVRES to ORVILLE arriving	JW
		6.15 p.m.		
ORVILLE			A.D.M.S. 20 Div. No. S.251 dated 16.8.16 received.	

Army Form C. 2118

Sheet 5.

WAR DIARY
or
INTELLIGENCE SUMMARY
(Erase heading not required.)

Instructions regarding War Diaries and Intelligence Summaries are contained in F. S. Regs., Part II. and the Staff Manual respectively. Title Pages will be prepared in manuscript.

Place	Date	Hour	Summary of Events and Information	Remarks and references to Appendices
ORVILLE	17/8/16	.	60 Inf. Bde. No. A 7654 dated 16.8.16 received.	JWO
			60 Inf. Bde. O.O. 131 and L 352 dated 17.8.16 received.	
	18/8/16	.	Unit leave ORVILLE and marches via DOULLENS, CANDAS, FIENVILLERS to GORGES arriving 2 p.m.	JWO
GORGES	19/8/16	.	60 Inf. Bde. O.O. 131 dated 18.8.16 received.	JWO
			A.D.M.S. 20 Div. M 8/162 dated 19.8.16 received.	
			XIV th. Corps Operating Station at AUTHIE handed over to 100th S.Amb. Personnel of 61 S.Amb. report sick at Headquarters.	
			A.D.M.S. 20 Div. S 254 & S 255 dated 19-8-16 received.	
	20/8/16		Unit entrains at CANDAS & proceeds via AMIENS to MERICOURT.	JWO
			detrains, marches to VILLE-SOUS-CORBIE. All transport proceeds by road on 19/8/16 – 20/8/16 via DAOURS to VILLE-SOUS-CORBIE.	

WAR DIARY
or
INTELLIGENCE SUMMARY
(Erase heading not required.)

Army Form C. 2118

Sheet 6.

Place	Date	Hour	Summary of Events and Information	Remarks and references to Appendices
VILLE-SOUS-CORBIE	21/8/16		60 Inf. Bde. O.O. No. 134 dated 21-8-16 received.	
	21/8/16		Unit marches to MEAULTE arriving 11 a.m.	
MEAULTE		3 pm	A.D.M.S. M 8/173 dated 21-8-16 received, instructing W.O.C. 137/8 Sanitary 20 Div. D.C. 61st D.Ans. to take over command of XIVth Corps Main Dressing Station at DIVE COPSE – J. 24. b. Ref Sheet (contoured) ALBERT tsoooo. Two tent sub-divisions of 61 D.Ans. proceed to DIVE COPSE to form part of XIVth Corps Main Dressing Station.	
DIVE COPSE			44619 Pte Brandon W. adt. 35291 Pte Shopperth P.W. evacuated sick & struck off the strength. D.Ans. at DIVE COPSE on 21.8.16 No. 7.8.106.107. D.Ants. nursing on 21.8.16 Nos 60, 61, 62.	

Army Form C. 2118

WAR DIARY
or
INTELLIGENCE SUMMARY
(Erase heading not required.)

Sheet 7.

Place	Date	Hour	Summary of Events and Information	Remarks and references to Appendices
DIVE COPSE	22/8/16		A.D.M.S. 20 Div. No. S 261 dated 22.8.16 received. Return of J.Amb. notes from MEAULTE to BRONFAY FARM. F.29.a (Ref Sheet (contined) ALBERT 1/40,000). (On the out division and there went out advance). 60, 61, and 62 J.Amb. open Dressing stations in their Dressing station. No. 7 J.Amb. Reserve. No. 8 J.Amb. leaves.	J.W.
	23/8/16		A.D.M.S. 20 Div. No. O.O 54 dated 23.8.16 received.	J.W.
	24/8/16		72 J.Amb. arrives and opens Dressing station.	J.W.

Army Form C. 2118

WAR DIARY
or
INTELLIGENCE SUMMARY
(Erase heading not required.)

Sheet 8.

Instructions regarding War Diaries and Intelligence Summaries are contained in F. S. Regs., Part II. and the Staff Manual respectively. Title Pages will be prepared in manuscript.

Place	Date	Hour	Summary of Events and Information	Remarks and references to Appendices
DIVE COPSE	25/8/16		Casualties in personnel to 12 noon 25.8.16. Wounded at Duty 50354 Pte Duffy J. 30249 Pte have R/s. 50662 Pte Parkes J. Wounded and evacuated 61619 Pte Shackelton J	JW
	26/8/16		N° 3 and 4 F.Amb. arrive and open Dressing Stations. N° 72 F.Amb. leaves.	JW
			Remainder Staff of 5th Division (12.O.R.) arrive	JW
			Remainder Staff of 24th Division (12.O.R.) depart. Casualties to 12 noon 26.8.16 :- Wounded at Duty 35919 Pte Seymour W.A.	JW

1875 Wt. W593/826 1,000,000 4/15 J.B.C. & A. A.D.S.S./Forms/C. 2118.

Army Form C. 2118

WAR DIARY
or
INTELLIGENCE SUMMARY
(Erase heading not required.)

Sheet 9.

Place	Date	Hour	Summary of Events and Information	Remarks and references to Appendices
DIVE COPSE	27/8/16		Evacuation to 12 noon 27-8-16 :-	JW
	28/8/16		Wounded at Duty 82141 Pte Green R.L. 38989 Pte Whitefoot A.	
			A.D.M.S. / 20 Div. N° O.O. 55 and M.E/232 dated 28.8.16 received.	JW
			Evacuation to 12 noon 28.8.16	
			Wounded and evacuated 39257 Pte Thompson W.	
			31234 A/Sgt. Lee H.B. and 37694 A/Sgt. Hooper R. appointed Sergeants. (Authority Reg.S. Records. 205/50 Orders N° 31 dated 14/8/16.)	
			Dressing stations O.N°s 106 + 107 J.Andro closed.	
	29/8/16		A.D.M.S. / 20 Div. N° S 276/1 dated 29.8.16 received.	JW
			XIV Corps Medical arrangements N° 1 dated 28.8.16 received.	
			Evacuation to 12 noon 29-8-16	
			Wounded and evacuated 50808 Pte Wade A.E.	

Army Form C. 2118

WAR DIARY
or
INTELLIGENCE SUMMARY
(Erase heading not required.)

Sheet 10.

Place	Date	Hour	Summary of Events and Information	Remarks and references to Appendices
DIVE COPSE	30/8/16		No. 30249 Pte Lee Rfl. reported wounded on duty on 25.8.16 re-admitted to hospital and evacuated Edn. Shock Shell (M). Nos 106 & 107 J.Amre. leave.	J.W.

J.Lowrey
Lieut. Col.
O.C. Main Dressing Station
XIVth Corps.

140/1734

War Diary

61st Field Ambulance R.A.M.C.

September 1916

COMMITTEE FOR THE
MEDICAL HISTORY OF THE WAR
Date 30 OCT. 1915

Army Form C. 2118

WAR DIARY
or
INTELLIGENCE SUMMARY
(Erase heading not required.)

Sheet 1.

Instructions regarding War Diaries and Intelligence Summaries are contained in F. S. Regs., Part II. and the Staff Manual respectively. Title Pages will be prepared in manuscript.

Place	Date	Hour	Summary of Events and Information	Remarks and references to Appendices
DIVE COPSE	30/8/16	—	D.D.M.S. XIV Corps. Medical Arrangements No. 1 dated 28-8-16 received.	Junior Colonel
	31/8/16		A.D.M.S. 20 Div. No. M8/247 dated 30-8-16 received.	Jell
			A.D.M.S. 16 Div. O.O. 9 dated 30-8-16 received.	
			A.D.M.S. 20 Div. M8/250 dated 31-8-16 received.	
			No. 111 & 112 St Andr. (16th Division) arrive at DIVE COPSE and open Dressing Station.	
	12 p.m.		39262 S/pte Williams J. appointed Acting Sergt. with pay. (D.D.M.S. XIV Corps. 58/64/16 actd Inq.16)	Jell
			37944 L/cpl Norman G.W. " " " "	
			31417 " Church Y. " " " " D.D.M.S. XIV Corps. 58/65/16 actd 1916
			36045 Pte Nelson B. " " " "
			50410 " Sermon A. " " " " L/cpl
			45794 " Hunter J. " " " " A.D.M.S. 20 Bri
			39243 " Delmar B. " " " " 106 actd 1-9-16

WAR DIARY
or
INTELLIGENCE SUMMARY
(Erase heading not required.)

Army Form C. 2118

Sheet 2.

Place	Date	Hour	Summary of Events and Information	Remarks and references to Appendices
DIV. COPSE.	1/9/16		T/30290 Dvr. Batus L.E. A.S.C. (H.T.) attached 61 F.Amb. evacuated sick & struck off the strength.	JLD
	2/9/16		38917 Pte Moore J. R.A.M.C. evacuated wounded & struck off the strength.	JLD
			51539 A/Cpl Shaugan Sidon D. joined the unit and taken on the strength.	
			A.D.M.S. 20 Div. M.9/1 dated 19-16 received.	
			A.D.M.S. 20 Div. M.9/7 and O.O. 55 (continuation) received.	JLD
	3/9/16		A.D.M.S. 20 Div. S.281/1 dated 2.9.16 received.	
			37700 Pte Watts J.B.K. evacuated wounded & 50618 Pte Parkes J. evacuated sick and struck off the strength.	

WAR DIARY
or
INTELLIGENCE SUMMARY
(Erase heading not required.)

Sheet 3.

Army Form C. 2118

Place	Date	Hour	Summary of Events and Information	Remarks and references to Appendices
DIVE COPSE	4/9/16		A.D.M.S. 20 Div. M.9/17 dated 3-9-16 received.	J.W.D.
	5/9/16		A.D.M.S. 20 Div. O.O. 56 & O.O. 57 dated 4-9-16 and M.9/24 dated 3-9-16 received.	J.W.D.
			A.D.M.S. 20 Div. O.O. 58 dated 5-9-16 received.	
			LIEUT. F. G. HACK R.A.M.C. (T.C.) reported his arrival & taken on the strength.	
			2/101 London & 2/3rd London F.Ambs. arrived and Open Dressing Stations.	
			37168 Pte Ogden J, 37162 Pte Reynolds V.S. and 47778 Pte Beaumont H. evacuated wounded on 4-9-16, struck off the strength. 38947 Pte Hoare I evacuated wounded on 2-9-16, returned to Duty & taken on the strength.	
	6/9/16		No remarks.	J.W.D.

Army Form C. 2118

WAR DIARY
or
INTELLIGENCE SUMMARY
(Erase heading not required.)

Place	Date	Hour	Summary of Events and Information	Remarks and references to Appendices
DIVE COPSE	7/7/16		Route taken by 37th Divn. from BRONFAY FARM to BOIS de TAILLES. K.18.a (Ref sheet ALBERT 57050).	
			27392 L/Cpl Antram A 80008 Pte Bracewell R.L. 77402 " Beckett S. 74582 " Bentham J.W. 77882 " Brook D. } Joined the unit from the Base & taken on the strength.	
			357 Pte Clarke E.N. R.A.M.C. transferred to 12th Siege Battery R.G.A. to army & struck off the strength.	
			6299 Pte Phillips R. R.A.M.C. transferred from 12th Siege Battery R.G.A. and taken on the strength.	
			73813 Pte Victory J.C. R.A.M.C. and 30562 Pte Dunn B.W. Rayter evacuated sick on 30-6-16 and 5-7-16 respectively and struck off the strength.	

WAR DIARY
or
INTELLIGENCE SUMMARY

(Erase heading not required.)

Army Form C. 2118

Shur S.

Place	Date	Hour	Summary of Events and Information	Remarks and references to Appendices
DIVE COPSE	7/7/16		A.D.M.S. 30 Div. O.O. 59 dated Sq.th received.	JWD
	8/7/16		BEARER SECTION 61 F.Amb. having return from BOIS du TAILLES to CORBIE.	JWD
			Commenced move of FM hdqrs. than Dressing Station from DIVE COPSE to BRONFAY FARM.	
BRONFAY FARM.	9/7/16		Main Dressing station closed in DIVE COPSE at 12 noon 9 Opened at BRONFAY FARM (F.29.a.7.0 Ref. Sheet ALBERT woods). at 12 noon.	JWD
	10/7/16		Completion of move of main Dressing Station to BRONFAY FARM.	JWD
	11/7/16		Bearer divisions of 61 F.Amb. have from CORBIE to MEAULTE.	JWD

WAR DIARY
or
INTELLIGENCE SUMMARY

(Erase heading not required.)

Army Form C. 2118

Thur 6

Place	Date	Hour	Summary of Events and Information	Remarks and references to Appendices
BRONFAY FARM.	12/9/16		A.D.M.S. 20 Div — No. M.9/69 dated 11-9-16 received.	JLB
			A.D.M.S. 20 Div — No. M.9/23 and M.9/65 dated 12.9.16 received. Remaining tent sub sections of 60 & 61 F.Amb. arrive at Main Dressing Station. BRONFAY FARM from Reserve Divisions. Two tent sub sections of 62 F.Amb. at BRONFAY FARM leave Main Dressing Station to rejoin Reserve Division of 62 F.Amb. Lieut. J. Harvey R.A.M.C. (T.C.) transferred to Lucknow C.C.S. and struck off the strength.	
	13/9/16		A.D.M.S. 20 Div. No. M.9/93 dated 13-9-16 received. 37967 Pte Parker J.P. and 37965 Pte Pike Ed Rame wounded each on 13.9.16 and struck off the strength.	JLB

WAR DIARY
or
INTELLIGENCE SUMMARY
(Erase heading not required.)

Army Form C. 2118

Sheet 7.

Place	Date	Hour	Summary of Events and Information	Remarks and references to Appendices
BRONFAY FARM	14/9/16		A.D.M.S. / 6 Div. — D.O.17 dated 13-9-16 and Amendment dated 14-9-16 received.	JD
			A.D.M.S. / 30 Div. — No. M9/100 dated 14-9-16 received.	
			A.D.M.S. / XIV Corps — Medical Arrangements No 2 dated 13-9-16 received.	
			A.D.M.S. / 20 Div. — No. S.299 and D.O. 60 dated 14-9-16 received.	
			Lieut. Lindsay R.A.M.C. transferred from 62 F.Amb. and taken on the strength.	
	15/9/16		Bearer sections 61 F.Amb. move from MEAULTE to CITADEL (F. 21 Central) in short abrupt moves (25,000).	JW
			80008 Pte Brewster R.S. R.A.M.C. evacuated wounded — struck off the strength.	

WAR DIARY or INTELLIGENCE SUMMARY

Army Form C. 2118

Place	Date	Hour	Summary of Events and Information	Remarks and references to Appendices
BRONFAY FARM.	15/9/16		The re-inforcements received from the Base and taken on the strength. 73513 Pte Rotero J.E. 2862 Pte Donald R. 34573 Pte Larton N. 61248 - Medwing J. 72019 - Leigh V.R. 8820 - Harvey J.	
	16/9/16		A.D.M.S. No M9/112 dated 15-9-16 received. 30 Div. Been down hours to Advanced Dressing Station at S. 30. 5. S. 6. (By Lieut Allwood U5000) Major E.P. Leahy R.A.M.C. evacuated dangerously wounded. 37939 Pte Newry A., 31818 Pte Ellacott A.E., and 75290 Pte Yolonde J. evacuated wounded struck off the strength.	

Army Form C. 2118

WAR DIARY
or
INTELLIGENCE SUMMARY
(Erase heading not required.)

Year 9.

Place	Date	Hour	Summary of Events and Information	Remarks and references to Appendices
BRONFAY FARM.	17/9/16		D.D.M.S. XIV Corps. No. 658/4/16 dated 17-9-16 received.	JW
	18/9/16		A.D.M.S. 20 Div. No. M.9/130 and S 302 dated 17-9-16 received. No remarks	JW
	19/9/16		Capt. E.D. Leahy R.A.M.C. evacuated wounded on 16-9-16, and 7 wounded at 2/2 nom L.F.L. struck off the strength.	JW
	20/9/16		A.D.M.S. 20 Div. O.O. 61 dated 20-9-16 received. B.D.M.S. XIV Corps. Judicial Arrangements No. 3 dated 19-9-16 received. A.D.M.S. 20 Div. No. S 307 dated 20-9-16 received.	JW

Army Form C. 2118

WAR DIARY
or
INTELLIGENCE SUMMARY
(Erase heading not required.)

Sheet 10

Instructions regarding War Diaries and Intelligence Summaries are contained in F.S. Regs., Part II. and the Staff Manual respectively. Title Pages will be prepared in manuscript.

Place	Date	Hour	Summary of Events and Information	Remarks and references to Appendices
BRONFAY FARM.	20/9/16		7760-9 Pte. Slack J. Rance killed in action on 20-9-16 and struck off the strength.	JEW
			M/33603 2/Lieut. Botting N. A.S.C. (M.T.) transferred to 20th Div. supply column on 23-9-16 struck off the strength.	
			M2/031603 Supp. Nicholas N.S. A.S.C. (M.T.) transferred from 20th Div. supply column and taken on the strength.	
	21/9/16		Bearer Sections 61 F.Amb. move to CITADEL F.21.central (Refs Sheet Albert 1/20000)	JEW
	22/9/16		Bearer Sections 61 F.Amb move to VILLE-SUR-ANCRE.	
			111 + 112 F.Ambs. (16th Division) have Main Dressing Station.	
	23/9/16		No movements	JEW
	24/9/16		No movements	JEW
	25/9/16		Bearer Sections 61 F.Amb, move to CITADEL.	JEW

Army Form C. 2118

WAR DIARY
or
INTELLIGENCE SUMMARY
(Erase heading not required.)

Sheet 11

Instructions regarding War Diaries and Intelligence Summaries are contained in F. S. Regs., Part II. and the Staff Manual respectively. Title Pages will be prepared in manuscript.

Place	Date	Hour	Summary of Events and Information	Remarks and references to Appendices
BRONFAY FARM.	26/9/16		Bearer Sections 61.2 Amb. move to Advanced Dressing Station at T.19.c.9.3. Ref Sheet Albert 1/10000.	JWO
			A.D.M.S. 20 Div. O.O. 62 & S.310 dated 25-9-16 received.	
			A.D.M.S. 20 Div. O.O. 62 (Amend.) dated 26-9-16 received.	
			The reinforcements from R.A.M.C. (T.F. ESSEX) found were on 26-9-16 were taken on the strength.	
			1954 Pte Nicholls L.D. 2366 Pte Scheein N.A. 2060 " Phillips B. 2563 " Mayho J. 1994 " Blackman R.	
	27/9/16		Lieut C.M. Ireland R.A.M.C. (T.C.) reported arrival from No 4 General Hospital taken on the strength.	JWO
	28/9/16		A.D.M.S. 20 Div. O.O. 63 dated 27-9-16 received. Permanent staff of 5th Div leave M.D.S. and previous staff of 4th Bde arrive.	JWO

Army Form C. 2118

WAR DIARY
or
INTELLIGENCE SUMMARY
(Erase heading not required.)

March 17.

Instructions regarding War Diaries and Intelligence Summaries are contained in F.S. Regs., Part II. and the Staff Manual respectively. Title Pages will be prepared in manuscript.

Place	Date	Hour	Summary of Events and Information	Remarks and references to Appendices
BRONFAY FARM.	28/9/16		Beamy Lieutenant 61 F.Amb. went to DUBLIN TRENCH re A.L.d. Ref Shew Alvers (town) J. ADMS 23 Div. Nº S 315 and D.O. 64 dated 28-9-16 received.	JW
	29/9		7/S/7308 Sj Smith Sloan S. R.A.M.C. (N.T.) joins the unit from the Base & taken on the strength.	JW
			MILITARY MEDAL awarded to 4pr.Sergt. Grierson W.J. and S0774 Pte Sharp A R.A.M.C. (Authority: XIV Corps 693/69d dated 22-9-16).	
	30/9/16		Removed staff of Europa Division whatever 3rd + 4th F.Amb. (Guards Division) leave the Main Dressing Station.	JW

J. Berrie
Lieut-Col.
O.C. 61st F.Amb.
R.A.M.C.

61st FIELD AMBULANCE
No.
Date 30-9-16
R.A.M.O.

Oct. 1916 / 5

War Diary

61st Field Ambulance Rouen.

October 1916

140/121

COMMITTEE FOR THE
MEDICAL HISTORY OF THE WAR
Date -9 DEC. 1916

Army Form C. 2118.

INTELLIGENCE SUMMARY

or

(Erase heading not required.)

Instructions regarding War Diaries and Intelligence Summaries are contained in F. S. Regs., Part II. and the Staff Manual respectively. Title Pages will be prepared in manuscript.

Sheet I. 2

Place	Date	Hour	Summary of Events and Information	Remarks and references to Appendices
BRONFAY FARM.	30/9/16		A.D.M.S. / 20 Div. O.O. 65 dated 30-9-16 received.	Alken P.C.C.
	1/10/16		A.D.M.S. / 20 Div. N° M 10/4 dated 1-10-16 received.	JWD
	2/10/16		A.D.M.S / 20 Div. N° 261/1 dated 1-10-16 received.	JWD
	3/10/16		A.D.M.S. / 20 Div. O.O. 66 (Prelim) and S 323 dated 2-10-16 received.	
			A.D.M.S. / 20 Div. O.O. 11 dated 29-9-16 received.	JWD
			XIV K. Corps Main Dressing Station at BRONFAY FARM moved to new site at CARNOY (A. 13. b. 9. 4. Ref. Sheet Albert 40000).	
CARNOY			Reserve Section 61 J.Amb. move to BERNAFAY WOOD.	

2449 Wt. W14957/M90 750,000 1/16 J.B.C. & A. Forms/C.2118/12.

INTELLIGENCE SUMMARY

(Erase heading not required.)

Sheet 2.

Place	Date	Hour	Summary of Events and Information	Remarks and references to Appendices
CARNOY	4/10/16		Lieut. J.G. Heath R.A.M.C. transferred to hospital charge of 12th. Rifle Brigade and struck off the strength.	file
	5/10		A.D.M.S. D.O. 67 dated 4-10-16 received. 20 Div. 2366 Pte Jenner R.A.M.C. (T.F. Weare) attached 61 2Amb. somewhat wounded on 5-10-16 and struck off the strength. 69065 Pte Neil W.S. and 76492 Pte Owens W.R. R.A.M.C. join the unit and taken on the strength.	file
	6/10		1954 Pte Nicholls T.A. R.A.M.C. (T.F. Weare) attached 61 2Amb. killed in action on 6/10; struck off the strength.	file
			A.D.M.S. No. G 336 dated 6-10-16 received. 20 Div. 2063 Pte Hayles J. (R.A.M.C.T.F. Weare) and 53889 Pte Ferguson N R.A.M.C. evacuated wounded and struck off the strength.	

INTELLIGENCE SUMMARY

(Erase heading not required.)

Sheet 3.

Place	Date	Hour	Summary of Events and Information	Remarks and references to Appendices
CARNOY	6/10		A.D.M.S. N° 10/40 dated 6-10-16 received. 2° Bri.	JWD
	7/10		P.O.28th Ste Homme J.G. Rame evacuated sick on 10/9/16 struck off the strength.	JWD
	8/10		A.D.M.S. N° M 10/41 dated 7-10-16 received. 2° Bri.	JWD
	9/10		A.D.M.S. D.O. 68 dated 8-10-16 received. 2° Bri.	JWD
	10/10		Tent Section 12th J.Amb. arrive at M.D.S. Beau Division by 2.Amb. move to SANDPITS, nr MEAULTE. Lieut E.A. Barker R.A.M.C. joins unit and taken on the strength.	JWD
	11/10		tups C.M Bullock R.A.M.C. transferred to Medical charge of the 6th K. Shrop. L.I. and struck off the strength. tups J.R. Tannet R.A.M.C. joins unit and taken on the strength.	JWD

INTELLIGENCE SUMMARY

Sheet 4.

Place	Date	Hour	Summary of Events and Information	Remarks and references to Appendices
CARNOY	12/10/16		No weather.	JWO
	13/10/16		7688 Pte Rowland R. 72935 - Hay S. 36650 - A.S. Dunlop J.W. 64081 - W.C. Bennick J. } join the unit and taken on the strength.	JWO
	14/10/16		A.D.M.S. No M 10/77 dated 13-10-16 received 20 Div. A.D.M.S. O.O. 69 dated 14-10-16 received. 20 Div.	JWO
	15/10/16		36275 S/Sgt Onions A.S. R.A.M.C. evacuated sick on 26-9-16 and struck off the strength. No 2 auxiliary Beam Lactria 61 Fond. move to DAOURS.	JWO
	16/10/16		Capt L.D. Reid transferred to medical charge of Sgt. Heavy Artillery Group on 16-10-16 and struck off the strength.	JWO

Army Form C. 2118.

WAR DIARY
INTELLIGENCE SUMMARY

(Erase heading not required.)

Sheet 5.

Place	Date	Hour	Summary of Events and Information	Remarks and references to Appendices
CARNOY	16/10		Permanent Staff of 8th Division arrive at M.D.S.	JW
	17/10		25 + 26 F.Ambs (8th Division) arrive at M.D.S.	JW
			72610 Pte Todd T.R. and 70272 Pte Lawrence H. R.A.M.C. join the unit and taken on the strength.	JW
	18/10		2/1st and 2/3rd London F.Ambs. and Permanent Staff of 9th Division leave Main Dressing Station.	JW
			Bearer Sections 61 F.Amb. move to COISY.	
			A.D.M.S. 8 Div. — O.O. 46 actd 17-10-16 received.	
			D.D.M.S. XIV Corps. No. T 133 actd 18-10-16 received.	
	19/10		Bearer Sections 61 F.Amb. move to MONTONVILLERS.	JW

INTELLIGENCE SUMMARY

(Erase heading not required.)

Sheet 6.

Place	Date	Hour	Summary of Events and Information	Remarks and references to Appendices
CARNOY	20/10		No remarks.	
	21/10		Permanent staff of 33rd Division arrive at A.D.S.	J.W.
	22/10		Lent lectures to 19th, 99th, and 101st 2/Ambs. arrive at A.D.S. Command of Main Dressing Station 14th Corps handed over from Lt.Col. Artf. J. Kenny R.A.M.C. O.C. 61 F.Amb. to Lt.Col. J.G. Fitzgerald R.A.M.C. O.C. 12 F.Amb.	J.W.
			D.D.M.S. No M994 dated 22.10.16 received. XIV Corps	
			Permanent staff of 6th Division leave A.D.S.	
			Permanent staff of 20th Division leave A.D.S. withdrawn.	
			D.D.M.S. No M999 dated 22.10.16 received. XIV Corps	
			D.A.M.S. No M1001 dated 22.10.16 received. XIV Corps	

INTELLIGENCE SUMMARY

Sheet 7.

Place	Date	Hour	Summary of Events and Information	Remarks and references to Appendices
CARNOY	23/10/16		Sent sections 61 and 60 2.Amb. and other 20 t Division details down main Amiens Station XIV Corps and march to DAOURS.	JW
	24/10/16		Sent section 61 2.Amb. move to station at VAUX - en - AMIENOIS.	JW
DAOURS				
VAUX.			Beau Section rejoins headquarters 7 61 2Amb. at VAUX. 35756 Acpl bede ? promoted Staff Sergeant. (Auth: Rome Order N° 37 dated 7-10-16).	JW
	25/10/16		Capt. J.R. Young Rome. transferred to Reserve strength ?	JW
			6th Oct + strike L.S. and struck off the strength.	
	26/10/16		1463 Pte Fisher J.C. and 83263 Pte Hopper A.C. Rome.	JW
			Join the unit and taken on the strength.	
	28/10/16		20th Div. disposition report dated 27-10-16 received.	JW

A.D.M.S. No M 10/125 dated 28.10.16 received.
20 Div.

ns regarding War Diaries and Intelligence
Summaries are contained in F. S. Regs., Part II.
and the Staff Manual respectively. Title Pages
will be prepared in manuscript.

INTELLIGENCE SUMMARY

or

(Erase heading not required.)

Sheet 2.

Place	Date	Hour	Summary of Events and Information	Remarks and references to Appendices
VAUX.	29/10/16		A.D.M.S. 20 Div. No. M10/126 dated 29-10-16 received.	Jeo
	30/10/16		60 Inf. Bde. No. G 834 dated 30-10-16 received	Jeo
			A.D.M.S. 20 Div. No. M10/129 and M10/130 dated 30-10-16 received.	

J. Brown
Lieut. Col.
O.C. 61 F.Amb.
R.A.M.C.

61st FIELD AMBULANCE
Date 31-10-16
R.A.M.C.

140/1862

61st FIELD AMBULANCE
R.A.M.C.
Date 30.11.16.

Vol 14

COMMITTEE FOR THE
MEDICAL HISTORY OF THE WAR
Date -3 JAN. 1917

20th Divn

War Diary
61st Field Ambulance R.A.M.C.

November 1916

Army Form C. 2118

WAR DIARY
or
INTELLIGENCE SUMMARY

(Erase heading not required.)

Instructions regarding War Diaries and Intelligence Summaries are contained in F. S. Regs., Part II. and the Staff Manual respectively. Title Pages will be prepared in manuscript.

Sheet 1.

Place	Date	Hour	Summary of Events and Information	Remarks and references to Appendices
VAUX.	31/10		A.D.M.S. / 20 Div. S 345 dated 31/10 received.	
			A.D.M.S. / 20 Div. O.O. 40 dated 31/10 received.	
	1/11/16		60 Inf. Bde. O.O. 163 dated 31/10 received.	
			3rd Field Ambulance from VAUX and marches via BREILLY-SUR-SOMME and PICQUIGNY to SOUES.	
SOUES	2/11/16		No remarks.	
	3/11/16		Field Ambulance moves to station 3/4 mile from SOUES on SOUES-HANGEST road, (CHATEAU de BICHECOURT).	
HANGEST	4/11/16		No remarks.	
	5/11/16		No remarks.	
	6/11/16		34513 Pte Hewton, R. Rams. evacuated sick and struck off the strength.	
			20th Recs Station opened by 61st Field Ambulance.	

WAR DIARY or INTELLIGENCE SUMMARY

Army Form C. 2118.

Sheet 2.

Place	Date	Hour	Summary of Events and Information	Remarks and references to Appendices
HANGEST	7/11/16		311456 Pte Bendens P.R. R.A.M.C. evacuated sick and struck off the strength.	E.Epsom
	8/11/16		72019 Pte Leigh V.R. R.A.M.C. evacuated sick and struck off the strength.	C.B.
	9/11/16		20 Div. Disposition Report dated 8-11-16 received	C.B.
			A.D.M.S. 20 Div. N° S 350 dated 9-11-16 received.	C.B.
			Lieut: Quartermaster B/ Lile R.A.M.C. transferred to 60th Division and struck off the strength.	
	10/11/16		Major A. Bone R.A.M.C. evacuated sick and struck off the strength.	
			73/025124 Dvr. Stroud J.E. A.S.C. (H.T.) attached 61 F.Amb. evacuated sick and struck off the strength.	C.B.
	11/11/16		A.D.M.S. 20 Div. N° 351 dated 11-11-16 received.	
			60 Inf Bde N° G 941/2 dated 11-11-16 received.	

Army Form C. 2118.

WAR DIARY
or
INTELLIGENCE SUMMARY

(Erase heading not required.)

Instructions regarding War Diaries and Intelligence Summaries are contained in F. S. Regs., Part II. and the Staff Manual respectively. Title Pages will be prepared in manuscript.

Sheet 3.

Place	Date	Hour	Summary of Events and Information	Remarks and references to Appendices
HANGEST.	11/11/16		T2/024113 Dvr. Brunt E.E. A.S.C. (M.T.) attached 61 D.Ans. evacuated sick and struck off the strength.	c/opp
	12/11/16		R.A.M.S. 2o Div. No. M.11/40 acted 11-11-16 received.	c/2
			60 Inf. Bde. No. B.941/8 acted 12-11-16 received.	
			A.D.M.S. 2o Div. No. S.252 acted 12-11-16 received.	
	13/11/16		60 Inf. Bde. O.O. 165 acted 13-11-16 received.	c/2
	14/11/16		T2/015991 Dvr. Antonio Ak. ⎫ A.S.C. (M.T.) attached 61 D.Ans. transferred	c/2
			T3/022704 „ Ansley J. ⎬ to 160 Coy A.S.C. and struck off the	
			T1/4612 „ Lee A. ⎭ strength.	
			T3/024104 Dvr. Epps E.C. ⎫ A.S.C. (M.T.) transferred from	
			T4/093955 „ Mahoney W.S. ⎬ 160 Coy A.S.C. and taken on the	
			T2/016344 „ Moore T.J.P. ⎭ strength.	
			M2/104971 Pte Newham J.L. A.S.C (M.T) attached 61 D.Ans. evacuated with Tarsor Bar 15220 to 1st A.S.C. Repair Shop PARIS and struck off the strength.	

Army Form C. 2118
Sheet 4.

WAR DIARY
or
INTELLIGENCE SUMMARY
(Erase heading not required.)

Instructions regarding War Diaries and Intelligence Summaries are contained in F.S. Regs., Part II. and the Staff Manual respectively. Title Pages will be prepared in manuscript.

Place	Date	Hour	Summary of Events and Information	Remarks and references to Appendices
HANGEST	15/11/16		Lieut T. Whitehead R.A.M.C. joined the unit and taken on the strength.	
			Transport of 61 F.Amb. leaves HANGEST and proceeds by road via PICQUIGNY to AILLY-SUR-SOMME.	
	16/11/16		Transport of 61 F.Amb. leaves AILLY-SUR-SOMME & proceeds via AMIENS to CORBIE.	
			61 F.Amb. leaves HANGEST and moves to CORBIE by train.	
			20 Div. Disposition report dated 15-11-16 received.	
			88622 Pte Imperly } R.A.M.C. join the unit from the Base and 75960 " Jones } } are taken on the strength.	
CORBIE	17/11/16		60 Inf.Bde. N° G 941/988 dated 17-11-16 received.	
			A.D.M.S. / 20 Div. O.O. 41 dated 17-11-16 received.	

Army Form C. 2118

WAR DIARY
or
INTELLIGENCE SUMMARY

(Erase heading not required.)

Sheet 5.

Instructions regarding War Diaries and Intelligence Summaries are contained in F. S. Regs., Part II. and the Staff Manual respectively. Title Pages will be prepared in manuscript.

Place	Date	Hour	Summary of Events and Information	Remarks and references to Appendices
CORBIE	18/11		Demands staff of 4 O.R. despatched to XIV Corps Grain Drying Station and 1 Officer 20 O.R. to XIV Corps M.N.C.P.	c.B. appx
	19/11		20 Div. Deposition Report dated 19-11-16 received. A.D.M.S. N°. S 354 dated 16/11 received. 20 Div.	c B.
	20/11		No remarks	c.B.
	21/11		No remarks	c.B.
	22/11		M2/118946 Pte Kemp C.J.C. R.S.C. (M.T.) attached to 61 Chb. transferred to South Army T.S.C. and struck off the strength. One Talbot Ambulance Car transferred to South Army T.S.C. and three Leslie Army Ambulance transferred to Fifth Army. Five Wolseley Ambulances received in exchange. M2/163778 Pte Bennett R.W. M1/06268 Pte Earle W. R.S.C. (M.T.) transferred from South Army T.S.C. on 22-11-16 and taken on the strength.	c.B.

Army Form C. 2118.

WAR DIARY
or
INTELLIGENCE SUMMARY

(Erase heading not required.)

Sheet 6.

Instructions regarding War Diaries and Intelligence Summaries are contained in F. S. Regs., Part II. and the Staff Manual respectively. Title Pages will be prepared in manuscript.

Place	Date	Hour	Summary of Events and Information	Remarks and references to Appendices
CORBIE	23/11		A.D.M.S. / 20 Div. Nº. S 274 dated 23-11-16 received.	E.J. Baynon Capr
	24/11		A.D.M.S. / 20 Div. Nº. S 357 received.	C.62
			20 Div. Disposition Report dated 24-11-16 received.	
	25/11		No remarks	C.62
	26/11		A.D.M.S. / 20 Div. Nº. M 20/227 dated 26-11-16 received.	C.62
	27/11		T2/018135 Dvr. Bransford J.J. } A.S.C. (H.T.) transferred from 160 Bde A.S.C. and taken on the strength.	C.62
			T4/123476 – Privis M. }	
			40581 Rfn Shannon J. appointed acting Sergeant with Pay from 26/10/16	
			53902 Pte Quy L. " " Corporal " " " "	
			(Authority A.D.M.S. 20 Div. 20 Corps)	

Army Form C. 2118.

WAR DIARY
or
INTELLIGENCE SUMMARY

(Erase heading not required.)

Sheet 7.

Place	Date	Hour	Summary of Events and Information	Remarks and references to Appendices
CORBIE	27/11		A.D.M.S. N° 20/279 dated 27-11-16 received. 20 Div.	c.3.
	28/11		53283 Pte Atkinson Y.J. R.A.M.C. evacuated sick and struck off the strength.	c.3.
	29/11		No remarks.	c.3.
	30/11		2820 Pte Harvey J. R.A.M.C. evacuated to Base Depot for Dental treatment and struck off the strength.	c.3.
			N° 88955 Pte Powell R.W. R.A.M.C. joins the unit from the Base and taken on the strength.	

C. B. [signature]
Capt. R.A.M.C.
A/O.C. 61 F.Amb.

[Stamp: 61st FIELD AMBULANCE R.A.M.C. 30-11-16]

20th Div.

140/1903

"War Diary"

61st Field Ambulance Rare.

December 1916.

COMMITTEE FOR THE
MEDICAL HISTORY OF THE WAR
Date 31 JAN. 1917

Army Form C. 2118.

WAR DIARY
or
INTELLIGENCE SUMMARY

(Erase heading not required.)

Instructions regarding War Diaries and Intelligence Summaries are contained in F. S. Regs., Part II. and the Staff Manual respectively. Title Pages will be prepared in manuscript.

Sheet 1.

Place	Date	Hour	Summary of Events and Information	Remarks and references to Appendices
CORBIE	1/12/16		20th Div. Disposition Report dated 1.12.16 received.	Appendix Dec C16 JW
	2/12/16		60 Inf. Bde. No 2/1152/3 dated 2.12.16 received.	JW
	3/12/16		No remarks.	JW
	4/12/16		Lieut. & Qr Mr R. Knappan Reeve joins the unit and is taken on the strength.	JW
	5/12/16		No remarks.	JW
	6/12/16		59123 Pte Robinson J. Raine joins the unit and is taken on the strength.	JW
	7/12/16		A.D.M.S. O.O.42 dated 7.12.16 received. 20 Div.	
			60 Inf. Bde. O.O. 167 dated 7.12.16 received.	
			20th Div. Disposition report dated 8.12.16 received.	JW
	8/12/16		A.D.M.S. S.365 dated 8.12.16 received. 20 Div.	JW

Army Form C. 2118.

WAR DIARY
or
INTELLIGENCE SUMMARY

(Erase heading not required.)

Sheet 2.

Place	Date	Hour	Summary of Events and Information	Remarks and references to Appendices.
CORBIE	8/12/16		34839 Pte Heavey J. R.A.M.C. evacuated sick and struck off the strength.	
	9/12/16		Unit leaves CORBIE and proceeds by road via MERICOURT to MEAULTE	
MEAULTE			D.D.M.S. 20 Div. O.O. 92 (Amendment) dated 9.12.16 received.	
			60 Inf. Bde. O.O. 167 (Amendment) dated 9.12.16 received.	
	10/12/16		Unit leaves MEAULTE and proceeds to CARNOY. (A.2.a.5.5. Rf Sheet Albert).	
CARNOY	11/12/16	2 pm	89th Field Ambulance relieved by 61st Field Ambulance. Headquarters of Unit at CARNOY. Bearer Division camp at TRONES WOOD. Advanced Dressing Station at GINCHY. Three Bearer Relay Posts and four Regt. Aid Posts. Bearer Divisions of 60 and 62 F.Ambs. attached to 61 Field Ambulance. O.C. 61 F.Amb. becomes responsible for collection of all casualties on 20th Div. Front.	

Army Form C. 2118.

WAR DIARY
or
INTELLIGENCE SUMMARY

(Erase heading not required.)

Sheet 3.

Instructions regarding War Diaries and Intelligence Summaries are contained in F. S. Regs., Part II and the Staff Manual respectively. Title Pages will be prepared in manuscript.

Place	Date	Hour	Summary of Events and Information	Remarks and references to Appendices
CARNOY	12/12/16		A.D.M.S. N° S.367 dated 11.12.16 received. 20 Div.	g/o
	13/12/16		No remarks.	g/o
	14/12/16		44372 Pte Lockie T. R.A.M.C. joins the unit and is taken on the strength	g/o
			34839 Pte Heavy J. R.A.M.C. rejoins unit from 21 M.A.L. and is taken on the strength.	
	15/12/16		A.D.M.S. N° S.368 dated 15.12.16 received. 20 Div.	g/o
	16/12/16		20th Div. Disposition report dated 15.12.16 received.	g/o
	17/12/16		No remarks.	g/o
	18/12/16		No remarks.	g/o

Army Form C. 2118.

WAR DIARY
or
INTELLIGENCE SUMMARY

(Erase heading not required.)

Sheet 4.

Instructions regarding War Diaries and Intelligence Summaries are contained in F.S. Regs., Part II. and the Staff Manual respectively. Title Pages will be prepared in manuscript.

Place	Date	Hour	Summary of Events and Information	Remarks and references to Appendices
CARNOY	19/12/16		M2/082126 Pte Pickering E. A.S.C. (M.T.) attached to 61 Field Ambulance transferred to 3rd A.S.C. Repair Shop and struck off the strength.	—
	20/12/16		A.D.M.S. 20 Div. S.340 dated 19.12.16 received.	—
	21/12/16		A.D.M.S. 20 Div. O.O. 93 dated 20.12.16 received.	—
			A.D.M.S. 20 Div. S.342 dated 21.12.16 received.	
	22/12/16		Bearer Division 60 F.Amb. reports to 60 F.Amb.	—
	23/12/16		No remarks	—
	24/12/16	11 am	61st Field Ambulance relieved by 51st Field Ambulance 14th Division. Unit proceeds by road via MEAULTE to TREUX. Bearer Division 62 F.Amb. detached and proceeds to MEAULTE.	—

Army Form C. 2118.

WAR DIARY
or
INTELLIGENCE SUMMARY

(Erase heading not required.)

Sheet 5

Instructions regarding War Diaries and Intelligence Summaries are contained in F. S. Regs., Part II. and the Staff Manual respectively. Title Pages will be prepared in manuscript.

Place	Date	Hour	Summary of Events and Information	Remarks and references to Appendices
TREUX	25/12/16		20 Div. Aid. Report dated 25.12.16 received.	JW
	26/12/16		No remarks.	JW
	27/12/16		M2/046732 Pte Sellar R.A.S.C. (M.T.) joins the unit and is taken on the strength.	JW
	28/12/16		No remarks.	JW
	29/12/16		A.D.M.S. 20 Div. O.O. 94 dated 28.12.16 and S 373 dated 28.12.16 received. 60 Inf Bde. O.O. 190 dated 29.12.16 received.	JW
	30/12/16		A.D.M.S. 20 Div. S 376 dated 28.12.16 received.	JW

J Bowen
Lieut. Col.
O.C. 61 F.Amb.

War Diary, January 1914.

61st Field Ambulance R.A.M.C.

Army Form C. 2118.

WAR DIARY
or
INTELLIGENCE SUMMARY

(Erase heading not required.)

Sheet 1.

Instructions regarding War Diaries and Intelligence Summaries are contained in F. S. Regs., Part II. and the Staff Manual respectively. Title Pages will be prepared in manuscript.

Place	Date	Hour	Summary of Events and Information	Remarks and references to Appendices
TREUX	31/12/16		A.D.M.S. 20 Div. Nº 377 dated 31-12-16 received.	[initials]
	1/1/17		A.D.M.S. 20 Div. Amendment to O.O. 190 dated 1-1-17 received.	[initials]
			51529 Lieut. Trapp Siron N. Rame proceeds to England as candidate for a commission and is struck off the strength.	
	2/1/17		A.D.M.S. 20 Div. Nº S 398 dated 2-1-17 received.	[initials]
	3/1/17		Unit moves from TREUX to bivouac near TRONES WOOD. (S.30.b.6.5. Rft Sheet 57 West edtn.), relieving Reserve Division 2Amb.	[initials]
GUILLEMONT			Advanced Dressing Station at COMBLES. Forward Adv. Dressing Station at HAIE WOOD. Two Rgtl Aid Posts, two Bearer Relay Posts also Bearer Post at COMBLES. Bearer Divisions Nº 60 & 62 D.Amb. attached to 61 D.Amb.	

Army Form C. 2118.

WAR DIARY
or
INTELLIGENCE SUMMARY

(Erase heading not required.) Sheet 2.

Instructions regarding War Diaries and Intelligence Summaries are contained in F. S. Regs., Part II. and the Staff Manual respectively. Title Pages will be prepared in manuscript.

Place	Date	Hour	Summary of Events and Information	Remarks and references to Appendices
GUILLEMONT	4/1/7		No remarks.	JW
	5/1/7		M2/131603 Dvr. Nicholson N.S. (A.S.C. M.T.) attached to 61 S.Amm. transferred to 20 Div. Supply Column on 5/17 and struck off the strength.	JW
	6/1/7		No remarks.	JW
	7/1/7		R.A.M.S. N.S. 343 dated 6-1-17 received. 20 Div.	JW
			A.A.M.S. N.S. 380 dated 7-1-17 received. 20 Div. 39150 Pte. Walpole J. R.A.M.C., 46205 Pte. Burns O. R.A.M.C. and 44948 Pte. Beckett D. R.A.M.C. evacuated sick on 1/17, 2/17, 4/17 respectively and struck off the strength.	
	8/1/7		No remarks.	JW
	9/1/7		No remarks.	JW

Army Form C. 2118.

WAR DIARY
or
INTELLIGENCE SUMMARY

(Erase heading not required.) Sheet 3.

Place	Date	Hour	Summary of Events and Information	Remarks and references to Appendices
GUILLEMONT	10/1/17		60 O.R. Btn. D.O. 171 acted 10-1-17 received.	ful
	11/1/17		No remarks.	ful
	12/1/17		42019 Pte Keigh V.R. Ranc. injure nui from N.Z. Gen. Hosp. and is taken on the strength.	ful
	13/1/17		37694 Sergt. Hospth. R. Ranc. evacuated sick struck off the strength.	ful
	14/1/17		Lieut E.G. Burtur Ranc. proceed to England on 14th on completion of term of contract struck off the strength.	ful
	15/1/17		No remarks	ful
	16/1/17		No remarks	ful
	17/1/17		90329 Pte McKenzie K. and 90330 Pte McKenzie M. Ranc join the unit from the Base and are taken on the strength.	ful

WAR DIARY or INTELLIGENCE SUMMARY

Army Form C. 2118.

(Erase heading not required.)

Sheet 4.

Place	Date	Hour	Summary of Events and Information	Remarks and references to Appendices
GUILLEMONT	18/1/17		60 Inf.Bde. O.O. 172 dated 17-1-17 received.	q10
	19/1/17		50302 Pte Bell M. R.A.M.C. evacuated sick on 11/1/17 & struck off the strength.	q10
			61st Inf.Bde. O.O. 151 dated 19-1-17 received.	q10
	20/1/17		No remarks	
	21/1/17		Sgt. Major Desmond S. R.A.M.C. joins the Unit from the Base and is taken on the strength.	q10
	22/1/17		38992 A/L/Cpl Nelson D.J. R.A.M.C. evacuated sick & struck off the strength.	q10
			A.D.M.S. No M1/24 dated 22-1-17 received. 20 Div	q10
	23/1/17		Capt R. G. Norrey R.A.M.C. joins the Unit and is taken on the strength.	q10
	24/1/17		A.A.M.S. O.O. 45 dated 24-1-17 received. 20 Div.	q10

Army Form C. 2118.

WAR DIARY
or
INTELLIGENCE SUMMARY

(Erase heading not required.)

Sheet 5.

Place	Date	Hour	Summary of Events and Information	Remarks and references to Appendices
GUILLEMONT	24/1/17		T3/02402 Dvr King S.D. A.S.C. (H.T.) attached to 61 J.Amb. transferred to 160 Coy A.S.C. and struck off the strength.	gro
			T1/4318 Dvr Shell N. A.S.C. (H.T.) transferred from 160 Coy and taken on the strength.	
			Rec'd Divisions 60 & 62 J.Amb. upon their respective units.	
			60 Inf.Bde. O.O. 173 dated 23-1-17 received.	
	25/1/17		A.D.M.S. Nº S 325 dated 24-1-17 received.	gro
			20 Div.	
	26/1/17		No remarks.	
	27/1/17		61 J.Amb. relieved by 17th Division J.Amb.	gro
MEAULTE			and move to MEAULTE.	
			A.D.M.S. Nº S 389 dated 27-1-17 received.	
			20 Div.	

Army Form C. 2118.

WAR DIARY
or
INTELLIGENCE SUMMARY

(Erase heading not required.)

March 6.

Place	Date	Hour	Summary of Events and Information	Remarks and references to Appendices
MEAULTE	22/1/17		No remarks	9w
	24/1/17		No remarks.	9w
	30/1/17		A.D.M.S. No. S 390 dated 29-1-17 received. 20 Div.	9w
			M2/120236 Pte Freeman W. of A.S.C. (M.T.) transferred from 20th D.S.C. taken on the strength.	
			W/W. 107/S. Strong Rooms, commanding 61st F.Amb. was congeted to D.S.O. in the London Gazette dated 1-1-17.	

61ST FIELD AMBULANCE.
Ro............
Date 31-1-17

J. S. Brown
Lieut. Col.
O.C. 61 F.Amb.
R.A.M.C.

War Diary.

61st Field Ambulance. R.A.M.C.

February, 1917.

WAR DIARY or INTELLIGENCE SUMMARY

Army Form C. 2118.

Place	Date	Hour	Summary of Events and Information	Remarks and references to Appendices
MEAULTE	1/2/17		To A.A. Daily Report week ending 31-1-17 received.	Filed in Orders
			76224 Pte Manning J. R.A.M.C. transferred to 38 A.A.L.G. struck off the strength.	
			63334 Pte Busby J. R.A.M.C. transferred from 38 A.A.L. taken on the strength.	
			38098 Pte Race W. and 214188 Pte Bovington M.A. R.A.M.C. appointed acting Lance Corporals without pay from 31/1.	
			37942 Pte Wilson D. J. R.A.M.C. received addn on 22/1 & struck off the strength.	
		2/2/17	3147 a/L/cpl Marsh L. R.A.M.C. appointed acting L/sgt with pay from 31/1.	
			115976 Pte Saunders J. R.A.M.C. appointed acting corporal with pay from 31/1.	
			To Air. Daily Report dated 1-2-17 received.	Filed

Army Form C. 2118.

WAR DIARY
or
INTELLIGENCE SUMMARY

(Erase heading not required.)

Sheet 2.

Place	Date	Hour	Summary of Events and Information	Remarks and references to Appendices
MEAULTE	2/2/17		2060 Pte Phillips B. Rane (I.F. Nozzes) and 35927 Pte Taylor J.M., R.A.M.C. evacuated sick returned off the strength.	
	3/2/17		No movements	
	d/o		A.D.M.S. / 20 Div. O.O. 76 noted 4.2.17 received.	
			60 Inf. Bde. O.O. 176 and 4.2.17 received	
	5/2/17		A.D.M.S. / 20 Div S 395 noted 5.2.17 received.	
			60 Inf Bde Amendments to O.O. 176 and 5.2.17 received.	
	6/2/17		A.D.M.S. / 20 Div S 395 noted 5.2.17 received.	
	7/2/17		Unit moved from MEAULTE to camp at A.2.d.5.5 (Ref Sheet 57nnw)(4.0000)	

WAR DIARY or INTELLIGENCE SUMMARY

Army Form C. 2118.

Sheet 3

Place	Date	Hour	Summary of Events and Information	Remarks and references to Appendices
P.2.A.5.5. (CARNOY)	7/2/17		Remainder of 24th Anzacs Brit Listening posts by 20th Aus Brit Anzacs completed at Noon. Brit Anzacs D 60 & 62 9 Anzac attached to 61 2 Anzac. Anzacs Stations (Aid) at GINCHY and FLANK AVENUE. 2nd Rgtl Aid Post, 3rd Ware relay posts. Bent stab near GUILLEMONT (S.30.4.)	JW
			A.D.M.S. 20 Div. S 397 dated 7.2.17 received.	
	9/2/17		Capt. R.L.G. Worsley R.A.M.C. evacuated sick rejoined Hd Qrs Strength.	JW
			A.D.M.S. 20 Div. S 450 dated 9.2.17 received.	
	10/2/17		31972 Pte Burns E. R.A.M.C. evacuated sick rejoined Hd Qrs strength.	JW

Army Form C. 2118.

WAR DIARY
or
INTELLIGENCE SUMMARY
(Erase heading not required.)

Army Form C. 2118.

Instructions regarding War Diaries and Intelligence Summaries are contained in F. S. Regs., Part II. and the Staff Manual respectively. Title Pages will be prepared in manuscript. Arch 1.

Place	Date	Hour	Summary of Events and Information	Remarks and references to Appendices
CARNOY	11/2/17		No Remarks.	JWD
	12/2/17		No Remarks.	JWD
	13/2/17		A.D.M.S. 20 Div. C.C.2. dated 13.2.17 received	JWD
			33202 A/L/Cpl Wood M.E. R.A.M.C. appointed L/Cpl with P.C. from 13/2/17	
			69853 Pte New J.J. } Joined Unit to be taken 65003 Wallworth M.F. } on strength 62001 Hughes C.O.	
			387 A/Serj. Supf. Bentley D. R.A.M.C. Wounded (at Duty) Return Thigh R (A) struck off the strength	JWD
			62337 Pte Brady F R.A.M.C. evacuated sick	
	15/2/17		No remarks	JWD
	16/2/17			JWD
	17/2/17		36001 Pte Duncan R.A.H.P. R.A.M.C. joined unit on 17/2/17 and taken on the strength	JWD

2449 Wt. W14957/M90 750,000 1/16 J.B.C. & A. Forms/C.2118/12.

Army Form C. 2118.

WAR DIARY
or
INTELLIGENCE SUMMARY

(Erase heading not required.)

Sheet 5

Instructions regarding War Diaries and Intelligence Summaries are contained in F. S. Regs., Part II. and the Staff Manual respectively. Title Pages will be prepared in manuscript.

Place	Date	Hour	Summary of Events and Information	Remarks and references to Appendices
CARNOY	18/2/17		No minutes	g.r.o
	19/2/17		No minutes	g.r.o
	20/2/17		190 Inf. Bde. O.O. 17] dated 20.2.17 received	g.r.o
	21/2/17		No minutes	g.r.o
	22/2/17		Lieut. B.N. Ludge Rance joined Bn. on 22/2/17 taken on the strength	g.r.o
	23/2/17		60 Inf. Bde. No. B. 2069 dated 23.2.17 received	g.r.o
			61 Inf.Bn. O.O. 150 dated 22.2.17 received	g.r.o
	24/2/17		20 Bde. Adm. Report dated 23.2.17 received	g.r.o
	25/2/17		61 Inf. Bn. O.O. 161 dated 25.2.17 received	g.r.o
	26/2/17		O.B.M.S. No S. 404 dated 26.2.17 received	g.r.o
			20 Bde.	

Army Form C. 2118.

WAR DIARY
or
INTELLIGENCE SUMMARY

(Erase heading not required.)

Instructions regarding War Diaries and Intelligence Summaries are contained in F. S. Regs., Part II. and the Staff Manual respectively. Title Pages will be prepared in manuscript.

Place	Date	Hour	Summary of Events and Information	Remarks and references to Appendices
CARNOY	27/2/17		Lieut. B.W. Smith R.A.M.C. transferred temporarily to Corps Depot at 12th K.R.R. for Rept.	
	28/2/17		No remarks.	
			Lieut. J.S. Stanford R.A.M.C. 61 F.Amb. was gazetted Captain from 11.2.17 in the supplement to the London Gazette dated 23/2/17.	

J. Stanning
Lieut. Col.
O. C. 61 F. Amb.

61ST FIELD AMBULANCE.
No. R-1/154
Date. 28.2.17

140/2042.

Nov 18

20th Div

War Diary.

61st Field Ambulance. Rare.

March 1917.

Mar 1917.

S

COMMITTEE FOR THE
MEDICAL HISTORY OF THE WAR
Date 11 MAY 1917

Army Form C. 2118.

WAR DIARY or INTELLIGENCE SUMMARY

(Erase heading not required.)

Instructions regarding War Diaries and Intelligence Summaries are contained in F. S. Regs., Part II. and the Staff Manual respectively. Title Pages will be prepared in manuscript.

Place	Date	Hour	Summary of Events and Information	Remarks and references to Appendices
CARNOY	28/2/17		60 S.I. Bde. O.O. M8 dated 28-2-17 received	Appendix
	1/3/17		A.D.M.S. S.114/1 dated 1-3-17 received. 20 Div.	App.
	2/3/17		61st Inf Bde. O.O. 152 dated 1-3-17 received	App
			60th Inf Bde. O.O. 199 dated 2-3-17 received	
	3/3/17		A.A.& Q.M.G. C.R.S.Rout. No./882. dated 3.3.17 received	App
			20 Div.	
			61st Inf Bde. O.O. 162/1 dated 2.3.17 received	
			61st Inf Bde. location table dated 3.3.17 received	
	4/3/17		No remarks	
	5/3/17		Recognition of enemy horses from CARNOY (A.21.d.5.5.) to GUILLEMONT	App
			(S.30.A.5.6.) Report Chief Observer (enclosed)	
			20 Div. B.Operation Report Ommiecourt dated 4.3.17 received	App
			60 Inf Bde. O.O. 160 dated 5.3.17 received	App
	6/3/17		61st Inf Bde. O.O. 163 dated 5.3.17 received	App

WAR DIARY or INTELLIGENCE SUMMARY

Army Form C. 2118.

Week 2

Place	Date	Hour	Summary of Events and Information	Remarks and references to Appendices
GUILLEMONT	6/3/17		31451 A/Cpl Milne W. Rome evacuated sick wounded on 6.3.17 and struck off the strength. (K.I.R. Neck severe)	
	7/3/17		32493 Pte Stocks N.J. Rope gun shot wound and taken on the strength	
			A/Capt J.C. Limebeer R.A.M.C. transferred from 60th Field Ambulance to this unit and taken on the strength.	yes
	8/3/17		No remarks	yes
	9/3/17		No remarks	yes
	10/3/17		A.A.M.S. S.14 dated 6.3.17 received 2nd Bn	yes
			2nd Arm. Inspection Report dated 9.3.17 received	
	11/3/17		No remarks	
	12/3/17		60th Inf. Bde. S.O. 181 dated 12.2.16 received	yes
			61st Inf. Bde. O.O. 165 dated 11.3.16 received	yes
			60th Inf. Bde. O.O. 182 dated 12.3.16 received	
	13/3/17		A.A.M.S. S.18 and S.19 dated 13.3.17 received	yes

Army Form C. 2118.

WAR DIARY or INTELLIGENCE SUMMARY

(Erase heading not required.)

Instructions regarding War Diaries and Intelligence Summaries are contained in F. S. Regs., Part II. and the Staff Manual respectively. Title Pages will be prepared in manuscript. Sheet 3

Place	Date	Hour	Summary of Events and Information	Remarks and references to Appendices
GUILLEMONT	13/3/17		B.G.R.S. / 20 Div. S.20 dated 13.3.17 received	[initials]
	15/3/17		59th Inf Bde. O.O. 16 dated 13.3.17 received	[initials]
	16/3/17		A.D.M.S. / 20 Div. S.21 dated 15.2.17 received	[initials]
			59th Inf Bde. O.O. 17 dated 15.3.17 received	[initials]
	17/3/17		A.A.H.S. / 20 Div. S.26 dated 16.3.17 received	[initials]
			A.A. & Q.M.G. / 20 Div. S.22 & S.29 dated 17.3.17 received	
			20 Div. Arty. Report dated 16.3.17 received	
			59th Inf Bde. N.425 dated 17.3.17 received	
			A.D.M.S. / 20 Div. O.O. Instr. dated 17.3.17 received	
	18/3/17		61st Inf Bde. O.O. 166 dated 17.3.17 received	[initials]
			59th Inf Bde. O.O. 18 dated 17.3.17 received	

Army Form C. 2118.

WAR DIARY
or
INTELLIGENCE SUMMARY

(Erase heading not required.)   Sheet 4

Place	Date	Hour	Summary of Events and Information	Remarks and references to Appendices
GUILLEMONT	18/3/17		61st Inf. Bri. Amendment to S.O. 166 dated 12.3.16 received	JWO
	19/3/17		60th Inf. Bri. D.O. 125 dated 18.3.17 received. Copy of Service Rifle Practice to temporary Musketry Course by K. Sharp. R.9.	JWO
	20/3/17		60th Inf. Bri. D.O. 126 dated 18.3.17 received. Amendment to 20th Div. Inf. Reports dated 18.3.17 received. Lieut. T. Hinchcliffe Rance assumed ack acte struck off strength.	JWO
	21/3/17		Amendment to 20th Div. Inf. Reports dated 20.3.17 received. No movements	JWO
	22/3/17		60th Inf. Bri. O.O. 183 dated 21.3.17 received A.A.H.S. S.35 dated 21.3.17 received 2nd Army	JWO
	23/3/17		No movements	JWO

Place	Date	Hour	Summary of Events and Information	Remarks and references to Appendices
GUILLEMONT	24/3/17		59th Inf. Bde. B.O. 10 dated 23.3.17 received	(A)
			60th Inf. Bde. B.O. 100 dated 23.3.17 received Rank	
			10215 Pte Stanford R.F. [On leave returns taken on]	
			102636 " Slater A. "	
			101436 " Sproston H. " [the strength]	
			21965 " Williams E. "	
			21966 " Shand Ja. "	
	25/3/17		61st Inf. Bde. O.O. 167 dated 22-3-17 and Brig. Report dated 23.3.17 received	(A)
			59th Inf. Bde. Reconnaissance and Observation Instructions dated 24.3.17 received	
			61st Inf Bde Amendments to O.O. 167 dated 24.3.17 received	
	26/3/17		61st Inf. Bde. O.O. 168 dated 25.3.17 received	(A)
			HQrs of Unit moved from GUILLEMONT to COMBLES (T.28.d.7.8 Ref Sheet Albert 62cSW)	

Army Form C. 2118.

WAR DIARY
or
INTELLIGENCE SUMMARY

(Erase heading not required.) Sheet 6.

Place	Date	Hour	Summary of Events and Information	Remarks and references to Appendices
COMBLES	26/3/17		20 Div. Dialy Report dated 26.3.17 received.	f(a)
			59 Bde. D.O. 20 dated 26.3.17 received.	
	a		T2/S.R./0139 4/Sgt Supt. Major Munroy N.J. A.S.C. (H.T.) attached to Unit died on 25-3-17 (Natural causes).	f(b)
	27/3/17		61st Inf. Bn. D.O. 189 dated 26.3.17 received.	f(c)
			59th Inf. Bn. D.O. 21 dated 27.3.17 received.	
	28/3/17		60th Inf. Bn. D.O. 192 dated 28.3.17 received.	
			61st Inf. Bn. D.O. 170 dated 28.3.17 received.	
			20th Div. O.O. 150 dated 28.3.17 received.	
			A.D.M.S. S 48 & S 49 dated 27.3.17 received. 20 Div.	f(d)
	29/3/17		20th Div. O.O. 152 dated 29.3.17 received.	
	30/3/17		59th Inf. Bn. D.O. 22 dated 30.3.17 received.	f(e)

Army Form C. 2118.

WAR DIARY
or
INTELLIGENCE SUMMARY

(*Erase heading not required.*)

Instructions regarding War Diaries and Intelligence Summaries are contained in F. S. Regs., Part II. and the Staff Manual respectively. Title Pages will be prepared in manuscript.

Month 7.

Place	Date	Hour	Summary of Events and Information	Remarks and references to Appendices
COMBLES	30/3/17		20 Aus. Div. Recip. Report dated 30-3-17 received	JLS

61st FIELD AMBULANCE.
No. ....
Date 31-3-17

J. Stoerner
Lieut Col.
O. C. 61 3 Aust. Rans.

War Diary

61st Field Ambulance – 20th Div

R.A.M.C.

April 1917

140/086

9 M 19

COMMITTEE FOR THE
MEDICAL HISTORY OF THE WAR
Date -6 JUN. 1917

Army Form C. 2118.

WAR DIARY
or
INTELLIGENCE SUMMARY

(Erase heading not required.)

Sheet 1.

Instructions regarding War Diaries and Intelligence Summaries are contained in F. S. Regs., Part II. and the Staff Manual respectively. Title Pages will be prepared in manuscript.

Place	Date	Hour	Summary of Events and Information	Remarks and references to Appendices
COMBLES	31/3		A.D.M.S. / 20 Div. S. 54 dated 31-3-17 received.	Appx. E.C.C
	1/4		59 Inf.Bde. O.O. 23 dated 31-3-17 received.	Jw
			60 Inf.Bde. O.O. 193 dated 31-3-17 received.	
			3rd.Dn. of Divis. hours from COMBLES to BUS.	
BUS	2/4		A.D.M.S. / 20 Div. S. 55 & S 56 and 1st & 20th received.	Jw
			A.D.M.S. / 20 Bus. O.O. 47 and 2.4.17 received.	
	3/4		59 Inf.Bde. O.O. 24 dated 2.4.17 received.	Jw
			60 Inf.Bde. O.O. 194 dated 3-4-17 received.	
	4/4		A.D.M.S. / 20 Div. S 58 dated 4.4.17 received.	Jw
			59th Inf.Bde. O.O. 25 dated 4.4.17 received.	
			General Staff 20th Div. G 73 dated 4.4.17 received.	
	6/4		A.D.M.S. / 20 Div. S 62 dated 4.4.17 received.	Jw

Army Form C. 2118.

WAR DIARY
or
INTELLIGENCE SUMMARY

(Erase heading not required.)

Sheet 2.

Place	Date	Hour	Summary of Events and Information	Remarks and references to Appendices
BUS	5/4/17		59 Inf. Bde. O.O. 26 dated 5.4.17 received.	Yes
			A.D.M.S. S.63 & S.64 dated 5.4.17 received. 20 Div.	
			60 Inf. Bde. O.O. 195 dated 5.4.17 received.	
			61 Inf. Bde. O.O. 172 dated 5.4.17 received.	
	6/4/17		No movements	
	7/4/17		20 Div. Disposition Report dated 6.4.17 received	
			A.D.M.S. S.66, S.69, S.71 and O.O. 78 dated 7.4.17 received. 20 Div.	yes
			35958 Pte Palmer C.J. R.A.M.C. } Apptd of three Corporals without pay	
			50446 - Stephenson J. " } from 7.4.17.	yes
			M2/103895 A/Cpl Bromley E.H. A.S.C. (M.T.) attached 61 I.Amm. appointed Acting Sgt. with pay from 7/4/17.	
			M2/116652 A/Cpl M°Shale J. A.S.C. (M.T.) attached 61 I.Amm. appointed Acting Cpl with pay from 7/4/17.	

Army Form C. 2118.

WAR DIARY
or
INTELLIGENCE SUMMARY

(Erase heading not required.)

Sheet 3.

Instructions regarding War Diaries and Intelligence Summaries are contained in F. S. Regs., Part II. and the Staff Manual respectively. Title Pages will be prepared in manuscript.

Place	Date	Hour	Summary of Events and Information	Remarks and references to Appendices
B.U.S.	7/4/17		73/02460 A/Sgt. Gill A.T. A.S.C. (H.T.) attached 61 S.Aus. Proceeded dispmt. from 28.3.17.	Jus
	8/4/17		A.D.M.S. 20 Aus. O.O. 79 dated 8.4.17 received. 60 Inf.Bde. O.O. 196 dated 8.4.17 received. T4/250282 Dvr. L.M. Watson J.S. A.S.C. (H.T.) joined unit & taken on the strength.	Jus
	9/4/17		A.D.M.S. 20 Aus. S.17 dated 8.4.17 received. 37694 Sgt. Hogarth R. R.A.M.C. rejoined unit from Base on 9.4.17. & taken on the strength.	Jus
	10/4/17		No matters	Jus
	11/4/17		Capt. J.F.M. Adams R.A.M.C. and Lieut K.L. Bates R.A.M.C. joined unit on 11-4-17 and taken on the strength. 60 Inf.Bde. O.O. 198 dated 11-4-17 received. 59 Inf.Bde. O.O. 27 dated 11-4-17 received.	Jus

WAR DIARY
or
INTELLIGENCE SUMMARY
(Erase heading not required.)

Army Form C. 2118.

Sheet 4.

Place	Date	Hour	Summary of Events and Information	Remarks and references to Appendices
B.U.S.	12/4/17		60 Inf. Bde. O.O. 192 dated 12.4.17 received.	JW
			61 Inf. Bde. O.O. 174 dated 12.4.17 received.	
			A.D.M.S. O.O. 80 dated 12.4.17 and S.84 dated 12.4.17 received. 20 Div.	
	13/4/17		59 Inf. Bde. O.O. 22 dated 12.4.17 received.	JW
			61 Inf. Bde. O.O. 175 dated 13.4.17 received.	JW
	14/4/17		A.A.M.S. C.1 and 14.4.17 received. 20 Div.	
	15/4/17		50110 L/Cpl Meacher D. Rame appears acting sgt with pay from 7/3/17. No remarks.	JW
	16/4/17		39196 Pte White C.C. Rame received wound return of the strength.	JW
	17/4/17		No remarks.	
	18/4/17		59 Inf. Bde. O.O. 30 dated 18.4.17 received.	JW
			A.A.M.S. S.93 dated 18.4.17 received. 20 Div.	JW

WAR DIARY
or
INTELLIGENCE SUMMARY

Army Form C. 2118.

Sheet 5.

Place	Date	Hour	Summary of Events and Information	Remarks and references to Appendices
B.U.S.	18/4/17		64081 Pte M: Cormack (¿ Rens transferred to 62 J.Amm. and cancel M the strength.	JHS
	19/4/17		Capt. N.J.M. Warden R.A.M.C. proceeded to temporary French change a —2154 D.A.L.	JHS
	20/4/17		A.D.M.S. S.94 dated 19.4.17 received. 20 Div.	JHS
			A.D.M.S. S.96 dated 20.4.17 received. 20 Div.	
	22/4/17		A.D.M.S. S.98 dated 22.4.17 received. 20 Div.	JHS
			59 Inf Bde. O.O. 31 dated 22.4.17 received.	
			A.D.M.S. O.O. 61 dated 22.4.17 received. 20 Div.	
	23/4/17		No remarks	JHS
	24/4/17		A.D.M.S. O.O. 62 and S.105 + S.106 dated 24.4.17 received. 20 Div.	JHS

Army Form C. 2118.

WAR DIARY
or
INTELLIGENCE SUMMARY

(Erase heading not required.)

Army Book 6.

Place	Date	Hour	Summary of Events and Information	Remarks and references to Appendices
BwS	24/4/17		61st Inf. Bde. O.O. 179 and 20-4-17 received.	JW
	25/4/17		59th Inf. Bn. O.O. 35 and 20-4-19 received	JW
	26/4/17		Capt. M. Annen Reme joined Unit taken on the strength.	JW
			36169 Lu. Lift. Channey J.G. Reme proceeded to England as candidate for a Commission. Struck off the strength.	JW
	27/4/17		A.D.M.S. O.O. 23 and S 110 & S 112 dated 27.4.17 received.	JW
			2o Dre.	
	28/4/17		59 Inf Bn. O.O. 33 dated 27-4-17 received	JW
			31456 Spt Bernard P.H. Reme injured Units on 27-4-17 & taken on the strength.	
			38098 A/L.Spl. Peace H. Reme appointed Lance Corporal with pay from 27/4/17	
			A.D.M.S. S 115 & S 117 dated 28.4.17 received.	JW
			2o Dre.	
	29/4/17		37800 Pte Shannon C.J Reme revived wounded and struck off the strength.	JW

Army Form C. 2118.

WAR DIARY
or
INTELLIGENCE SUMMARY

(Erase heading not required.)

Instructions regarding War Diaries and Intelligence Summaries are contained in F. S. Regs., Part II. and the Staff Manual respectively. Title Pages will be prepared in manuscript.

Army 7.

Place	Date	Hour	Summary of Events and Information	Remarks and references to Appendices
BuS.	29/4/17		Capt. M. Lewis Rome transferred to Medical charge of 12th K.R. Rif.C. vice Capt. B.J. Mullini to LE TREPORT. Capt. C.M. Mallard Rome. returns to Medical charge of 6th K.S.L.I. vice Capt. J.C. Turnbull to 61 F.Amb.	JML

J Bennene
Lieut. Col.
O.C. 61 F.Amb.

61st FIELD AMBULANCE.
No. RU/270
Date. 30.4.17

WAR DIARY

OF

61ST FIELD AMBULANCE — 20th Div.

MAY 1917.

Army Form C. 2118

WAR DIARY
or
INTELLIGENCE SUMMARY
(Erase heading not required.)

Sheet I.

Place	Date	Hour	Summary of Events and Information	Remarks and references to Appendices
BUS	1/5/17		No remarks	February Scale
	2/5/17		A.D.M.S. S.127 dated 2.5.17 received.	Jul
			20 Div	
			Capt. C.J. ROGERSON R.A.M.C. took over temporary command of Units during absence of Lt. Col. N.J.S. HARVEY D.S.O. on leave to U.K.	
			59th Inf. Bde. O.O.'s 34 and 35 dated 2.5.17 received.	
			60th Inf. Bde. O.O. 210 dated 2.5.17 received.	
	3/5/17		Capt. J.C. TURNBULL R.A.M.C. proceeded to temporary medical charge of 20th Div. Train A.S.C. vice Capt. C.W. WALKER R.A.M.C. evacuated sick.	Jul
	4/5/17		37694 Sgt. NORFOLK R. R.A.M.C. transferred to Office of D.D.M.S. 2nd Echelon for temporary duty on 4/5/17	Jul
			31116 Pte CLARKE T. R.A.M.C. evacuated sick on 29/4/17 + struck off the strength.	
			Capt. H.F.N. ADAMS R.A.M.C. returned to Unit from temp. med. charge of 2104 H.A.G.	

Army Form C. 2118

WAR DIARY
or
INTELLIGENCE SUMMARY
(Erase heading not required.)

Sheet 2.

Place	Date	Hour	Summary of Events and Information	Remarks and references to Appendices
BUS.	5/17	3 p.m	Adv. Qrs. of Unit moved to ROYAULCOURT.	yes
ROYAULCOURT	6/17		A.D.M.S. S130 dated 5/17 received.	yes
	7/17		No remarks	yes
	8/17		No remarks	yes
	8/17		31456 A/Cpl BENSTEAD P.W. R.A.M.C transferred to 62nd Div. and struck off the strength.	yes
	9/17		Lieut K L BATES R.A.M.C transferred to "Camp" and change of 10th Rif. Bde.	yes
	9/17		60 Inf. Bde. O.O. 211 dated 9/17 received.	
	10/17		61 Inf. Bde. O.O. 182 dated 10/17 received.	yes
			61 Inf. Bde. O.O. 182 dated 10/17 cancelled.	

Army Form C. 2118

WAR DIARY
or
INTELLIGENCE SUMMARY

(Erase heading not required.)

Sheet 3.

Instructions regarding War Diaries and Intelligence Summaries are contained in F. S. Regs., Part II. and the Staff Manual respectively. Title Pages will be prepared in manuscript.

Place	Date	Hour	Summary of Events and Information	Remarks and references to Appendices
RUYAULCOURT		11/5/17	A.D.M.S. 20 Div. O.O. 80 dated 11/5/17 received. 61st Inf.Bde. G 61/176 dated 11/5/17 received.	gds
		12/5/17	A.D.M.S. 20 Div. S 132 dated 11/5/17 received. T/106288 Pte GOBLE M A.S.C. (M.T.) evacuated sick and struck off the strength. A.D.M.S. 20 Div. S 143 dated 12/5/17 received. 61st Inf.Bde. O.O. 183 dated 12/5/17 received. 59th Inf.Bde. O.O. 36 dated 12/5/17 received.	gds
		13/5/17	A.D.M.S. 20 Div. S 144 dated 13/5/17 received. A.D.M.S. 20 Div. S 147 dated 13/5/17 received.	gds

Army Form C. 2118

WAR DIARY
or
INTELLIGENCE SUMMARY
(Erase heading not required.)

Sheet 4

Place	Date	Hour	Summary of Events and Information	Remarks and references to Appendices
RUYAULCOURT	13/5/17		O.C. 61 I.Bde. becomes responsible for collection of casualties from 2nd Bttn. of left Brigade (61st Bde.) and left Bttn. and Reserve Bttn. of Centre Brigade (59th Bde.) on re-adjustment of Div. Front. (Lantern maps & system of evacuation attached)	JW see appendix I.
	14/5/17		A.D.M.S. 20 Div. S 150 dated 14th received.	JW
	15/5/17		No matter	JW
	16/5/17		D.D.M.S. 20 Div. S 153 dated 15th received: S 154 and 16th received.	JW
	17/5/17		61 Inf. Bde. O.O. 124 dated 17.5.17 received.	JW
			A.D.M.S. 20 Div. O.O. 85 dated 17.5.17 received.	
			Major N.J.S. HARVEY D.S.O. re-assumed command of Unit.	

Army Form C. 2118

WAR DIARY
or
INTELLIGENCE SUMMARY
(Erase heading not required.)

Sheet 5

Place	Date	Hour	Summary of Events and Information	Remarks and references to Appendices
ROYAULCOURT	19/5/17		Capt. H.F.M. ADAMS RAMC proceeded to "Temp" Medical charge R.14th Bde. L.J.	JWO
	18/5/17		A.D.M.S. 20 Bde. S 162 dated 18.5.17 received.	JWO
			BM7/163973 Pte ELDER J. R.A.C. (M.T.) joined Unit and taken on the strength.	
	19/5/17		61 Inf. Bde. O.O. 185 dated 19.5.17 received.	JWO
			Recces of 61 Bde 7 Ambs. by 1/2nd E. LANCS F.Amb. completed by 6 p.m.	
		6 pm	2nd Gen. of Units moved from ROYAULCOURT to BUS.	
			Unit attached temporarily to 61st Inf. Bde.	
			20th Bde. O.O. 86 dated 19.5.17 received.	
BUS	20/5/17		A.D.M.S. 20 Bde. S 167 & S165 dated 19.5.17 received.	JWO
			A.D.M.S. 20 Bde. S 169 dated 20.5.17 received.	

Army Form C. 2118

WAR DIARY
or
INTELLIGENCE SUMMARY
(Erase heading not required.)

Instructions regarding War Diaries and Intelligence Summaries are contained in F. S. Regs., Part II. and the Staff Manual respectively. Title Pages will be prepared in manuscript.

Place	Date	Hour	Summary of Events and Information	Remarks and references to Appendices
BOS	20/5/17		Bearer Division of Unit proceeded by Ambulance car to 1^{ing} two him Dressing Stn. 5th Aust. Div, 1st ANZAC. Tent Div. remainder of Unit moves by road with 61st Inf Bde to temp A. m. BEAULENCOURT. Unit attached to 5th Aust Div. 1st ANZAC.	JW
BEAULENCOURT	5/7		Bearer + Tent Division of Unit moved Org road to Walking Wounded main Dressing Station at H.12.6.B.3. Relief of 8th Aust. Fld. Ambulance complete by 12 noon. Bearer Division of Unit relieves 8th Aust 3^{Amb}. in Rifle Butts of Aust. front. (Sketch map of system of evacuation attached) Beauville Advancing Bearer at H.26.a.5.d. taken over from 8th Aust 3^{Amb}. by 12 noon. 61st Inf Bde. O.O. 126 dated 20-5-17 received.	JW see Appendix II.

WAR DIARY
INTELLIGENCE SUMMARY

Army Form C. 2118

Sheet 7

Place	Date	Hour	Summary of Events and Information	Remarks and references to Appendices
H.12.b.3.3.	22/5/17		5th Aust. Div. A.A.M.C. 33 dated 22nd received.	JWO
			Lt/pl. H.F.M. ADAMS Rame returns to Units from Temp? hrs.	
			charge of 71th Aus. L.J.	
			44372 Pte LOCKIE T. Rame } Evacuees arrived & struck off the	
			31862 - O'NEILL P. } strength.	
			R.O.M.S. S.112 dated 21.5.17 received.	
			35958 a/2/6pl PALMER E.T. Rame allowed to 4th Rath. t/Borgen. Pay	
			to cost from 10/5/17 (Auth. Rampscorps Orders 14 dr. 10/5/17).	
	23/5/17		No remarks.	JWO
	24/5/17		Owing to repeated and intentional shelling of camp, Units is moved	JWO
			from H.12.c.3.3 to tents at H.16.a.9.2.	
			About 17 shells from high velocity gun were fired at camp during	
			night of 23/24th.	

Army Form C. 2118

WAR DIARY
or
INTELLIGENCE SUMMARY
(Erase heading not required.)

Sheet 2.

Instructions regarding War Diaries and Intelligence Summaries are contained in F. S. Regs., Part II. and the Staff Manual respectively. Title Pages will be prepared in manuscript.

Place	Date	Hour	Summary of Events and Information	Remarks and references to Appendices
H.16.a.9.2.	24/5/17		A.D.M.S. / 20 Div. S.124 dated 24.5.17 received.	J.21
	25/5/17		A.D.M.S. / Flanders Div. U16/50 dated 24.5.17 received.	J.20
			A.D.M.S. / Flanders Div. R.A.M.C. 3d March 24.5.17 received.	
			A.D.M.S. / 20 Div. S.191 dated 25.5.17 received.	
			A.D.M.S. / 20 Bn. S.192 dated 25.5.17 received.	
	26/5/17		34936 Pte BRUCE W.F. R.A.M.C. evacuated sick and struck off the strength.	J.W
			9 And C attached to 20th Div.	
	27/5/17		No. numbers.	J.20
	28/5/17		60 Sept Bn. O.O. 217 dated 27.5.17 received.	J.M
			61 " " 187 " " "	

WAR DIARY
or
INTELLIGENCE SUMMARY

Army Form C. 2118

(Erase heading not required.)

Place	Date	Hour	Summary of Events and Information	Remarks and references to Appendices
H.Q.61 F.A.	29/5/17		Lieut. K.L. BATES R.A.M.C. returns to Unit from Temp'y Duty charge of 10th Rif. Bde.	jud
	30/5/17		Capt. J.S. CRAWFORD R.A.M.C. evacuated sick. 61 Inf. Bde. O.O. 188 dated 29.5.17 received.	jud
			Strength of Unit at end of May 1917 : Officers 10 Other Ranks 226.	
			All map references are to Sheet 57.c. 1/40000.	

J. Brunney
Lieut. Col.
O.C. 61 F.Amb.

61ST FIELD AMBULANCE.
R5/253
31-5-17

61ST FIELD AMBULANCE.
No. R6/221
Date 30-6-17

14d/2230

War Diary
of
61st Field Ambulance France.

June 1917.

COMMITTEE FOR THE
MEDICAL HISTORY OF THE WAR
Date -7 AUG. 1917

Army Form C. 2118

WAR DIARY
or
INTELLIGENCE SUMMARY

(Erase heading not required.)

Sheet 1

Instructions regarding War Diaries and Intelligence Summaries are contained in F.S. Regs., Part II. and the Staff Manual respectively. Title Pages will be prepared in manuscript.

Place	Date	Hour	Summary of Events and Information	Remarks and references to Appendices
Beugnatre	1st.		61st. Inf. Bde. G 4o 61/233 dated 1-6-17 received.	[sig]
	2nd.		M1/06288 Pte Geble W. A.S.C.(M.T.) rejoined Unit from C.C.S. and taken on the strength.	[sig]
			31862 Pte. O'Neill P.R.A.M.C. rejoined Unit from C.C.S. and taken on the strength.	
			60th. Inf. Bde. 0.0.219 dated 1-6-17 received.	
	3rd.		A.D.M.S. 20th. Division S.208 & 209 received.	[sig]
			Capt. H.F.W. Adams R.A.M.C. proceeded to temporary Medical charge of 12th. R.B.	
			A.D.M.S. 20th. Division S.210 dated 3-6-17 received.	
			A.D.M.S. 20th. Division S.211 dated 3-6-17 received.	
	4th.		30702 Pte. Parsons H. R.A.M.C. and 26654 Pte. Nolan P. R.A.M.C. evacuated wounded and struck off the strength.	[sig]
	5th.		A.D.M.S. 20th. Division S.212 and S.213 dated 4th. and 5th. respectively received.	[sig]
	6th.		27372 Sergt. Andersen A. R.A.M.C. wounded (returned to duty).	[sig]
	7th.		No remarks.	[sig]
	8th.		No remarks.	
	9th.		No remarks.	
	10th.		No remarks.	
	11th.		A.D.M.S. 20th. Division S. 215 dated 11-6-17 received.	[sig]
	12th.		60th. Inf. Bde. 0.0.221 dated 12-6-17 received.	[sig]

Army Form C. 2118

WAR DIARY
or
INTELLIGENCE SUMMARY

(Erase heading not required.)

Sheet 2.

Instructions regarding War Diaries and Intelligence Summaries are contained in F.S. Regs., Part II. and the Staff Manual respectively. Title Pages will be prepared in manuscript.

Place	Date	Hour	Summary of Events and Information	Remarks and references to Appendices
BEUGNATRE	12th.		A.D.M.S. 20th. Division S.217 dated 11-6-17 received.	
			1st. Lieut. P.H.Zinkhan and 1st. Lieut. W.B.Sappington United States Medical Corps reported their arrival and taken on the strength.	
	13th.		38983 Pte. Wedekind E. R.A.M.C. evacuated sick and struck off the strength.	
	14th.		A.D.M.S. 20th. Division S.219 dated 14-6-17.	
			" " " S.220 dated 14-6-17.	
	15th.		34716 Pte. Bardsley J.E. R.A.M.C. evacuated sick on 15th. and struck off the strength.	
	16th.		No remarks.	
	17th.		Cases from A.D.S. Right Sector cease to be evacuated through Main Dressing Station : cases evacuated direct from A.D.S. to H.Q. of Field Ambulance at H.16.d.9.2.	
			A.D.M.S. 20th. Division S.227 dated 16-6-17 received.	
	18th.		Ambulance Car Leading Post established at C.26.d.3.6. Cases evacuated from A.D.S. to Leading Post by Horsed Ambulance or Hand Carriage : thence to Field Ambulance H.Q. at H.16.d.9.2. by Motor Ambulance.	
	19th.		A.D.M.S. 20th. Division S.232 received.	
			" " " S.234 and S.235 dated 19-6-17 received.	
	20th.		61st. Inf. Bde. O.O.192 dated 20-6-17 received.	
			A.D.M.S. 20th. Division S.289 dated 20-6-17 received.	

Army Form C. 2118

WAR DIARY
or
INTELLIGENCE SUMMARY
(Erase heading not required.)

Sheet 3.

Instructions regarding War Diaries and Intelligence Summaries are contained in F. S. Regs., Part II. and the Staff Manual, respectively. Title Pages will be prepared in manuscript.

Place	Date	Hour	Summary of Events and Information	Remarks and references to Appendices
Beugnatre.	21st.		No remarks.	JW
	22nd.		No remarks.	JW
	23rd.		New Dug-out at Adv. Dressing Station Completed. (Sketch plan attached).	JW
			A.D.M.S. 20th. Division O.O.87 dated 23-6-17 received.	
			60th. Inf. Bde. O.O.222 dated 23-6-17 received.	
			A.D.M.S. 20th. Division S.248 dated 23-6-17 received.	
			38985 Pte. Wedekind E. R.A.M.C. returned to Unit from C.C.S. and taken on the strength.	JW
	24th.		A.D.M.S. 20th. Division S.251 dated 24-6-17 received.	JW
	25th.		Field Ambulance Bearers, Advanced Dressing Station, and Motor Ambulance Loading Post relieved by 2/1st. West Riding Field Ambulance.	JW
	26th.		A.D.M.S. 20th. Division O.O.85 dated 26-6-17 received.	
			" " " S.256 dated 26-6-17 received.	
			Unit moves by road from H.16.d.9.2. to Camp at G.9.a.7.7. (Ref. Map Sheet 57c 1/40000.)	
			Camp at H.16.d.9.2. handed over to 2/1st. West Riding Field Ambulance.	JW
	27th.		60th. Inf. Bde. G3479/83 dated 26-6-17 received.	
			A.D.M.S. 20th. Division S. 258 dated 27-6-17 received.	
			60th. Inf. Bde. O.O.224 dated 27-6-17 received.	
	28th.		A.D.M.S. 20th. Division S.258 dated 27-6-17 received.	JW

1875. Wt. W593/826 1,000,000 4/15 J.B.C. & A. A.D.S.S./Forms/C. 2118.

Army Form C. 2118

WAR DIARY
or
INTELLIGENCE SUMMARY

(Erase heading not required.)

Sheet 4.

Place	Date	Hour	Summary of Events and Information	Remarks and references to Appendices
ACHIET-le-GRAND.	29th.		No remarks.	
			Capt. J.P. QUINN R.A.M.C. was awarded the MILITARY CROSS in the "Birthday Honours" Gazette, June, 1917.	
			All Map References are to Sheet 57c 1/40,000.	
			Strength of Unit at end of June 1917	
			Officers 11 O.R. R.A.M.C. 174 " A.S.C.(H.T.) 36 " A.S.C.(M.T.) 15 Total. 236	

30th. June 1917.

J. Brown
Lieutenant Colonel
O.C. 61st. Field Ambulance.

APPENDIX I.   SHEET 57c. 1/40,000.

+ REGTL. AID. POST.
⊕ F.AMB. ADV. DRESSING STATION.
⊕ AMBULANCE LOADING POST.
--→--- Evacuation from R.A.P. to A.D.S.
----- Evacuation from A.D.S. to June 18th.
- - - - Evacuation from June 18th.
(a) Arrived 17/7.
(b) Evacuated 18/7.

APPENDIX II.

PLAN of ADV. DRESSING STATION   C.29.c.5.9.

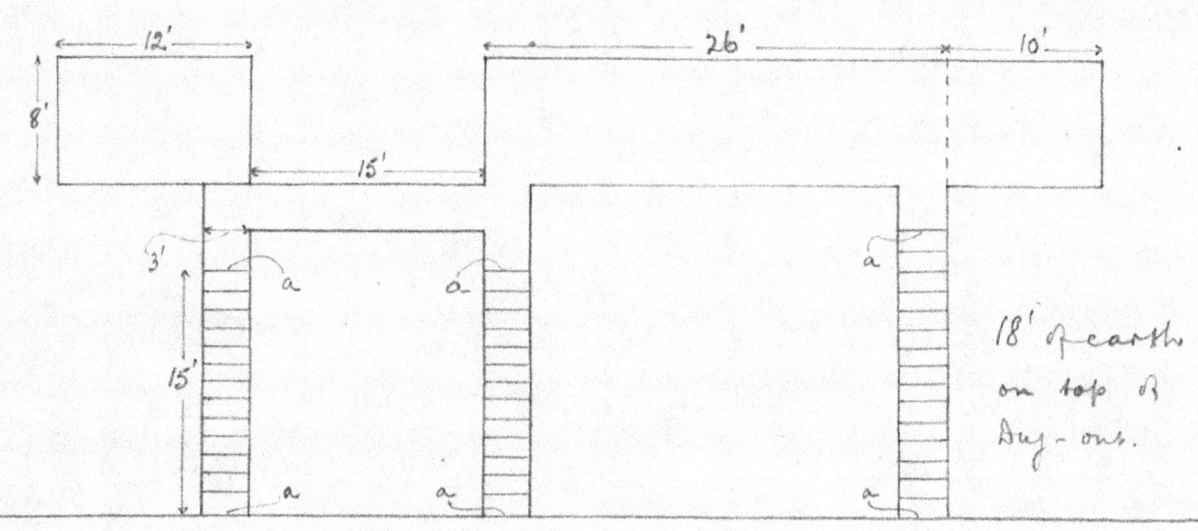

18' of earth on top of Dug-outs.

ROAD.

(a) Gas proof blankets.

Accommodation for 20 stretcher cases.

War Diary

of

61st Field Ambulance

July 1917.

B.E.F.

SUMMARY OF MEDICAL WAR DIARIES FOR

61st F.A. 20th Divn. 14th Corps, 5th Army.
from 21.7.17.

WESTERN FRONT. July- Sept. 1917.

O.C. Lt. Col. V.S. Harvey.

SUMMARISED UNDER THE FOLLOWING HEADINGS.

Phase "D" 1. Passchendaele Operations July- Nov. 1917.
(a) Operations commencing 1st July 1917.

B.E.F. 1.

61st F.A. 20th Divn. 14th Corps, 5th Army.   WESTERN FRONT.
O.C. Lt. Col. V.S. Harvey.   July-Aug. '17.

Phase "D" 1. Passchendaele Operations July-Nov. 1917.
(a) Operations commencing 1/7/17.

1917.	Headquarters.	At E.18.b.2.8. (27)
July 21st.	Moves and Transfer.	Unit transferred with 20th Divn. from 4th Corps, 4th Army to 14th Corps 5th Army. and arrived at E.18.b.2.8. (27)
25th.	Moves:Det.	1 T.S.D. to 46th C.C.S. for duty.
31st.	Moves:	To F.10.c.8.6. (27.)

B.E.F. 1.

61st F.A. 20th Divn. 14th Corps, 5th Army.   WESTERN FRONT
O.C. Lt. Col. V.S. Harvey.   July-Aug. '1

Phase "D" 1. Passchendaele Operations July-Nov. 1917.
(a) Operations commencing 1/7/17.

1917.	Headquarters. At E.18.b.2.8. (27)
July 21st.	Moves and Transfer. Unit transferred with 20th Divn. from 4th Corps, 4th Army to 14th Corps 5th Army. and arrived at E.18.b.2.8. (27)
25th.	Moves:Det. 1 T.S.D. to 46th C.C.S. for duty.
31st.	Moves: To F.10.c.8.6. (27.)

Army Form C. 2118.

WAR DIARY
or
INTELLIGENCE SUMMARY.
(Erase heading not required.) Sheet 1.

Instructions regarding War Diaries and Intelligence Summaries are contained in F.S. Regs., Part II. and the Staff Manual respectively. Title pages will be prepared in manuscript.

Place	Date	Hour	Summary of Events and Information	Remarks and references to Appendices
ACHIET-LE-GRAND.	30th		Field Ambulance moves by rail to CANAPLES, Transport proceeding by road.	
CANAPLES	1st		37694 Sergt. WORFOLK R. R.A.M.C. transferred to Directorate of D.G.M.S. 2nd Echelon on 26/6/17 and struck off the strength.	
	2nd		No remarks	
	3rd		No remarks	
	4th		77661 Pte. WALDOCK H. R.A.M.C.) 74355 " ASHPLANT F. ") 47463 " MORTLOCK G.W. ") joined the Unit and taken on the strength. 10209 " POLLEY W.S. ") 70052 " STAGG G.F. ")	
	5th		No remarks	
	6th		39176 Pte. WRIGHT F.M. R.A.M.C. appointed acting Lance Corporal without pay.	
	7th		A.D.M.S. 20th Division No.S.261 dated 7/7/17 received.	
	8th		No remarks	
	9th		No remarks	
	10th		No remarks	
	11th		64188 Pte. WELLS J. R.A.M.C.) 73022 " WILSON T. ") joined the Unit and taken on the strength. 64827 " WRIGHT W. ") 73264 " WRIGHT W. ")	
	12th		No remarks.	

Army Form C. 2118.

WAR DIARY
or
INTELLIGENCE SUMMARY.
(Erase heading not required.) Sheet 2.

Instructions regarding War Diaries and Intelligence Summaries are contained in F.S. Regs., Part II. and the Staff Manual respectively. Title pages will be prepared in manuscript.

Place	Date	Hour	Summary of Events and Information	Remarks and references to Appendices
CANAPLES	13th		50291 Pte. BRIGHT R.R. R.A.M.C. transferred to H.Q. 20th Division and struck off the strength.	
			52933 Pte. TOES H. R.A.M.C. transferred to Unit from H.Q. 20th Division and taken on the strength.	
	14th		A.D.M.S. 20th Division No. S.264 dated 12/7/17 received.	
	15th		33421 Pte. BEDFORD H. R.A.M.C. evacuated sick and struck off the strength.	
	16th		No remarks.	
	17th		A.D.M.S. 20th Division No. S-267 dated 17/7/17 received.	
	18th		A.D.M.S. 20th Division Nos. M.7/54 & 55 and S.268 dated 18/7/17 received.	
			60 Inf. Bde. O.O.225 dated 18/7/17 received.	
	19th		89853 Pte. HEY F.J. R.A.M.C. evacuated sick and struck off the strength	
			35916 Cpl. RADBURN G. R.A.M.C. promoted acting Sergt. with pay from 6/7/17.	
			35958 Pte. PALMER C.J. R.A.M.C. promoted acting Corpl. with pay from 6/7/17.	
	20th		No remarks.	
	21st		Unit, with transport, proceeds by road via FIEFFES, MONTRELET, and CANDAS to DOULLENS South Station and entrains for HOPOUTRE.	
	22nd		Unit arrives at HOPOUTRE near POPERINGHE, detrains, and proceeds by road to camp at E.18.b.2.8. near PROVEN.	

Army Form C. 2118.

WAR DIARY
or
INTELLIGENCE SUMMARY. Sheet 3.
(Erase heading not required.)

Place	Date	Hour	Summary of Events and Information	Remarks and references to Appendices
PROVEN	23rd		A.D.M.S. 20th Division O.O.89 dated 23/7/17 received.	JW
	24th		A.D.M.S. 20th Division M.20/221 dated 24/7/17 received.	JW
			A.D.M.S. 20th Division No.S.273 dated 24/7/17 received.	
			60 Inf. Bde. No.G.3794 dated 24/7/17 received.	JW
	25th		One Tent Sub-division of Unit proceeds to 46 C.C.S. for duty.	
			A.D.M.S. 20th Division Nos. S.272, S.275, S.276 and S.277 dated 25/7/17 received.	
			60 Inf. Bde. O.O.226 dated 25/7/17 received.	
			T.4/250252 Stf.Sergt.Major WATSON J.S. A.S.C. (H.T.) evacuated to A.S.C. Base Depot by order of A.D.M.S. 20th Division and struck off the strength.	JW
	26th		A.D.M.S. 20th Division Nos. S.274, S.280, S.283, and M.7/97 dated 26/7/17 received.	
			60 Inf. Bde. No.B.M.15 dated 26/7/17 received.	JW
	27th		A.D.M.S. 20th Division Nos. S.288 and M.7/104 dated 27/7/17 received.	JW
	28th		A.D.M.S. 20th Division Nos. S.290, S.291, and S.303 dated 28/7/17 received.	JW
	29th		60 Inf. Bde. No. G.3882/3904 and amendment to O.O.226 dated 29/7/17 received.	JW
			75960 Pte. Janes W. R.A.M.C. appointed acting Lance Corporal without pay	

Army Form C. 2118.

WAR DIARY
or
INTELLIGENCE SUMMARY.

Sheet 4.

(Erase heading not required.)

Place	Date	Hour	Summary of Events and Information	Remarks and references to Appendices
PROVEN	30th		Capt. H.F.W.ADAMS R.A.M.C. transferred to Medical charge of 12th R.IF. BDE. and struck off the strength.	
			Capt. J.C.TURNBULL R.A.M.C. transferred to Medical charge of 20th Div. Train A.S.C. and struck off the strength.	
			Lieut. K.L.BATES R.A.M.C. transferred to Medical charge of 6th K.S.L.I. and struck off the strength.	
			A.D.M.S. 20th Division Nos. S.313 and M.7/123 dated 30/7/17 received.	
			80 Inf.Bde. O.O.227 dated 30/7/17 received.	
			**************************	
			During the period July 1st to 21st, Unit was in Rest Area; Programme of Training in Field Ambulance duties carried out.	
			**************************	
			All map references are to Sheet 27 1/40,000.	
			Strength of Unit at end of July 1917	
			Officers 8.	
			Other ranks R.A.M.C. 180.	
			A.S.C. (H.T) 35.	
			A.S.C. (M.T) 15.	
			238.	

Lieut.Col.
O.C.61st Field Amb.

61st
FIELD
AMBULANCE.
No. R7/231
Date 31.7.17.

Aug 1917 Vol 23

140/234

War Diary
of
61st Field Ambulance

August 1917.

COMMITTEE FOR THE
MEDICAL HISTORY OF THE WAR
Date -1 OCT. 1917

B.E.F.

SUMMARY OF MEDICAL WAR DIARIES FOR

61st F.A. 20th Divn. 14th Corps, 5th Army.
from 21.7.17.

WESTERN FRONT. July- Sept. 1917.

O.C. Lt. Col. V.S. Harvey.

SUMMARISED UNDER THE FOLLOWING HEADINGS.

Phase "D" 1. Passchendaele Operations July- Nov. 1917.
(a) Operations commencing 1st July 1917.

Aug. 5th.	"	To B.2.1.a.3.1.
12th.		Casualties R.A.M.C. 0 and 1 D. of W. 0 and 1 wounded.
16th.		Operations: Battle of Langemarck.

Assistance. 180 Divn. Str. Bearer attached to B.Ds. to assist evacuation.

Map Attached.

Casualties R.A.M.C. 0 and 1 killed   0 and 1 D. of W. 0 and 1 wounded.

17th   0 and 2 wounded   0 and 4 wounded (Gas)

Military Situation: Medical Arrangements: Relief of forward posts by 38th Divn. completed. All Bearers and B.D. rejoin their original units.

19th.   Casualties R.A.M.C.   0 and 1 wounded.

Moves: To Singapore Camp X.29.c.6.3. (19)

30th.   Decorations.   Pte. Bairston awarded the M.M.

Aug. 5th.	"	To B.2.1.a.3.1.
12th.		Casualties R.A.M.C. 0 and 1 D. of W. 0 and 1 wounded.
16th.		Operations: Battle of Langemarck.

Assistance. 180 Divn. Str. Bearer attached to B.Ds. to assist evacuation.

Map Attached.

Casualties R.A.M.C. 0 and 1 killed 0 and 1 D. of W. 0 and 1 wounded.

17th   0 and 2 wounded 0 and 4 wounded (Gas)

Military Situation: Medical Arrangements: Relief of forward posts by 38th Divn. completed. All Bearers and B.D. rejoin their original units.

19th.   Casualties R.A.M.C. 0 and 1 wounded.

Moves: To Singapore Camp X.29.c.6.3. (19)

30th.   Decorations. Pte.Bairston awarded the M.M.

Army Form C. 2118.

WAR DIARY
or
INTELLIGENCE SUMMARY
Sheet 1.

(Erase heading not required.)

Instructions regarding War Diaries and Intelligence Summaries are contained in F. S. Regs., Part II. and the Staff Manual respectively. Title pages will be prepared in manuscript.

Place	Date	Hour	Summary of Events and Information	Remarks and references to Appendices
PROVEN	31st		A.D.M.S. No. S.319 dated 30-7-17 received.	
	1st		Unit moves to camp at F.10.c.8.6.	
	2nd		A.D.M.S. No. S.314 dated 30-7-17 received.	
			No remarks.	
	3rd		60 Infantry Brigade O.O.228 dated 2-8-17 received	
			A.D.M.S. 20th Division O.O.90 dated 3-8-17 and S.329 dated 3-8-17 received.	
	4th		60 Infantry Brigade O.O.230 dated 4-8-17 received.	
	5th		77882 Pte. BROOK H. R.A.M.C.) Evacuated sick and struck off the strength.	
			61848 Pte. McInerney F. R.A.M.C.)	
PELLISSIER FARM.			Unit moves to camp at B.21.a.3.1.	
			Bearer Divisions of 60 and 62 Field Ambulances attached to Unit.	
			Relief of 38th Division bearers and Relay Posts and Advanced Dressing Stations completed.	
	6th		No remarks	
	7th		A.D.M.S. 20th Division S.346 dated 7-8-17 received.	
	8th		No remarks	
	9th		A.D.M.S. 20th Division S.350 dated 9-8-17 received.	
			1st/Lieut. W.T.FENKER U.S.M.C. joins Unit and is taken on strength.	

Army Form C. 2118.

WAR DIARY
or
INTELLIGENCE=SUMMARY.

Sheet 2.

(Erase heading not required.)

Instructions regarding War Diaries and Intelligence Summaries are contained in F. S. Regs., Part II. and the Staff Manual respectively. Title pages will be prepared in manuscript.

Place	Date	Hour	Summary of Events and Information	Remarks and references to Appendices
PELLISSIER FARM.	9th		A.D.M.S. 20th Division S.354 dated 9-8-17 received.	
	10th		A.D.M.S. 20th Division S.360 dated 10-8-17 received.	
			A.D.M.S. 20th Division S.358 dated 10-8-17 received.	
	11th		A.D.M.S. 20th Division S.363 dated 11-8-17 received.	
			1st/Lieut W.T.FENKER U.S.M.C. transferred to 38th Division and struck off the strength.	
			Capt. R.B.WALLACE B.S.O.,M.C., R.A.M.C. joins unit and is taken on the strength.	
	12th		A.D.M.S. 20th Division S.366, S.367, S.368, and S.369 dated 12-8-17 received.	
			A.D.M.S. 20th Division S.373 dated 12-8-17 received.	
			102748 Pte. NEEDHAM L. R.A.M.C. } joined Unit and taken on the strength.	
			29170 Pte. NEWBOLD F.H. R.A.M.C. }	
			37937 Pte. NASH E.S.E. R.A.M.C. evacuated wounded and struck off the strength.	
			T2/11653 Dvr. SWIFT J. A.S.C. (H.T) died of wounds. Struck off the strength.	
	13th		A.D.M.S. 20th Division S.374 dated 13-8-17 received.	
			A.D.M.S. 20th Division S.379 and S.383 dated 13-8-17 received.	
	14th		61st Infantry Brigade 00.206 dated 14th received.	
			60th Infantry Brigade 00.234 dated 14-8-17 received.	
			A.D.M.S. 20th Division S.387 and S.389 dated 14-8-17 received.	

Army Form C. 2118.

WAR DIARY Sheet 3.
or
INTELLIGENCE SUMMARY.

(Erase heading not required.)

Instructions regarding War Diaries and Intelligence Summaries are contained in F.S. Regs., Part II. and the Staff Manual respectively. Title pages will be prepared in manuscript.

Place	Date	Hour	Summary of Events and Information	Remarks and references to Appendices
PELLISSIER FARM.	14th		60 Infantry Brigade O.O.234 and O.O.235 dated 14-8-17 received.	gto
	15th		A.D.M.S. 20th Division S.390 and S.394 dated 15-8-17 received.	gto
	16th		BATTLE OF LANGEMARCK	gto
			Positions of Advanced Dressing Stations, Relay Posts and Reg't'l Aid Posts and Scheme of Evacuation from R.A.P's to A.D.S. are shown on sketch map attached. (See appendix 1.) GALLWITZ FARM Forward A.D.S. had to be evacuated during the day owing to continued heavy shelling.	
			180 Divisional Stretcher Bearers attached to Bearer Divisions to assist in the work of evacuation	
			10209 Pte. POLLEY W.S. R.A.M.C. killed in action. Struck off the strength.	
			73513 Pte. VICKERS J.C. R.A.M.C. evacuated wounded. " " "	
			73022 Pte. WILSON T. R.A.M.C.) (Died of wounds at 47 C.C.S. on 17-8-17.)	
			37953 " OWEN J.M. ") evacuated wounded and struck off the strength.	
			59627 " NORRIE J.M. ")	
			81658 " EDWARD J. ")	
			1st/Lieut W.F.SAPPINGTON U.S.M.C. wounded (at duty)	
	17th		A.D.M.S. 20th Division O.O.91 dated 17-8-17 received.	gto
			A.D.M.S. 20th Division S.400 and S.401 dated 17-8-17 received.	
			36056 Sergt. THORNHILL A.L. wounded (at duty)	
			78388 Pte. BAREHAM T.H. " " "	
			73648 Pte. BANNISTER H. R.A.M.C. wounded (gas) (at duty)	

Army Form C. 2118.

WAR DIARY
or
INTELLIGENCE SUMMARY.

Sheet 4.

(Erase heading not required.)

Instructions regarding War Diaries and Intelligence Summaries are contained in F. S. Regs., Part II. and the Staff Manual respectively. Title pages will be prepared in manuscript.

Place	Date	Hour	Summary of Events and Information	Remarks and references to Appendices
PELLISSIER FARM.	17th		39785 Pte. HEDGER G.A. R.A.M.C.) 37971 " PHILLIPS W. " ") wounded (gas) (at duty) 50107 " SMITH S. " ")	JW
			8241 Pte. GREEN R.L. R.A.M.C. evacuated sick and struck off the strength.	JW
	18th	6 p.m.	60 Infantry Brigade O.O. 241 dated 18-7-18 received.	
		6 p.m.	Relief of Bearers, Forward Posts and Advanced Dressing Stations by 38th Division completed. Bearer Divisions 60 and 62 Field Ambulances rejoin their respective Units	
	19th		Capt. R.B.WALLACE D.S.O.,M.C., R.A.M.C. transferred to 62 Field Amb. and struck off the strength.	JW
			Capt. C.M.STALLARD R.A.M.C. joins Unit and taken on the strength.	
			73648 Pte. BANNISTER H. R.A.M.C.) 35966 Pte. SCOTT L. " ") evacuated sick and struck off the strength.	
			31770 Pte. PASCOE V. R.A.M.C. evacuated wounded and struck off the strength.	
			Unit moves to Reserve Area entraining at ELVERDINGHE, detraining at PROVEN and marching to SINGAPORE CAMP near ST.SIXTE (X.29.c.6.3. Sheet 19)	JW
	20th		A.D.M.S. 20th Division S.402 and S.403 dated 20-8-17 received.	
			73578 Pte. BELL G. R.A.M.C. evacuated sick and struck off the strength.	JW
			M.4/060892 Pte. WALLIS C. A.S.C. (M.T) joined Unit and taken on the strength.	
	21st		No remarks	

Army Form C. 2118.

WAR DIARY

Sheet 5.

INTELLIGENCE SUMMARY.

(Erase heading not required.)

Place	Date	Hour	Summary of Events and Information	Remarks and references to Appendices
SINGAPORE CAMP.	22nd		T.4/268748 Dvr. WELFORD R. A.S.C. (H.T.) joined Unit and taken on the strength.	pro
	23rd		60 Infantry Brigade O.O.242 dated 23-8-17 received.	pro
			A.D.M.S. 20th Division S.404 dated 23-8-17 received.	
			11873 Pte. BYRNE W. R.A.M.C.) 11457 " BEECH A. ") 1380 " CROSS F. ") joined Unit and taken on the strength. 51426 " GODBY W. ") 53541 " HUNTER R.B. ") 2616 " MARTIN B.J. ") 76023 " MOORE G.E. ")	
			35858 Pte. PALMER J.W. R.A.M.C. evacuated sick and struck off the strength.	pro
	24th		No remarks	
	25th		39785 Pte. HEDGER G.A. R.A.M.C.) evacuated sick and struck off the strength. 50107 " SMITH S. ")	pro
	26th		No remarks	pro
	27th		60 Infantry Brigade O.O.243 dated 27-8-17 received.	pro
	28th		52933 Pte. TOES H. R.A.M.C evacuated sick and struck off the strength.	pro
	29th		No remarks.	pro
	30th		73416 Pte. BAIRSTOW P. R.A.M.C. awarded the Military Medal	pro

Army Form C. 2118.

WAR DIARY
or
INTELLIGENCE SUMMARY.

Sheet 6.

(Erase heading not required.)

Place	Date	Hour	Summary of Events and Information	Remarks and references to Appendices
SINGAPORE CAMP.	31st		Strength of Unit at end of August 1917 :- Officers 9 O.R. R.A.M.C. 171 O.R. A.S.C.(H.T) 34 O.R. A.S.C.(M.T) 13 Total 227 (signature) Lieut.Col., O.C. 61 Field Ambulance.	

Hops. detached and placed with

Summary: War Diary

of

61st Field Ambulance

September 1917

COMMITTEE FOR THE
MEDICAL HISTORY OF THE WAR
Date -5 NOV. 1917

B.E.F.

61st F.A. 20th Divn. 14th Corps, 5th Army.   WESTERN FRONT.
O.C. Lt. Col. V.S. Harvey.   Aug.-Sept.'17

Phase "D" 1 (Cont.)

1917.
Sept. 9th.   Moves: To A.18.a.8.6.
10th.   Moves: Medical Arrangements: To Canada Farm. Taking over part 14th C.M.D.S. from 131st Field Ambulance 38th Divn.
11th.   Casualties U.S.M.C. 1 and 0 wounded.
20th.   Casualties R.A.M.C. 0 and 11 wounded 0 and 1 Died of W.
21st.   do.   0 " 2   "
22nd.   do.   0 " 2   "
23rd.   do.   0 " 1   "
28th.   do.   0 " 4   "   0 and 1 A.S.C. W.

61st F.A. 20th Divn. 14th Corps, 5th Army.   WESTERN FRONT.
O.C. Lt. Col. V.S. Harvey.   Aug.-Sept.'17

Phase "D" 1 (Cont.)

1917.
Sept. 9th.   Moves: To A.18.a.8.6.
10th.   Moves: Medical Arrangements: To Canada Farm. Taking over part 14th C.M.D.S. from 131st Field Ambulance 38th Divn.
11th.   Casualties U.S.M.C. 1 and 0 wounded.
20th.   Casualties R.A.M.C. 0 and 11 wounded 0 and 1 Died of W.
21st.   do.   0 " 2   "
22nd.   do.   0 " 2   "
23rd.   do.   0 " 1   "
28th.   do.   0 " 4   "   0 and 1 A.S.C. W.

Army Form C. 2118.

WAR DIARY
or
INTELLIGENCE SUMMARY.
Sheet 1.

(Erase heading not required.)

Instructions regarding War Diaries and Intelligence Summaries are contained in F. S. Regs., Part II. and the Staff Manual respectively. Title pages will be prepared in manuscript.

Place	Date	Hour	Summary of Events and Information	Remarks and references to Appendices
SINGAPORE CAMP	31st		60 Infantry Brigade O.O.244 dated 31-8-17 received.	
	1st		72362 Pte WOODLEY H.G. R.A.M.C. joined Unit and taken on the strength.	
	2nd		A.D.M.S. 20th Division No. S.417 dated 2-9-17 received.	
	3rd		A.D.M.S. 20th Division No. S.418 dated 1-9-17 received.	
			A.D.M.S. 20th Division No. S.421 dated 3-9-17 received.	
	4th		A.D.M.S. 20th Division No. O.O.92 dated 4-9-17 received.	
			A.D.M.S. 20th Division No. S.423 dated 4-9-17 received.	
			40460 Pte. ARCHBOLD J.H. D.L.I.)	
			21/528 Pte. BROWN W. ")	
			42196 Pte. DOLPHIN E. ") Permanent Base men.	
			277215 Pte. GRANGER W. ") Joined Unit to replace A.S.C. Batmen	
			47820 Pte. HAWTHORNE R.J. ") on 4-9-17 and taken on the strength.	
			205145 Pte. HELDEN R. ")	
			201478 Pte. LONGSTAFFE A. ")	
			251863 Pte. SHAW J. ")	
			32653 Pte. SLEEP W. ")	
			52261 Pte. WALTERS W. ")	
	5th		T.2/018135 Dvr. CRAWFORD J.I. A.S.C. (H.T))	
			T.3/024133 Dvr. PICKETT W. ")	
			T.4/263748 Dvr. WELFORD R. ") Transferred to A.S.C.(H.T.) Base Depot	
			T.1/ 3878 Dvr. SMITH J.H. ") and struck off the strength.	
			T.3/024028 Dvr. GRIFFITHS F. ")	
			T.3/033926 Dvr. HOLLOWAY R. ")	
			T.3/033997 Dvr. LLOYD E. ")	

Army Form C. 2118.

WAR DIARY
or
INTELLIGENCE SUMMARY. Sheet 2.
(Erase heading not required.)

Place	Date	Hour	Summary of Events and Information	Remarks and references to Appendices
SINGAPORE CAMP.	6th		60 Infantry Brigade O.O. 245 dated 6-9-17 received.	fw
			A.D.M.S. 20th Division No. S.426 dated 6-9-17 received.	
			60 Infantry Brigade G.4422/3 dated 6-9-17 received.	fw
			Lieut. & Quartermaster R.MOFFAT R.A.M.C. evacuated to R.A.M.C. Base Depot and struck off the strength.	fw
	7th			
	8th		No remarks.	
	9th		60 Infantry Brigade Table "C" for O.O. 245 received.	
			T.3/027678 Dvr. COOPER H. A.S.C. (H.T)) Transferred to A.S.C. (H.T) Base Depot	
			T.3/024024 Dvr. RANDLES R. " ") and struck off the strength.	
			1768 Pte. SLATOR J. R.A.M.C. evacuated sick and struck off the strength.	
			T/Lieut. W.A.WILLIAMS U.S.M.C. joined Unit and taken on the strength.	
			T/343529 S.S.M. GOLTON S.R. A.S.C. (H.T) joined Unit and taken on the strength.	
NUTZA FARM			Unit moves to camp at A.18.a.8.6. XIV	
CANADA FARM.	10th		Unit moves to and takes over part of Corps Main Dressing Station from 131 Field Ambulance (38 Division)	fw
			60 Infantry Brigade Amendment No. 1 to O.O. 246 dated 10-9-17 received.	
			A.D.M.S. 20th Division No. S.340 dated 10-9-17 received.	

Army Form C. 2118.

WAR DIARY
or
INTELLIGENCE SUMMARY.
Sheet 3.

(Erase heading not required.)

Instructions regarding War Diaries and Intelligence Summaries are contained in F.S. Regs., Part II. and the Staff Manual respectively. Title pages will be prepared in manuscript.

Place	Date	Hour	Summary of Events and Information	Remarks and references to Appendices
CANADA FARM.	10th		49273 Pte. BARROW P. R.A.M.C.) 62005 Pte. BEESLEY W. ") 5269 Pte. GILBERT H.C. ") 64256 Pte. GOODWIN E.G. ") Joined Unit and taken 88055 Pte. LEATHERDALE S.J. ") on the strength. 27246 Pte. LEE A. ") 10202 Pte. MILLHOUSE A. ") 8937 Pte. NEWLUN J. ") 15998 Pte. PAGE V. ") 52076 Pte. ROBERTS A.A. ")	Jno
	11th		1/Lieut W.F.SAPPINGTON U.S.M.C. evacuated wounded and struck off the strength.	
			40581 Sergt. HARRISON F. R.A.M.C. evacuated sick and struck off the strength.	Jno
	12th		39785 Pte. HEDGER G.A. R.A.M.C. returned to Unit from C.C.S. and taken on the strength.	Jno
			60 Infantry Brigade O.O.247 dated 12-9-17 received.	Jno
	13th		A.D.M.S. 20th Division S.433 dated 12-9-17 received.	
			A.D.M.S. 20th Division S.434 dated 13-9-17 received.	
			30853 Pte. READER F. R.A.M.C. transferred from 1/3rd South Midland Field Ambulance and taken on the strength.	
			74355 Pte. ASHPLANT F. R.A.M.C. transferred to 1/3rd South Midland Field Ambulance and struck off the strength.	
	14th		T.4/123976 Dvr. HIRST N. A.S.C. (H.T) transferred to A.S.C.H.T Base Depot and struck off the strength.	Jno
			A.D.M.S. 20th Division S.435 dated 14-9-17 received.	
			A.D.M.S. 20th Division S.436 dated 14-9-17 received.	

Army Form C. 2118.

WAR DIARY
or
INTELLIGENCE SUMMARY. Sheet 5.
(Erase heading not required.)

Instructions regarding War Diaries and Intelligence Summaries are contained in F. S. Regs., Part II. and the Staff Manual respectively. Title pages will be prepared in manuscript.

Place	Date	Hour	Summary of Events and Information	Remarks and references to Appendices
CANADA FARM.	15th		D.D.M.S. XIV Corps 658/128/17 dated 14-9-17 received.	
	16th		A.D.M.S. 20th Division S.438 dated 15-9-17 received.	
			60 Infantry Brigade G.3882/4589 dated 15-9-17 received.	
	17th		T.3/024059 Corpl. McGUIRE H. A.S.C. (H.T) joined Unit and taken on the strength.	
			60 Infantry Brigade G.3882/4615 and G.3882/4616 dated 17-9-17 received.	
	18th		60 Infantry Brigade O.O.248 dated 17-9-17 received.	
			60 Infantry Brigade G.3882/4626 and G.3882/4635 dated 18-9-17 received.	
			A.D.M.S. 20th Division S.454 and S.455 dated 18-9-17 received.	
			60 Infantry Brigade O.O.249 dated 18-9-17 received.	
			T.3/024069 Dvr. DALE E.W. A.S.C. (H.T) wounded and returned to duty.	
	19th		60 Infantry Brigade G.3882/4648 dated 19-9-17 received.	
			60 Infantry Brigade O.O.250 dated 19-9-17 received.	
	20th		A.D.M.S. 20th Division S.458 dated 20-9-17 received.	
			73264 Pte. WRIGHT W. R.A.M.C.)	
			64827 Pte. WRIGHT W. R.A.M.C.) Wounded and returned to duty.	
			6299 Pte. PHILLIPS R.T. R.A.M.C.)	

Army Form C. 2118.

WAR DIARY
or
INTELLIGENCE SUMMARY.   Sheet 6.
(Erase heading not required.)

Instructions regarding War Diaries and Intelligence Summaries are contained in F. S. Regs., Part II. and the Staff Manual respectively. Title pages will be prepared in manuscript.

Place	Date	Hour	Summary of Events and Information	Remarks and references to Appendices
CANADA FARM.	20th		73416 Pte. BAIRSTOW P. R.A.M.C. ⎫	
			78388 Pte. BAREHAM T.H. R.A.M.C. ⎬	
			49273 Pte. BARROW P. R.A.M.C. ⎬ Evacuated wounded and struck off the strength.	
			33781 Pte. DEAMER A. R.A.M.C. ⎬	
			51426 Pte. GODBY W. R.A.M.C. ⎬	
			65043 Pte. HOLLANDS H.L. R.A.M.C. ⎬	
			102151 Pte. STANFORD A.P. R.A.M.C. ⎬	
			*50774 Pte. THORPE H. R.A.M.C. ⎭ *Died of wounds at No.4 C.C.S. 22-9-17.	
	21st		36025 Pte. WHYTE O. R.A.M.C. evacuated wounded and struck off the strength.	
			A.D.M.S. 20th Division S.459 and S.460 dated 21-9-17 received.	
			10203 Pte. MILLHOUSE A. R.A.M.C. evacuated wounded and struck off the strength.	
	22nd		37175 Pte. PLUM A.C. R.A.M.C. evacuated sick and struck off the strength.	
			T.3/023910 Dvr. BERRY A.V. A.S.C. (H.T) evacuated sick and struck off the strength.	
			31137 Pte. HORNBY J. R.A.M.C. ⎫ Wounded and returned to	
			50530 Pte. LAWSON W. R.A.M.C. ⎭ duty.	
			A.D.M.S. 20th Division S.461 and S.462 dated 22-9-17 received.	
	23rd		60 Infantry Brigade Z.O.80 dated 22-9-17 received.	
			60 Infantry Brigade O.O.253 dated 23-9-17 received.	
			101736 Pte. SPROSTON W. R.A.M.C. wounded and returned to duty.	
	24th		8937 Pte. NEWLUN J. R.A.M.C. evacuated sick and struck off the strength.	

Army Form C. 2118.

WAR DIARY
or
INTELLIGENCE SUMMARY.

(Erase heading not required.) Sheet 7.

Instructions regarding War Diaries and Intelligence Summaries are contained in F. S. Regs., Part II. and the Staff Manual respectively. Title pages will be prepared in manuscript.

Place	Date	Hour	Summary of Events and Information	Remarks and references to Appendices
CANADA FARM.	24th		A.D.M.S. 20th Division S.464 dated 24-9-17 received.	Jno
	25th		A.D.M.S. 20th Division O.O.93 dated 25-9-17 received.	Jno
			A.D.M.S. 20th Division S.469 dated 25-9-17 received.	
	26th		60 Infantry Brigade O.O.254 dated 25-9-17 received.	Jno
			60 Infantry Brigade Table & Amendment to O.O.254 dated 26-9-17 received.	Jno
	27th		No remarks.	
	28th		A.D.M.S. 20th Division S.475 dated 28-9-17 received.	Jno
			A.D.M.S. 20th Division S.476 dated 28-9-17 received.	
			34468 Pte. SMITH T.H. R.A.M.C.) 31862 Pte. O'NEILL P. R.A.M.C.) Wounded and returned to duty. 40430 Pte. BYRAM H. R.A.M.C.) 50322 Pte. CLARK W.F. R.A.M.C.)	
			T.3/024062 Dvr. DEEBANK A. A.S.C.(H.T) wounded and returned to duty.	

			Strength of Unit at end of September 1917 :- Officers R.A.M.C. 6
			                                       Officers U.S.M.C. 2
			                                       O.R. R.A.M.C. 169
			                                       A.S.C.(H.T) O.R. 38
			                                       A.S.C.(M.T) O.R. 13
			                                       Durham L.I. O.R. 10
			                                                                     238	

J. Ebenn
Lieut.Col.,
O.C. 61 Field Ambulance

APPENDIX I.

Parts of
Sheet 28 N.W.
20 S.W.
1/20,000

BATTLE of
LANGEMARCK

Positions on
Zero.

———— Hand carriage
– – – – Wheeled stretcher
or horsed ambulance
— - — - Trolley

BATTLE of LANGEMARCK map showing: Steenbecque R., R. BDE BATTLE RAP, L BDE BATTLE RAP, IRON CROSS, IRON POST, OLD BROAD GAUGE LINE, CORNER HOUSE, GALLWITZ FARM F.A.D.S., RELAY POST, RELAY POST, CANAL, FUSILIER A.D.S.

War Diary

61st Field Ambulance.

October 1917.

B.E.F. 1.

SUMMARY OF MEDICAL WAR DIARIES FOR
61st F.A., 20th Divn. 14th Corps, 5th Army.
To 3rd Corps, 3rd Army on 2/10/17.

WESTERN FRONT Oct. 1917.

O.C. Lt. Col. J.S. Harvey.

SUMMARISED UNDER THE FOLLOWING HEADINGS.

Phase "D" 1. Passchendaele Operations July-Dec. 1917.

(b) Operations commencing 1/10/17.
Canadians attacked Passchendaele Oct. 30th.
Canadians took Passchendaele Nov. 6th.

B.E.F.

<u>61st F.A., 20th Divn. 14th Corps, 5th Army.</u> <u>WESTERN FRONT.</u>

<u>O.C. Lt. Col. J.S. Harvey.</u> <u>Oct. 1917.</u>

<u>3rd Corps, 3rd Army from 2/10/17.</u>

<u>Phase "D" 1. Passchendaele Operations July-Dec. 1917.</u>

    (b) Operations commencing 1/10/17.
        Canadians attacked Passchendaele Oct. 30th.
        Canadians took Passchendaele Nov. 6th.

1917.   <u>Headquarters.</u> At Singapore Camp X.29.c.6.3. (Sheet 19)

Oct. 2nd.   <u>Moves and Transfer.</u> Unit transferred with 20th Divn. to 3rd Corps, 3rd Army and moved Bapaume en route for new area.

B.E.F. 1.

SUMMARY OF MEDICAL WAR DIARIES FOR
61st F.A., 20th Divn. 14th Corps, 5th Army.
To 3rd Corps, 3rd Army on 3/10/17.

WESTERN FRONT Oct. 1917.

O.C. Lt. Col. J.S. Harvey.

SUMMARISED UNDER THE FOLLOWING HEADINGS.

Phase "D" 1. Passchendaele Operations July-Dec. 1917.

(b) Operations commencing 1/10/17.
Canadians attacked Passchendaele Oct. 30th.
Canadians took Passchendaele Nov. 6th.

B.E.F. 1.

61st F.A., 20th Divn. 14th Corps, 5th Army. XWESTERN FRONT.

O.C. Lt. Col. J.S. Harvey.   Oct. 1917.

3rd Corps, 3rd Army from 2/10/17.

Phase "D" 1. Passchendaele Operations July-Dec. 1917.

    (b) Operations commencing 1/10/17.
        Canadians attacked Passchendaele Oct. 30th.
        Canadians took Passchendaele Nov. 6th.

1917.   Headquarters. At Singapore Camp X.29.c.6.3.(Sheet 19)

Oct. 2nd.   Moves and Transfer. Unit transferred with 20th Divn. to 3rd Corps, 3rd Army and moved Bapaume en route for new area.

Army Form C. 2118.

WAR DIARY
or
INTELLIGENCE SUMMARY.

Sheet 1.

(Erase heading not required.)

Instructions regarding War Diaries and Intelligence Summaries are contained in F. S. Regs., Part II. and the Staff Manual respectively. Title pages will be prepared in manuscript.

Place	Date	Hour	Summary of Events and Information	Remarks and references to Appendices
CANADA FARM.	29th		Bearer Division rejoins Unit.	[initials]
			XIV Corps Main Dressing Station at CANADA FARM (A.18.a.1.7: sheet 28.) handed over to 10th Field Ambulance.	
SINGAPORE CAMP.			Unit moves to SINGAPORE CAMP (X.29.c.6.3. sheet 19.)	
			A.D.M.S., 20th Division S.479 and S.480 dated 29-9-17 received.	fw
			60th Infantry Brigade O.O.256 dated 29-9-17 received.	fw
			M.2/077818 Pte. RISK R.H., A.S.C.(M.T.) evacuated sick and struck off the strength.	fw
			92141 Pte. GREEN R.L., R.A.M.C. rejoined Unit from C.C.S. and taken on the strength.	fw
	30th		No remarks	
	1st.		No remarks	
	2nd		Unit entrains at PROVEN and proceeds by rail to BAPAUME, detrains, and marches to BARASTRE.	
BARASTRE	3rd		60th Infantry Brigade W.O.257 dated 3-10-17 received.	
			A.D.M.S. 20th Division S.484 dated 3-10-17 received.	
			60th Infantry Brigade O.O.258 dated 3-10-17 received.	
			A.D.M.S., 20th Division O.O.94 dated 3-10-17 received.	
	4th		Unit moves by road to camp at V.18.c. : Sheet 57c.	fw
FINS	5th		A.D.M.S., 20th Division S.492, S.493, and S.494 dated 5-10-17 received.	fw
	6th		No remarks.	fw

Army Form C. 2118.

WAR DIARY
or
INTELLIGENCE SUMMARY.

Sheet 2.

(Erase heading not required.)

Instructions regarding War Diaries and Intelligence Summaries are contained in F.S. Regs., Part II. and the Staff Manual respectively. Title pages will be prepared in manuscript.

Place	Date	Hour	Summary of Events and Information	Remarks and references to Appendices
FINS	7th		A.D.M.S., 20th Division S.491 dated 7-10-17 received.	Jno
			M.2/101863 Pte. RISK R.H., A.S.C.(M.T.) rejoined Unit and taken on the strength.	
			M./S/1898 a/Corpl. GREEN W., A.S.C.(M.T.) rejoined Unit and taken on the strength.	
	8th		T.3/023010 Dvr. BERRY A.V., A.S.C.(H.T.) rejoined Unit and taken on the strength.	Jno
			40704 Corpl. JONES T.L., R.A.M.C. joined Unit and taken on the strength.	
			M/S/1898 a/Corpl. GREEN W., A.S.C.(M.T.) transferred to 20th Divisional Supply Column and struck off the strength.	
			T/38756 Dvr. PRATTENT S., A.S.C.(H.T.) joined Unit and taken on the strength.	
	9th		40th Divisional Main Dressing Station at v.18.c. Sheet 57c taken over from 137 Field Amb. R.A.M.C. bearers of 137 Field Ambulance attached to Regimental M.O's relieved.	Jno
			Advanced Dressing Station at VILLERS-GUISLAIN and Sick Collecting Post at HEUDICOURT taken over from 137 Field Ambulance.	
			60th Infantry Brigade O.O.260 dated 9-10-17 received.	
	10th		No remarks.	
	11th		A.D.M.S., 20th Division S.495 and S.497 dated 11-10-17 received.	Jno
			62001 Pte Hughes G.O., R.A.M.C. evacuated sick and struck off the strength.	Jno
	12th		A.D.M.S., 20th Division S.498 and S.499 dated 12-10-17 received.	Jno
			T.3/12300 Corpl. HAINES F., A.S.C.(H.T.) rejoined Unit and taken on the strength.	

Army Form C. 2118.

WAR DIARY
or
INTELLIGENCE SUMMARY. Sheet 3.

(Erase heading not required.)

Instructions regarding War Diaries and Intelligence Summaries are contained in F. S. Regs., Part II. and the Staff Manual respectively. Title pages will be prepared in manuscript.

Place	Date	Hour	Summary of Events and Information	Remarks and references to Appendices
FINS	13th		T.3/13300 Corpl. HAINES F., A.S.C. (H.T.) transferred to 20th Divisional Train A.S.C. and struck off the strength.	
	14th		80th Infantry Brigade B.O.261 dated 14-10-17 received.	
	15th		No remarks.	
	16th		No remarks	
	17th		1/Lieut. W.F.SAPPINGTON, U.S.M.C. rejoined unit from the Base and taken on the strength. 83263 Pte. MOFFAT W.C., R.A.M.C. transferred to ENGLAND as candidate for Infantry Commission and struck off the strength. A.D.M.S., 20th Division S.502 dated 17-10-17 received.	
	18th		40581 a/Sergt. HARRISON F., R.A.M.C. rejoined Unit from the Base and taken on the strength.	
	19th		80th Infantry Brigade B.O.262 dated 18-10-17 received. A.D.M.S. 20th Division S.504 dated 19-10-17 received.	
	20th		No remarks.	
	21st		Quartermaster & Hon.Lieut. G.DRUMMOND, R.A.M.C. joined Unit and taken on the strength.	
	22nd		No remarks.	
	23rd		No remarks.	
	24th		80th Infantry Brigade B.O.263 dated 24th received.	

Army Form C. 2118.

WAR DIARY
or
INTELLIGENCE SUMMARY.   Sheet 4.
(Erase heading not required.)

Instructions regarding War Diaries and Intelligence Summaries are contained in F. S. Regs., Part II. and the Staff Manual respectively. Title pages will be prepared in manuscript.

Place	Date	Hour	Summary of Events and Information	Remarks and references to Appendices
FINS	25th		No remarks.	
	26th		No remarks.	
	27th		No remarks.	
	28th		A.D.M.S., 20th Division S.513 dated 28-10-17 received.	
			A.D.M.S., 20th Division S.514 dated 27-10-17 received.	
			Capt. P.H.ZINKHAN, U.S.M.C. transferred to 60 Field Amb. and struck off the strength.	
			Capt. B.H.SWIFT, R.A.M.C. transferred to medical charge of 91st brigade R.F.A. and struck off the strength.	
			Capt. H.J.MILLIGAN, M.C., R.A.M.C., joined the Unit and taken on the strength.	
	29th		No remarks.	
	30th		60th Infantry Brigade B.O.264 dated 29-10-17 received.	
			During the month the following N.C.O's and men were awarded the Military Medal.-	
			387 a/Sergt. BAILEY F., R.A.M.C.	
			33202 a/Corpl. ADCOCK W.E. R.A.M.C.	
			24246 Private. LEE A. R.A.M.C.	
			54311 " WILLIAMS R.E. R.A.M.C.	
			Strength of Unit at end of October 1917 :-	
			Officers R.A.M.C. 7	
			Officers U.S.M.C. 2	
			O.R., R.A.M.C. 169	
			A.S.C. (H.T.)O.R. 27	
			A.S.C. (M.T.)O.R. 13	
			Durham L.I. O.R. 10	
			___	
			228	

J. [signature] Lieut.Col.,
C.O. 61 Field Ambulance.

24 Vol 26

40/2578

War Diary
of
61st Field Ambulance

Nov: 1914

COMMITTEE FOR THE
MEDICAL HISTORY OF
Date 17 JAN. 1918

Army Form C. 2118.

WAR DIARY
or
~~INTELLIGENCE SUMMARY.~~

(Erase heading not required.)

Sheet No. 1.

Instructions regarding War Diaries and Intelligence Summaries are contained in F. S. Regs., Part II. and the Staff Manual respectively. Title pages will be prepared in manuscript.

Place	Date	Hour	Summary of Events and Information	Remarks and references to Appendices
FINS	3rd		93263 Pte. MOFFAT W.C., R.A.M.C. (attd 12 Kings L'pools on probation) wounded September 28th evacuated October 1st. struck off the strength. (This cancels entry "Transferred to ENGLAND as candidate for infantry commission 17-10-17")	
	4th		A.D.M.S., 20th Division S.517 received.	
	5th		27372 Sergt. ANDERSON A., R.A.M.C. transferred to R.A.M.C. Base Depot. Auth: A.D.M.S. 20th Div. N.1173/227/17 dated 1-11-17.	
			No remarks.	
	5th		A.D.M.S., 20th Division S.519 received.	
	6th		60th Infantry Brigade B.O.265 dated 6-11-17 received.	
	7th		A.D.M.S., 20th Division S.520 dated 7-11-17 received.	
	8th		47212 Sergt. TESSEYMAN W.F. R.A.M.C. promoted acting staff sergeant from 19-9-17; assumed duty with pay from 8-11-17. Auth: D.G.M.S. E.1450/1578 dated 2-11-17.	
	9th		No remarks.	
	10th		A.D.M.S., 20th Division S.522 dated 9-11-17 received.	
	11th		No remarks.	
	12th		No remarks.	
	13th		61st Infantry Brigade O.O.231 dated 13-11-17 received.	
	14th		No remarks.	
	15th		A.D.M.S., 20th Division S.524 dated 15-11-17 received.	

Army Form C. 2118.

WAR DIARY
or
INTELLIGENCE SUMMARY.
Sheet No. 2.

(Erase heading not required.)

Instructions regarding War Diaries and Intelligence Summaries are contained in F.S. Regs., Part II. and the Staff Manual respectively. Title pages will be prepared in manuscript.

Place	Date	Hour	Summary of Events and Information	Remarks and references to Appendices
FINS	16th		A.D.M.S., 20th Division S.526 dated 16-11-17 received.	E.J.G.
	17th		60th Infantry Brigade B.U.269 dated 16th received.	E.J.G.
			A.D.M.S., 20th Division S.527 dated 17-11-17 received.	
			D.D.M.S. III Corps 249/223/2 dated 17-11-17 received.	
			D.D.M.S. III Corps 5968/17 and Medical Arrangements No. 17 received.	
			A.D.M.S., 20th Division S.529 dated 17-11-17 received.	
		12 noon.	20th Divisional Main Dressing Station becomes III Corps Main Dressing Station.	
			T.3/024160 Sergt. HILL A.T. A.S.C.(H.T) evacuated sick 17-11-17 and struck off the strength.	
			5269 Pte. GILBERT H.C., R.A.M.C. evacuated sick 17-11-17 and struck off the strength.	
	18th		TWO tent sub-divisions of 18th Field Ambulance and one tent sub-division of 17th Field Ambulance report for duty at Corps Main Dressing station.	E.J.G.
			Tent sub-division of 37th Field Ambulance arrives and takes over Corps Walking Wounded station and Corps Sick Collecting station with one tent sub-division of 16th Field Ambulance.	
			D.D.M.S., III Corps 5974/17 dated 18-11-17 received.	
			A.D.M.S., 20th Division S.545 dated 18-11-17 received.	
	19th		A.D.M.S., 20th Division S.549 dated 19-11-17 received.	E.J.G.
			73326 Pte. BROOKES W.A. R.A.M.C. evacuated sick 19-11-17 and struck off the strength.	
			37937 Pte. NASH E.S.E., R.A.M.C. joined Unit from Base 19-11-17 and taken on the strength.	

Army Form C. 2118.

WAR DIARY
or
INTELLIGENCE SUMMARY.

(Erase heading not required.)

Sheet No. 3.

Instructions regarding War Diaries and Intelligence Summaries are contained in F. S. Regs., Part II. and the Staff Manual respectively. Title pages will be prepared in manuscript.

Place	Date	Hour	Summary of Events and Information	Remarks and references to Appendices
FINS.	20th		A.D.M.S., 20th Division S.550 dated 20-11-17 received.	
	21st		35909 Pte. NOBLE J.E., R.A.M.C. evacuated wounded 20-11-17 and struck off the strength.	
	22nd		No remarks.	
	23rd		A.D.M.S., 20th Division S.552 dated 22-11-17 received.	
	24th		A.D.M.S., 20th Division S.554 dated 23-11-17 received.	
	25th		No remarks.	
			598138 Pte. Limwood H. R.A.M.C.)	
			341333 " McCabe C. ")	
			352238 " Nutter J.H. ")	
			1068834 " Pinkard W.T. ")	
			421317 " Abbott J. ") Joined Unit from Base 25-11-17 and taken on the strength.	
			3571171 " Atkinson J. ")	
			85961 " Hunt H. ")	
			103027 " Eastwood T. ")	
			24238 " Hodson E.G. ")	
			101950 " Jepson J.R. ")	
			112939 " Palmer J.W. ")	
			105801 " Colley R. ")	
			26392 " Emmett A.G. ")	
			473336 " Green F.E. ")	
			205145 Pte. HELDEN R. Dur.L.I. attd 61 Field Amb. transferred to Reinforcements ETAPLES in accordance with D.A.G. No. A.H.674.	
	26th		50530 Pte. LAWSON W. R.A.M.C. evacuated wounded 26-11-17 and struck off the strength.	
			40581 Sergt. HARRISON F., R.A.M.C. wounded and returned to duty 26-11-17.	

Army Form C. 2118.

WAR DIARY
or
INTELLIGENCE SUMMARY

(Erase heading not required.)   Sheet No. 4.

Place	Date	Hour	Summary of Events and Information	Remarks and references to Appendices
FINS.	27th		No remarks.	
	28th		No remarks.	
	29th		A.D.M.S., 20th Division S.559 dated 29-11-17 received.	
	30th		No remarks.	
			Strength of Unit at end of November 1917 :-	
			Officers R.A.M.C. 7	
			" U.S.M.C. 2	
			O.R., R.A.M.C. 179	
			O.R., A.S.C.(H.T) 26	
			O.R., A.S.C.(M.T) 13	
			Durham L.I., O.R. 9	
			236	

Capt. R.A.M.C.
a/O.C. 61 Field Ambulance.

War Diary

of

61st Field Ambulance

Month of December 1917.

Army Form C. 2118.

WAR DIARY
or
INTELLIGENCE SUMMARY.
(Erase heading not required.) Sheet 1.

Instructions regarding War Diaries and Intelligence Summaries are contained in F.S. Regs., Part II. and the Staff Manual respectively. Title pages will be prepared in manuscript.

Place	Date	Hour	Summary of Events and Information	Remarks and references to Appendices
FINS.	1st		Lieut. H.E. ORMDOFF, U.S.M.C. joined Unit and taken on the strength.	Jw (Appx)
			75960 a/L/Cpl. JANES W. R.A.M.C.) 50626 Pte. NISBET G.R. ") evacuated wounded and struck off the strength. 36795 " BLACKWOOD G.T. ")	Jw
	2nd		481261 Pte. BLACKMAN H. R.A.M.C. T.F. wounded and returned to duty.	
			52261 Pte. WALTERS W. D.L.I. evacuated sick and struck off the strength.	
			Bearer Division rejoin Unit from 60 Field Ambulance.	
	3rd		60 Infantry Brigade O.O.275 dated 3-12-17 received.	Jw
			54312 Pte. MITCHELL A. R.A.M.C. wounded and returned to duty.	Jw
	4th		Capt. H.J. MILLIGAN, R.A.M.C. transferred to 50 Sanitary Section and struck off the strength.	
			III Corps Main Dressing Station handed over to 2/1 South Midland Field Ambulance.	
			Bearer Division departs for ACHEUX: marching from FINS to YPRES, entraining at YPRES and detraining at BUIRE; proceeding from BUIRE to ACHEUX by bus.	
			Transport leaves for ACHEUX (by road)	
	5th		Headquarters move by bus to ACHEUX.	Jw
			Transport arrives at ACHEUX	
ACHEUX	6th		Headquarters and Ambulance move to MARESQUEL: marching from ACHEUX to AVELUY; entraining at AVELUY and detraining at HESDIN; marching from HESDIN to MARESQUEL	Jw
			Transport leaves ACHEUX.	

Army Form C. 2118.

WAR DIARY
or
INTELLIGENCE SUMMARY.

(Erase heading not required.) Sheet 2.

Instructions regarding War Diaries and Intelligence Summaries are contained in F. S. Regs., Part II. and the Staff Manual respectively. Title pages will be prepared in manuscript.

Place	Date	Hour	Summary of Events and Information	Remarks and references to Appendices
MARFSQUEL	7th		Headquarters and Ambulance move by road to SEHEN.	flo
SEHEN	8th		497398 Pte. SMITH S. R.A.M.C.T.F. ⎫	fll
			421330 " STOKES B. " ⎬ joined Unit and taken on the strength.	fll
			405337 " SHAW D. " ⎪	fll
			439291 " TURNER A. " ⎪	fll
			538387 " TRACEY H. " ⎪	fll
			337354 " TOMKINSON H. " ⎭	
	9th		Transport arrives SEHEN.	fll
	10th		A.D.M.S. 20th Division S.562 dated 10-12-17 received.	fll
			60 Infantry Brigade 840/1 dated 9-12-17 received.	fll
			60 Infantry Brigade 849/134 and 452/01 received.	
	11th		No remarks.	fll
	12th		No remarks.	fll
	13th		Ambulance moves to EBBLINGHEM: Personnel by bus, Transport by road.	fll
EBBLINGHEM	14th		No remarks.	fll
	15th		1/Lieut. W.B.READING, U.S.M.C. joined Unit and taken on the strength.	fll
	16th		No remarks.	fll
	17th		No remarks.	fll
	18th		A.D.M.S. 20th Division S.566 dated 18-12-17 received.	fll

Army Form C. 2118.

WAR DIARY
or
INTELLIGENCE SUMMARY.
(Erase heading not required.)   Sheet 3.

Instructions regarding War Diaries and Intelligence Summaries are contained in F. S. Regs., Part II. and the Staff Manual respectively. Title pages will be prepared in manuscript.

Place	Date	Hour	Summary of Events and Information	Remarks and references to Appendices
EBBLINGHEM	19th		No remarks.	
	20th		No remarks.	
	21st		47463 Pte. MORTLOCK G.W. R.A.M.C. evacuated sick and struck off the strength.	
	22nd		No remarks.	
	23rd		A.D.M.S. 20th Division S.567 dated 23-12-17 received.	
	24th		No remarks.	
	25th		60 Infantry Brigade 543/01 dated 24-12-17 received.	
	26th		No remarks.	
	27th		A.D.M.S. 20th Division S.568 and 569 dated 27-12-17 received.	
	28th		No remarks.	
	29th		A.D.M.S. 20th Division S.571 dated 29-12-17 received.	
	30th		A.D.M.S. 20th Division S.572 dated 29-12-17 received and passed on.	
			A.D.M.S. 20th Division S.573 dated 30-12-17 received.	
	31st		No remarks.	
			During the month 50426 Pte. HENSON G. R.A.M.C. and 53896 Pte. MUIR F. R.A.M.C. were awarded the MILITARY MEDAL.	

Army Form C. 2118.

WAR DIARY
or
INTELLIGENCE=SUMMARY.

(Erase heading not required.) Sheet 4.

Instructions regarding War Diaries and Intelligence Summaries are contained in F. S. Regs., Part II. and the Staff Manual respectively. Title pages will be prepared in manuscript.

Place	Date	Hour	Summary of Events and Information	Remarks and references to Appendices
EBBLINGHEM			Strength of Unit at end of December 1917 :-	
			Officers R.A.M.C. 6	
			" U.S.M.C. 3	
			O.R. R.A.M.C. 181	
			O.R. A.S.C. (H.T) 26	
			O.R. A.S.C. (M.T) 13	
			O.R. Dur. L.I. 8	
			237	
			[signature]	
			Lieut.Col.,	
			O.C. 61 Field Ambulance.	

War Diary

of

61st Field Ambulance

January 1918.

Army Form C. 2118.

WAR DIARY
or
INTELLIGENCE SUMMARY.

(Erase heading not required.) Sheet No. 1.

Instructions regarding War Diaries and Intelligence Summaries are contained in F. S. Regs., Part II. and the Staff Manual respectively. Title pages will be prepared in manuscript.

Place	Date	Hour	Summary of Events and Information	Remarks and references to Appendices
EBBLINGHEM	31st		A.D.M.S., 20th Division O.O.96 and S.576/1 dated 31-12-17 received.	
	1st		60th Infantry Brigade O.O.281 dated 1-1-18 received.	
			A.D.M.S., 20th Division S.579 and S.580 dated 1-1-18 received.	
	2nd		A.D.M.S., 20th Division S.583 dated 2-1-18 received.	
	3rd		A.D.M.S., 20th Division S.584 dated 3-1-18 received.	
			A.D.M.S., 20th Division S.585 dated 3-1-18 received.	
			60th Infantry Brigade 1087/1 dated 3-1-18 received.	
			Detachment of Unit relieves 98th Field Ambulance in charge of IX Corps Scabies Station.	
	4th		No remarks.	
	5th		Bearer Division attached to 62 Field Ambulance.	
			Headquarters move to WESTOUTRE, taking over Dressing Station at WESTOUTRE from 98 Field Amb. Dressing Station at LA CLYTTE also taken over from 98 Field Ambulance.	
			A.D.M.S., 20th Division S.588 dated 5-1-18 received.	
WESTOUTRE	6th		A.D.M.S., 20th Division M.20/66 dated 6-1-18 received.	
	7th		No remarks.	
	8th		A.D.M.S., 20th Division S.592, S.593 and S.594 dated 8-1-18 received.	
	9th		A.D.M.S., 20th Division S.594 and S.595 dated 9-1-18 received.	

Army Form C. 2118.

WAR DIARY
or
INTELLIGENCE SUMMARY.
(Erase heading not required.) Sheet No. 2.

Place	Date	Hour	Summary of Events and Information	Remarks and references to Appendices
WESTOUTRE	9th (cont)		59th Infantry Brigade O.O.85 dated 9-1-18 received.	
	10th		30853 Pte. READER F., R.A.M.C. evacuated wounded and struck off the strength.	
			A.D.M.S., 20th Division S.596 dated 10-1-18 received.	
			A.D.M.S., 20th Division S.598 dated 10-1-18 received.	
			Dressing Station at LA CLYTTE handed over to 62 Field Ambulance.	
	11th		A.D.M.S., 20th Division M.54 dated 10-1-18 received.	
			A.D.M.S., 20th Division M.59 dated 11-1-18 received.	
	12th		A.D.M.S., 20th Division S.599 and S.600 dated 12-1-18 received.	
	13th		59th Infantry Brigade O.O.86 dated 13-1-18 received.	
			T.1.S.R/305 Sergt. GRANTHAM W., A.S.C.(H.T) joined Unit and taken on the strength.	
			T.1/4318 Dvr. HALL W., A.S.C.(H.T) evacuated sick and struck off the strength.	
	14th		A.D.M.S., 20th Division S.602 and M.20/190 dated 14-1-18 received.	
	15th		No remarks.	
	16th		59th Infantry Brigade O.O.87 dated 16-1-18 received.	
			A.D.M.S., 20th Division S.604 dated 16-1-18 received.	
	17th		A.D.M.S., 20th Division S.605 dated 17-1-18 received.	
	18th		No remarks.	

Army Form C. 2118.

WAR DIARY
or
INTELLIGENCE SUMMARY.

(Erase heading not required.) Sheet No. 3.

Place	Date	Hour	Summary of Events and Information	Remarks and references to Appendices
WESTOUTRE	19th		No remarks.	
	20th		1/Lieut. H.E.ORMDOFF, U.S.M.C. transferred to Medical charge of 242 Army Brigade R.F.A. and struck off the strength.	
	21st		A.D.M.S., 20th Division S.611 and S.612 dated 21-1-18 received.	
	22nd		A.D.M.S., 20th Division S.614 dated 22-1-18 received.	
			59th Infantry Brigade O.O.89 dated 22-1-18 received.	
	23rd		No remarks.	
	24th		No remarks.	
	25th		No remarks.	
	26th		59th Infantry Brigade O.O.90 dated 26-1-18 received.	
	27th		A.D.M.S., 20th Division S.617 dated 26-1-18 received.	
			A.D.M.S., 20th Division S.618 dated 27-1-18 received.	
			A.D.M.S., 20th Division M.20/405 dated 27-1-18 received.	
	28th		A.D.M.S., 20th Division S.620 dated 28-1-18 received.	
	29th		59th Infantry Brigade O.O.91 dated 29-1-18 received.	
			A.D.M.S., 20th Division N.64/18 dated 29-1-18 received.	

Instructions regarding War Diaries and Intelligence Summaries are contained in F.S. Regs., Part II. and the Staff Manual respectively. Title pages will be prepared in manuscript.

Army Form C. 2118.

WAR DIARY
or
INTELLIGENCE SUMMARY.

Sheet No. 4.

(Erase heading not required.)

Place	Date	Hour	Summary of Events and Information	Remarks and references to Appendices
WESTOUTRE			HONOURS & REWARDS:-	
			Awarded during the month	
			Capt. C.J. ROGERSON, R.A.M.C. - MILITARY CROSS	
			Capt. J.P. JONES. R.A.M.C. - MILITARY CROSS	
			M.2/101863 Pte. WELLCOME W. A.S.C.(M.T) - DISTINGUISHED CONDUCT MEDAL.	
			Strength of Unit at end of January 1918 :-	
			Officers, R.A.M.C. 6	
			" U.S.M.C. 2	
			O.R. R.A.M.C. 180	
			O.R. A.S.C.(H.T) 26	
			O.R. A.S.C.(M.T) 13	
			O.R. Dur. L.I. 8	
			235	
			Lieut.Col.,	
			O.C. 61 Field Ambulance.	

Confidential

War Diary

of

61st Field Ambulance

for

January 1918.

COMMITTEE FOR THE
MEDICAL HISTORY OF THE WAR
Date -8 APR.1918

Army Form C. 2118.

WAR DIARY
or
INTELLIGENCE SUMMARY.

(Erase heading not required.) Sheet 1.

Instructions regarding War Diaries and Intelligence Summaries are contained in F. S. Regs., Part II. and the Staff Manual respectively. Title pages will be prepared in manuscript.

Place	Date	Hour	Summary of Events and Information	Remarks and references to Appendices
WESTOUTRE	31st		A.D.M.S., 20th Division S.632 dated 31-1-18 received.	
	1st		No remarks.	
	2nd		A.D.M.S., 20th Division S.633 and 639 dated 2-2-18 received.	
			Lieut. E.G.BUNBURY, R.A.M.C. joins Unit and is taken on the strength.	
	3rd		No remarks.	
	4th		59th Infantry Brigade O.O.92 dated 4-2-18 received.	
			59th Infantry Brigade O.O.93 dated 4-2-18 received.	
	5th		A.D.M.S., 20th Division S.640 and O.O.97 dated 5-2-18 received.	
			1/Lieut. W.B.READING, U.S.M.C. transferred to Medical Charge of 6th K.S.L.I. and struck off the strength.	
	6th		No remarks.	
	7th		509 Dvr. PAYNE R. and 9304 Dvr WEST J. R.F.A. (Category "B") join Unit and are taken on the strength.	
	8th		9304 Dvr. WEST J., R.F.A. evacuated sick and struck off the strength.	
			A.D.M.S., 20th Division S.646, 647, 648, 649, 650 and 651 dated 8-2-18 received.	
			Divisional Front extended to include parts of front occupied by 66th and New Zealand Divisions. Relief of forward posts in new area completed.	
	9th		A.D.M.S., 20th Division S.653 dated 9-2-18 received.	

Army Form C. 2118.

WAR DIARY
or
INTELLIGENCE-SUMMARY.   Sheet 2.
(Erase heading not required.)

Place	Date	Hour	Summary of Events and Information	Remarks and references to Appendices
WESTOUTRE	9th (cont.)		MENIN ROAD Main Dressing taken over from 2/2 East Lancs Field Ambulance	JH
	10th		Lieut. W.A.WILLIAMS, U.S.M.O. joined Unit from 6th Oxf. & Bucks L.I. and taken on the strength.	JH
			Field Ambulance and Hospital accommodation at RENINGHELST taken over from 2/2 East Lancs Field Ambulance.	
			Field Ambulance Headquarters moves to RENINGHELST.	
RENINGHELST	11th		32789 Pte. MOSS A., R.A.M.C.) wounded and returned to duty. 461261 Pte. BLACKMAN H., R.A.M.C.)	JH
			1/Lieut. W.A.WILLIAMS, U.S.M.C. transferred to Medical Charge of 12 Rifle Brigade and struck off the strength.	
			Capt. H.F.W.ADAMS, R.A.M.C. transferred to Unit from Medical Charge of 12 Rifle Brigade and taken on the strength.	
			A.D.M.S., 20th Division O.0.98 dated 11-2-18 received.	
			60th Infantry Brigade O.0.296 dated 11-2-18 received.	
			A.D.M.S., 20th Division S.658 dated 11-2-18 received.	
	12th		9093 Dvr. STIBBS J., R.F.A. (Category "B") joined unit and taken on the strength.	JH
	13th		Capt. W.F.SAPPINGTON, U.S.M.C. released from duty with British Forces to rejoin American Forces, and struck off the strength.	JH
			A.D.M.S., 20th Division S.659 and S.664 dated 13-2-18 received.	
	14th		A.D.M.S., 20th Division S.663 dated 13-2-18 received.	JH

Army Form C. 2118.

WAR DIARY
or
INTELLIGENCE-SUMMARY.

(Erase heading not required.) Sheet 3.

Place	Date	Hour	Summary of Events and Information	Remarks and references to Appendices
RENINGHELST	15th		Forward posts and MENIN ROAD Advanced Dressing Station handed over to 49th Field Amb.	
	16th		Field Ambulance site and Hospital accommodation at RENINGHELST handed over to 49th F.Amb.	
			Unit moves to BANDRINGHEM.	
BANDRINGHEM	17th		No remarks.	
	18th		No remarks.	
	19th		Lieut.Col W.J.S.HARVEY, D.S.O., R.A.M.C. transferred to command of 36 C.C.S. and struck off the strength	
			Capt. G.J.ROGERSON, M.C., R.A.M.C., assumes temporary command of the unit.	
			A.D.M.S., 20th Division S.682, S.683 and S.686 dated 19-2-18 received.	
			60 Infantry Brigade O.O.298 dated 19-2-18 received.	
	20th		A.D.M.S. 20th Division S.689 dated 20-2-18 received.	
	21st	1 p.m.	Unit moves to Fifth Army Area, by road to STEENBECQUE, entraining at STEENBECQUE, detraining at NESLE and marching to ROUY-LE-PETIT.	
ROUY-LE-PETIT	22nd	12 noon	Unit arrives at ROUY-LE-PETIT.	
			60 Infantry Brigade S.C.401 dated 23-2-18 received.	
	23rd		A.D.M.S. 20th Division M.102 dated 24-2-18 received.	
	24th		Unit moves to ESMERY HALLON by road.	

Army Form C. 2118.

WAR DIARY
or
INTELLIGENCE SUMMARY.

Sheet 4.

(Erase heading not required.)

Instructions regarding War Diaries and Intelligence Summaries are contained in F. S. Regs., Part II. and the Staff Manual respectively. Title pages will be prepared in manuscript.

Place	Date	Hour	Summary of Events and Information	Remarks and references to Appendices
ESBURY HALLON	24th		80th Infantry Brigade 1038/01 dated 24-2-18 received.	
	25th		No remarks.	
	26th		A.D.M.S., 20th Division S.697 dated 26th received.	
	27th		A.D.M.S., 20th Division S.699 dated 27th received.	
			Strength of Unit at end of February 1918 :—	
			Officers, R.A.M.C. 7.	
			O.R. " 180.	
			O.R.A.S.C. (H.T) 26	
			O.R.A.S.C. (M.T) 13	
			O.R. Dur.L.I. (Category "B") 8	
			O.R. R.F.A. (Category "B") 2	
			236	

[signature]
Capt. R.A.M.C.
a/O.C. 61 Field Ambulance.

Confidential

96 30
40/2900

COMMITTEE FOR THE
MEDICAL HISTO...
Date 6 JUN 1918

War Diary

61st Field Ambulance

March 1916.

61st
FIELD
AMBULANCE.
No.............
Date............

Army Form C. 2118.

WAR DIARY
or
INTELLIGENCE SUMMARY.

(Erase heading not required.) Sheet No. 1.

Instructions regarding War Diaries and Intelligence Summaries are contained in F.S. Regs., Part II. and the Staff Manual respectively. Title pages will be prepared in manuscript.

Place	Date	Hour	Summary of Events and Information	Remarks and references to Appendices
ESMERY HALLON	28th		Lieut.Col. F. McLENNAN, R.A.M.C. takes over command of Unit and is taken on the strength.	Init.
			34762 a/L/Cpl. EVANS D.L., R.A.M.C. transferred to 60 Field ambulance. Auth: A.D.M.S. M.20/847 dated 26-2-18.	
	1st		A.D.M.S., 20th Division S.700 dated 28-2-18 received.	Init.
			60 Infantry Brigade 1071/01, N.122, 1079/01, O.O.299 and 1084/01 dated 28-2-18 received.	Init.
			One Tent Sub-division detached for duty at 41 C.C.S.	
	2nd		A.D.M.S., 20th Division S.707 and 708 dated 1-3-18 received.	Init.
			60 Infantry Brigade 1084/01 dated 1-3-18 received.	Init.
	3rd		A.D.M.S., 20th Division S.714 dated 2-3-18 received.	Init.
			60 Infantry Brigade 1084/01 dated 2-3-18 received.	Init.
	4th		A.D.M.S., 20th Division S.722 dated 3-3-18 received.	Init.
			32789 Pte. MOSS A., R.A.M.C. appointed acting lance corporal without pay from 4-3-18.	Init.
	5th		A.D.M.S., 20th Division S.723 dated 3-3-18 received.	Init.
			60 Infantry Brigade O.O.556 dated 5-3-18 received.	Init.
	6th		Divisional Commander visited Unit with A.D.M.S. and inspected hospital and billets.	Init.
	7th		A.D.M.S., 20th Division S.729 dated 7-3-18 received	Init.
	8th		60 Brigade O.O.300 dated 8-3-18 received.	Init.

Army Form C. 2118.

WAR DIARY
or
INTELLIGENCE SUMMARY.

(Erase heading not required.) Sheet No. 2.

Instructions regarding War Diaries and Intelligence Summaries are contained in F. S. Regs., Part II. and the Staff Manual respectively. Title pages will be prepared in manuscript.

Place	Date	Hour	Summary of Events and Information	Remarks and references to Appendices
ESMERY HALLON	9th		Captains C.J.ROGERSON, M.C., R.A.M.C. Section Commander of "B" Section and J.P.QUINN, M.C., R.A.M.C, Section Commander of "C" Section appointed acting Majors with effect from 4-1-18 under the provisions of War Office letter No. 100/Medical/579 (A.M.D.1), dated 29th January, 1918.	J.McX.
	10th		A.D.M.S., 20th Division No. S.733 dated 10-3-18 received.	JmcX
	11th		A.D.M.S., 20th Division No. S.734 dated 11-3-18 received.	JmcX
	12th		No remarks	JmcX
	13th		No remarks	JmcX
	14th		No remarks	JmcX
	15th		A.D.M.S., 20th Division S.740 dated 15-3-18 received.	JmcX
			A.D.M.S., 20th Division S.746 dated 15-3-18 received.	JmcX
	16th		A.D.M.S., 20th Division S.750 and S.751 dated 16-3-18 received.	JmcX
			33496 Pte. WIGNALL G., R.A.M.C. evacuated sick and struck off the strength.	JmcX
	17th		A.D.M.S., 20th Division S.753 dated 17-3-18 received.	JmcX
	18th		No remarks.	JmcX
	19th		60 Infantry Brigade 1761/1 dated 19-3-18 received.	JmcX
			A.D.M.S., 20th Division S.758 dated 19-3-18 received.	JmcX

Army Form C. 2118.

WAR DIARY
or
INTELLIGENCE SUMMARY.

Sheet No. 3.

(Erase heading not required.)

Instructions regarding War Diaries and Intelligence Summaries are contained in F. S. Regs., Part II. and the Staff Manual respectively. Title pages will be prepared in manuscript.

Place	Date	Hour	Summary of Events and Information	Remarks and references to Appendices
ESMERY HALLON	19th		352034 Pte. BERESFORD E., R.A.M.C.) 366385 " COX B.E. ") 352058 " LITTLEWOOD A., ") Joined Unit and taken on the strength. 352275 " SMITH H., ") 371017 " SUMMERS I.J., ")	fwQ
	20th to 31st		Detailed account of Unit moves, etc., etc., during the operations of this period is given at end of Diary.	
St. SULPICE	22nd		40430 Pte. EYRAM H, R.A.M.C.) 88955 " POWELL R.H. ") reported "Missing, believed prisoners of war in German hands" and struck off the strength. 78362 " WOODLEY H.G. ")	fwQ fwQ fwQ
OMENCOURT	25th		M.2/103895 a/Sergt. BROMBY G.W., A.S.C.(M.T) evacuated wounded and struck off the strength.	fwQ
LE QUESNEL	26th		366385 Pte. COX B., R.A.M.C. wounded (returned to duty)	
SAINS	28th		1/Lieut. R.E.BLEY, M.O.R.C., U.S.A. joined Unit and taken on the strength.	
	29th		1/Lieut. M.M.GARDNER M.O.R.C., U.S.A. joined Unit and taken on the strength.	
			M.4/060892 Pte. WALLIS C., A.S.C.(M.T) evacuated sick and struck off the strength.	
			Lieut. E.G.BUNBURY, R.A.M.C. transferred to administration of A.D.M.S., CALAIS and struck off the strength.	

Army Form C. 2118.

WAR DIARY
or
INTELLIGENCE SUMMARY.

(Erase heading not required.) Sheet No. 4.

DETAILED ACCOUNT OF UNIT MOVES ETC., ETC., DURING OPERATIONS ON XVIII CORPS FRONT BETWEEN MARCH 20th and 31st inclusive.

Place	Date	Hour	Summary of Events and Information	Remarks and references to Appendices
ESMERY HALLON	20th		Orders received to have all transport loaded and ready to move at one hours notice. At 7-30 p.m. orders received to carry out marching out test; marching out test carried out at 8-30 p.m. and reported satisfactory to Brigade Headquarters. Unit stood to all night.	App.1.
	21st		Orders received from A.D.M.S. at 9 a.m. to send three large ambulance cars to report to O.C. 31 M.A.C. at HAM forthwith; cars despatched at once, leaving one Ford Car with Unit. 60 Infantry Brigade Order F.B.122 received at 3 p.m. ordering Unit to march out at 4 p.m. Unit prepared to march out. Second message (C.K.410) received at 3-30 p.m. ordering march out at 3-30 p.m. instead of 4 p.m. Unit marched out from ESMERY HALLON at 3-52 p.m. to AUBIGNY via VERLAINES and HAM. Sent Quartermaster on in advance with billetting party in Ford Car. Unit arrived at AUBIGNY at 6-20 p.m. Billets allotted were in Farmyard at K.11.d.O.5. (Sheet 66d). Interviewed Brigadier who explained the military situation:- Brigade in position on line FLUQUIERES - HAPPENCOURT. R.A.Ps. at following points: 12 K.R.R.C. at F.7.Central; 12 R.B. at F.20.d.3.1.; 6 K.S.L.I. at F.8.a.1.0. Called on O.C. 98th Field Ambulance at 7-30 p.m. who explained that he had established an Advanced Dressing Station and Walking Wounded Post at St. CHRISTOPHE about half a mile away and that he had already made arrangements for the evacuation of wounded from No. 2 R.A.P. Sent Major ROGERSON to visit No. 1 R.A.P., M.O. of which reported that he was evacuating through GERMAINE to Main Dressing Station of 30th Division there. Sent Major QUINN to visit No. 3 R.A.P. and sent forward one stretcher squad with a bicycle orderly to maintain communication with AUBIGNY. In view of the fact that the Field Ambulance was evacuating from one post only (i.e. No. 3 R.A.P.) and owing to the vagueness of the military situation, I suggested to the Brigadier the advisability of sending the Ambulance heavy transport back to St.SULPICE. He agreed, and the transport was accordingly sent back at 9-0 p.m. Reported action taken to A.D.M.S. and asked for two M.A.C. Cars for speedy evacuation of the Right Sector in the event of casualties. Receipt of message acknowledged by A.D.M.S. who added that O.C. 31 M.A.C. had been ordered to send two cars at once. Unit bivouacked at AUBIGNY all night.	App.2.
AUBIGNY				

Army Form C. 2118.

WAR DIARY
or
INTELLIGENCE-SUMMARY.
(Erase heading not required.)

Sheet No. 5.

Place	Date	Hour	Summary of Events and Information	Remarks and references to Appendices
AUBIGNY	22nd		Quiet night - no casualties. Called at Brigade Headquarters at 8 a.m. and saw Brigadier - no change in military situation, beyond the fact that enemy was advancing. Called on O.C. 98th Field Ambulance at ST.CHRISTOPHE who asked me for an officer to help at his A.D.S. Sent Lieut. BUNBURY, R.A.M.C. with two bearer squads to assist at No. 2 R.A.P. At 9 a.m. received a message from O.C.98th Field Ambulance that he was falling back and preparing to evacuate ST.CHRISTOPHE. Decided to retire Unit to St.SULPICE leaving two M.A.C. cars and A.D.S. party under Major QUINN at AUBIGNY. Issued orders to Unit to pack and drove in car to Div.H.Q. at HAM. Saw A.D.M.S. to whom I explained the situation and what I proposed doing. He acquiesced. Returned to AUBIGNY and marched the Unit back to St.SULPICE sending Major ROGERSON and QrMr on in advance with billetting party. Informed O.C. 98th Field Amb. that I was forming an A.D.S. at St.SULPICE and that he might evacuate wounded through me if he so desired. The Divisional Commander passed Unit en route and asked for details. I explained the medical military situation to him and he appeared to be satisfied. Unit arrived at St.SULPICE at 3-25 p.m. Dressing Station established in an Estaminet at the entrance to St.SULPICE on the main road to HAM. A.D.M.S. visited unit about 3-30 p.m. and ordered O.C. 31 M.A.C. to send cars to evacuate from St.SULPICE to C.C.S. at ROYE. The heavy transport was sent back across the river at OFFOY via TOULES and OFFOY. From 6 p.m. onwards wounded began to come in, mostly walking cases. With the aid of M.A.C. cars and some lorries, all were evacuated to C.C.S. at ROYE. The road became very congested with transport. Could obtain no definite information so called on A.D.M.S. at Div.H.Q. at HAM. Found H.Q. leaving for ESMERY HALLON. A.D.M.S. ordered unit to fall back on ESMERY HALLON at once. At 10 p.m. sent Unit under Major ROGERSON on to ESMERY HALLON via HAM and VERLAINES leaving Capt. JONES at St.SULPICE with two M.A.C. Cars and orders to evacuate wounded up to the last possible moment and rejoin Unit at ESMERY HALLON. I went personally in Ford Car to OFFOY via TOULES and picked up the heavy transport and gave orders for it to proceed at once to ESMERY HALLON where it arrived at 1-30 a.m. on 23rd. Unit arrived half an hour afterwards.	M172
ESMERY HALLON	23rd		Met A.D.M.S. who gave orders for Unit to proceed at once to OMENCOURT via ERCHEU and form a Main Dressing Station at the former place and for an A.D.S. to be formed at HOMBLEUX. Sent Major QUINN with nine squads and Divisional bearers with orders to form an A.D.S. at the latter place. Proceeded forthwith with Unit less A.D.S. party and arrived at OMENCOURT at 6 a.m.	

Army Form C. 2118.

WAR DIARY
or
INTELLIGENCE SUMMARY.
(Erase heading not required.)

Sheet No. 6.

Place	Date	Hour	Summary of Events and Information	Remarks and references to Appendices
OMENCOURT	23rd		Capt. JONES arrived at 9 a.m. and reported that all sick and wounded had been evacuated from St.SULPICE to ROYE. Major ROGERSON, who had been left behind at ESMERY HALLON with a number of sick collected there, also arrived at 9 a.m. and reported all sick evacuated to ROYE. Established the Main Dressing Station in OMENCOURT. At 2 p.m. movement of Divisional transport towards ROYE became marked and road very congested. Divisional Train passed and said that the Brigade Transport was hooked in at CRESSY and ready to move at moments notice. No message received from A.D.M.S. or Major QUINN and situation very vague. Decided to send back heavy transport at once under the QrMr; at 5-15 p.m. received report from the latter that the transport had halted and was parked at CHAMPIEN on main road to ROIGLISE. Sent back word that the transport was to remain there and await further orders. Unit kept standing to and remainder of transport with ambulance wagons kept ready to move off at a moments notice. At 6-15 p.m. received a message from Major QUINN, who reported that he had tried all day to find Brigade H.Q. and had at last found them established at J.36.b.9.8. R.A.Bs. were established at the following points:- 12 R.B. at J.19.b.9.5.; 12 K.R.R.C. at J.25.b.3.5.; 6 K.S.L.I. not heard of since last night and location unknown. At each of the above R.A.Ps there were two Field Amb. stretcher squads. A bearer and car post was established at J.31.c.1.8. Advanced Dressing Station formed at MOYENCOURT at 0.10.d.3.5. Five stretcher squads and Divisional bearers together with one Ford car and two large cars kept at MOYENCOURT. Sent message to O.C. 31 M.A.C. at ROYE to send two more cars to OMENCOURT, also message to O.C. C.C.S. at ROYE to send a load of stretchers by the above cars to form a stretcher dump at OMENCOURT. Sent Captn JONES to A.D.S. to assist Major QUINN. Up to this time have have no information as to location of Div. H.Q.> want of Motor Cycles was badly felt at this juncture. At 11 p.m. four M.A.C. cars arrived from ROYE with a note from the O.C. to the effect that in future demands for cars should be made through the A.D.M.S. A.D.M.S. however had previously given me verbal instructions to make demands direct to O.C. M.A.C. 25 stretchers were received with the cars in response to my request to the O.C. C.C.S. These were sent on at once to the A.D.S. at MOYENCOURT. FRENCH troops begin to arrive in the village.	
	24th		Quiet night except for moderate gun fire. No wounded during night. At 9-15 a.m. visited A.D.S. at MOYENCOURT. On arrival found Capt. JONES with all personnel leaving to form new A.D.S. at CRESSY. Capt. JONES informed me that on visiting the bearer post at HOMBLEUX at 9 a.m., that post was found to have been evacuated. Brigade H.Q. had also moved.	

Army Form C. 2118.

WAR DIARY
or
INTELLIGENCE SUMMARY.

(Erase heading not required.)

Sheet No. 7.

Place	Date	Hour	Summary of Events and Information	Remarks and references to Appendices
OMENCOURT	24th		No notification of these moves had been received by me or Major QUINN. On discovery of evacuation of post Major QUINN at once proceeded in car to BREUIL, to make enquiries but could find no trace nor information. It was accordingly decided to fall back to CRESSY where a new A.D.S. was formed at O.7.d.1.7. At 10 a.m. while at CRESSY, I received a message from Brigade H.Q. saying there were 100 wounded in HOMBLEUX and to evacuate them at once. I immediately sent Major QUINN and Capt. JONES with three cars to HOMBLEUX. No wounded could be found there, nor were there any wounded there. The A.D.M.S. visited me at this time, and I explained the situation to him; after visiting MOYENCOURT he proceeded to the M.D.S. at OMENCOURT and I remained at CRESSY. A car collecting post was formed at BREUIL for evacuation through CRESSY to OMENCOURT. At 2 p.m. I again visited the A.D.S. taking a supply of splints and dressings. Went on to BREUIL, which I found on the point of being evacuated as the enemy was now in HOMBLEUX. Brigade H.Q. had fallen back to CRESSY. Visited Brigade H.Q. and was informed that the Brigade was holding the Bridge heads across the canal at QUIQUERY, BACQUENCOURT and BUVERCHY respectively. Wounded from the former were being evacuated through the A.D.S. of a Field Amb. of the 61st Division establishment at LANGEVOISIN. A bearer post of two N.C.Os and three stretcher squads was left at BREUIL and ordered to work back to a car post at the fork roads at O.3.Central; two wheeled stretchers were also sent to BREUIL. I brought back Major QUINN to OMENCOURT and sent Major ROGERSON and Capt. TURNBULL to CRESSY with orders to send Capt. JONES back to OMENCOURT. was Throughout the day a steady flow of wounded was passing through the A.D.S. and M.D.S. - the flow becoming slightly less in the evening. At 11 p.m. 120 more stretchers arrived from the C.C.S.	
	25th		at ROYE. At 12 midnight Capt. JONES returned from CRESSY with a report from Major ROGERSON as follows:- 12 K.R.R.C. H.Q. and M.O. at I.34.d.3.5.4.; 12 R.B. H.Q. and M.O. at I.34 Central One N.C.O. and five squads are at I.34.d.3.3.; these will clear both R.B. and K.R.R.C. Car is kept at O.5.b.4.3. and the car can run direct across to CRESSY. 6 K.S.L.I. and 11 D.L.I. have no Regt'l M.O. - H.Q. at O.11.a.0.5. - Regimental bearers will carry back to car post at B.10.d.3.3. where there is one large car with a Corporal and four men. At 12-5 a.m. acknowledged the report from Major ROGERSON and sent him a message to say that should CRESSY become untenable and road to OMENCOURT become cut he was to fall back to BLARRE, report to me, and await orders there.	

Army Form C. 2118.

WAR DIARY
or
INTELLIGENCE SUMMARY.

(Erase heading not required.) Sheet No. 8.

Place	Date	Hour	Summary of Events and Information	Remarks and references to Appendices
OMENCOURT	25th		Quiet night. At 8 a.m. firing became very heavy with heavy bursts of machine gun fire. Capt. AVENT, R.A.M.C., M.O. 1/c 12 K.R.R.C. was brought in from the A.D.S. wounded in the buttock and hand - able to walk - sent him on to C.C.S. at ROYE. Artillery fire now became very heavy. Visited the A.D.S. ar CRESSY at 9 a.m. Visited Brigade H.Q. and was informed that in the event of further retirement Brigade H.Q. would be at BIARRE. Sent Capt. TURNBULL to Brigade H.Q. with orders to remain there until H.Q. moved and then inform me at once. Sent report to A.D.M.S. Returned to OMENCOURT at 10 a.m. Considerable shelling at cross roads leading to OMENCOURT. Again visited A.D.S. at 11 a.m. taking forty gallons of fresh water and a supply of cigarettes for patients. Again visited Brigade H.Q. and saw Brigadier who informed me that H.Q. would retire to OMENCOURT if they moved, and the Brigade would fall back on the line BILLANCOURT - CRESSY - MOYENCOURT. Shelling about CRESSY and cross roads getting steadily heavier. Sent further report to A.D.M.S. Visited A.D.S. again at 3-30 p.m. Could get no information from Brigade H.Q. but surmised that the military situation was not too favourable. In the event of retirement it was now decided to fall back on BIARRE - BALÂTRE BERLANCOURT, not OMENCOURT. At 4 p.m. O.C. 2/3rd South Midland Field Ambulance called at A.D.S.; he left Capt. COATSWORTH, R.A.M.C. with me also one car for duty at A.D.S. A bearer post of his Unit is still somewhere about BREUIL. At 4-30 p.m. returned to OMENCOURT from CRESSY. Shelling at CRESSY heavier but less at cross roads. Great congestion of transport moving to rear on OMENCOURT - SOLENTE Road. Shells began to fall in and around OMENCOURT and one or two wounded were brought in at cross roads. Fire began to get gradually hotter up to 5-30 p.m. when a large stream of soldiers mostly British mixed with a few French began to pour back across the fields on both sides of OMENCOURT towards SOLENTE. Situation looking very ugly. Shelling became very uncomfortable and shells fell all round the M.D.S. At 6 p.m. the last British battery passed OMENCOURT and the disorderly retreat across the fields still continued. A shell pitched in the centre of the road opposite the main entrance to the M.D.S. and wounded Sergt. BROMBY, A.S.C. (M.T) my M.T. Sergeant. I now decided to evacuate OMENCOURT and sent the transport under Capt. JONES down the SOLENTE Road and took the personnel at 6-10 p.m. through the rear of the M.D.S. picking up the transport half way between OMENCOURT and SOLENTE. All wounded were evacuated. A Staff Officer of the 30th Division came up and said that all British troops were to retire at once on ROIGLISE. The road continued to be shelled until the Unit passed SOLENTE but we were fortunate to escape without further casualties.	fuget

Army Form C. 2118.

WAR DIARY
or
INTELLIGENCE SUMMARY.   Sheet No. 9.
(Erase heading not required.)

Place	Date	Hour	Summary of Events and Information	Remarks and references to Appendices
ROIGLISE	25th		Arrived ROIGLISE at 7 p.m. having picked up the heavy transport on the way and was there directed by a Staff Officer of 30th Division to proceed to 20th Division rendezvous at BOUCHOIR. Having sent all ambulance cars back to pick up any wounded I proceeded with Unit towards BOUCHOIR via ROYE. Sent Major QUINN and QrMr with billetting party to BOUCHOIR in advance to arrange billets. An hour later Major QUINN reported that there were no 20th Division at BOUCHOIR so I sent him on to LE QUESNEL, in the meantime halting the unit on the further side of BOUCHOIR by the side of the road and close to a deserted Chinese Labour Camp where tents were still standing. After an hour, having received no message from billetting party, I decided to camp there for the night. At 11-30 p.m. Major QUINN returned and reported that there was Divisional transport in LE QUESNEL and also 31 M.A.C. but that H.Q. had not yet arrived.	
BOUCHOIR	26th		At 1 a.m. I visited the O.C. 31 M.A.C. at LE QUESNEL. He informed me that the A.D.M.S. had not yet arrived. Returned to camp. At 8-45 a.m. I saw Capt. HOBSON SCOTT D.A.D.M.S. XVIII Corps, passing in a car; I stopped the car and he informed that the A.D.M.S. was at ROYE and gave me his address. I proceeded in a Ford car to ROYE and saw the D.A.D.M.S. who informed me that the A.D.M.S. had just left for LE QUESNEL where H.Q. was to be established. Went back to LE QUESNEL, found the A.D.M.S. and gave him a verbal report of the evacuation of OMENCOURT and subsequent movements and then returned to camp. A.D.M.S. visited Unit at 9 a.m. and gave orders for Unit to move to LE QUESNEL. Marched out at 11 a.m.- road very congested with traffic. Sent Major QUINN and QrMr on in advance to find billets. Field Ambulance site found in a field by cross roads at North West corner of village where Unit halted. Major ROGERSON and Captain TURNBULL with A.D.S. party from CRESSY arrived and rejoined Unit. They left CRESSY at 6 p.m. on the 25th having previously evacuated all wounded and fell back via BIARRE - BALATTRE and ROYE, the line having been handed over to the French.	
LE QUESNEL			Visited Brigade H.Q. and was informed that it was the intention to hold a defensive line in front of LE QUESNEL. At 3-15 p.m. in company with Major ROGERSON visited A.D.M.S. re medical dispositions. A.D.M.S. decided that Unit should form an A.D.S. at LE QUESNEL and a M.D.S. at MEZIERES. Detailed Major QUINN for charge of A.D.S. and bearers, with Capt. TURNBULL to assist. A.D.M.S. to detail two other officers from another Field Amb. 62 Field Amb. to form a walking wounded post at FRESNOY. Evacuation to be to C.C.S. at HARGICOURT.	

Army Form C. 2118.

WAR DIARY
or
INTELLIGENCE SUMMARY. Sheet No. 10.
(Erase heading not required.)

Instructions regarding War Diaries and Intelligence Summaries are contained in F. S. Regs., Part II. and the Staff Manual respectively. Title pages will be prepared in manuscript.

Place	Date	Hour	Summary of Events and Information	Remarks and references to Appendices
LE QUESNEL MEZIERES	26th		A.D.S. established in a large barn close to halting place. Proceeded with Unit less A.D.S. party at 4 p.m. to MEZIERES and selected site for M.D.S. in a large house with out-buildings, PROVOTE FRANCIASE, ARMEE BRITTANIQUE in Rue de MOULINS on main road to MOREUIL. At 4-30 p.m. received verbal message at MEZIERES from A.D.M.S. that his H.Q. would be at the Chateau, LE QUESNEL. At 4-45 p.m. received R.A.M.C. O.O.1 giving Medical dispositions, route of evacuation, etc. Acknowledged receipt and gave site of M.D.S. At 5-30 p.m. A.D.M.S. visited M.D.S. At 6 p.m. I visited A.D.S. at LE QUESNEL and found it well established and everything going well. Returned to MEZIERES. Sent heavy transport on to MORISEL under QrMr in order to make us more mobile in case of further sudden retirement. Received message later that transport had parked on left hand side of MORISEL - AILLY Road at road junction South West of "S" in MORISEL.	final
	27th		At 5 a.m. received a message from A.D.M.S. that cases were to be evacuated to C.C.S. at HARGICOURT until 8 a.m. and after that all cases to go to C.C.S. at NAMPS. Quiet night and very few wounded. A few walking wounded found their way to M.D.S. without passing through A.D.S. Several sick reported from various Units. Evacuated all in two stray empty motor lorries to C.C.S. at HARGICOURT. At 10-15 a.m. visited A.D.S. at LE QUESNEL. Found that Brigade had advanced slightly in front of LE QUESNEL. More blankets and stretchers required at A.D.S. Visited A.D.M.S.: arranged that in the event of retirement, A.D.S. would fall back to MEZIERES, Div.H.Q. falling back to MEZIERES. Return to MEZIERES and send forward blankets and stretchers. At 12-35 p.m. Major QUINN applied for more cars as wounded were coming in from three divisions to A.D.S. Received R.A.M.C. O.O.2. Car relay post now changed to MEZIERES instead of FRESNOY. Received further message from Major QUINN saying he was sending back water cart and limber to MEZIERES as he expected to have to fall back shortly - personnel not yet moving. Saw A.D.M.S. and proceeded with him to MORISEL to find a site for a new M.D.S. no suitable place in MORISEL. Found suitable site at a farm on the MORISEL - AILLY-SUR-NOYE Road, one mile West of MORISEL. Ordered QrMr with heavy transport which was at MORISEL, to proceed forthwith to the farm and make preliminary arrangements for the formation of a M.D.S. Returned with A.D.M.S. to MEZIERES. Proceeded with Unit less Major ROGERSON and one tent sub-division to farm. Arrived about 5-30 p.m and at once made preparations for reception of wounded. At 6 p.m. D.D.M.S. XVIII Corps visited us and said that the French Authorities had stopped all traffic on the Road leading to the M.D.S. to allow French Troops to go through, and said we were to receive no more wounded.	final
Near MORISEL				

Army Form C. 2118.

WAR DIARY
or
INTELLIGENCE SUMMARY.

Sheet No. 11.

(Erase heading not required.)

Place	Date	Hour	Summary of Events and Information	Remarks and references to Appendices
Near MORISEL	27th		At that time we had sixteen stretcher and forty sitting; of the stretcher cases all except two were evacuated by cars before 11 p.m. and the sitting cases evacuated by lorry. Two stretcher cases died during the night. Received orders from A.D.M.S. to move next morning to Brigade area at HANGARD.	
DOMART	28th		Sent QrMr on in advance by Ford car to HANGARD to find Ambulance site. The two patients who had died during the night were buried in the orchard at the farm. Marched out at 9-30 a.m. with Unit via ROUVREL, THENNES, and DOMART. Arrived at DOMART at 12 noon and was informed that the Brigade was not yet at HANGARD. Passed Div.H.Q. transport in DOMART and was informed by the officer in charge that Div.H.Q. were at a wood beyond DOMART. Parked Unit in a small field at junction of DOMART - ROYE and DOMART - HANGARD Roads. A.D.M.S. visited Unit and instructed us to wait pending orders. Proceeded to Div.H.Q. and enquired for location of Brigade H.Q. Met Brigade Staff Captain who said that the position of Brigade H.Q. was not known. Returned to Ambulance and met A.D.M.S. who held a consultation with O.S.O. of 60 and 62 Field Ambulances and myself and informed us that he had received instructions to send all wheeled vehicles that could be spared to the rear towards ABBEVILLE, that it had been decided to send 60 and 62 Field Ambulances to the rear and retain 61 Field Ambulance with the Division, 61 Field Ambulance in the meantime to stand to and await further orders. Majors ROGERSON and QUINN with A.D.S. party from MEZIERES reported their arrival, having cleared all wounded and fallen back with the Brigade. At 2 p.m. sent heavy transport back to DOMART. At 2-30 p.m. saw A.D.M.S. who gave verbal instructions to fall back at once with whole Unit to BOVES.	
BOVES			A.D.S. under Major ROGERSON formed at BOVES, (Capt. TORNEULL	
SAINS			M.D.S. formed at SAINS. Capt. JONES with six stretcher squads and two cars were sent forward towards DOMART with instructions to get in touch with the Brigade and R.A.Ps. and form a collecting post, and evacuate all wounded to BOVES.	
	29th		Visited A.D.S. at 10 a.m. Saw D.A.Q.M.G. and explained to him the medical situation and arrangements. Advised the moving back of heavy transport to CREUSE, there to await further orders. Saw Capt. JONES who established a car and collecting post in DOMART and was in touch with R.A.Ps. Returned to SAINS and sent heavy transport under QrMr to CREUSE to await further orders. A.D.M.S. called at 2 p.m. and gave instructions that all Divisional Ambulance cars were to be exclusively employed in forward area, all wounded being evacuated back from DOMART through A.D.S. at BOVES to M.D.S. at SAINS and thence by M.A.C. cars to C.C.S. at NAMPs.	

Army Form C. 2118

WAR DIARY
or
INTELLIGENCE SUMMARY
(Erase heading not required.) Sheet No. 12.

Place	Date	Hour	Summary of Events and Information	Remarks and references to Appendices
SAINS	29th		At 4 p.m. received a message from Officer i/c A.D.S. that a large number of wounded were coming in. Road from BOVES to SAINS very congested with transport and refugees, greatly hindering the speed of evacuation.	[initials]
	30th		Busy night and large number of wounded passed through both lying and sitting cases. Road traffic still very congested but evacuation very good notwithstanding. All cases cleared back to C.C.S. at NAMPS by 8-30 a.m. Three American M.Os. reported their arrival. Fair number of casualties passing through all day. At 11 a.m. A.D.M.S. called. Later D.D.M.S. XVIII Corps called. At 3 p.m. sent medical comforts and supplies to A.D.S. Collecting post under Capt. JONES still in DOMART. Most of Divisional cars now working forward between DOMART and BOVES. At 4-15 p.m. sent two M.A.C. cars to BOVES with further supplies and dressings, also thirty stretchers and sixty blankets. At 8 p.m. large number of stretcher cases and our accommodation becoming crowded. Have asked for all available M.A.C. cars and lorries. At 8-30 p.m. received a supply of medical comforts and splints and dressings from NAMPS. At 8-35 p.m. D.D.M.S. XVIII Corps with O.C.31 M.A.C. called and made enquiries re accommodation and means of expansion and informed me he was to detail another Field Ambulance to takeover from us tomorrow.	[initials]
	31st		Very busy night, but all wounded cleared to NAMPS by 5 a.m. Wounded continued to come in steadily all night - many French among them. Wounded from three other divisions and a cavalry division in addition to our own were dealt with. At 11 a.m. A.D.M.S. called and said orders would probably be issued for us to move this evening. At 12 noon A.D.M.S. 18th Division called with a view to one of his Field Ambulances taking over. At 2-30 p.m. an officer of 54th Field Ambulance called. Showed him round M.D.S. and billets. At 4-30 p.m. received a message from A.D.M.S. 18th Division that Unit which was to relieve us had not turned up and was not expected until tomorrow morning. At 6-30 p.m. D.D.M.S. XVIII Corps called and said we were not to be relieved tonight. Sent Major QUINN and Capt. PROCTOR A.D.S. at BOVES relieved by 56 Field Ambulance; Major ROGERSON remaining in the meantime at BOVES to regulate the evacuation of wounded. Remainder of A.D.S. personnel arrived at SAINS from BOVES.	[initials]

Army Form C. 2118

WAR DIARY
or
INTELLIGENCE SUMMARY

Sheet No. 13.

(*Erase heading not required.*)

Instructions regarding War Diaries and Intelligence Summaries are contained in F. S. Regs., Part II. and the Staff Manual respectively. Title Pages will be prepared in manuscript.

Place	Date	Hour	Summary of Events and Information	Remarks and references to Appendices
SAINS	31st		Sent message to A.D.M.S. informing him of relief of Captains JONES and TURNBULL and bearers. At 6-45 p.m. message received from O.C.56 Field Ambulance, BOVES asking for M.A.C. cars and one lorry. Sent cars but no lorry available. At 9 p.m. Captains JONES and TURNBULL arrived at SAINS. At 11 p.m. all M.A.C. cars left SAINS in order to evacuate from BOVES via AMIENS to NAMPS, as BOVES - SAINS Road becoming impracticable. SAINS therefore ceases to be the M.D.S.	AM2

J.M.Kennan
Lieut.Col.,
O.C.61 Field Ambulance.

Confidential.

Vol 31
1401902

War Diary
of
61st Field Ambulance
for
April 1918.

COMMITTEE FOR THE
MEDICAL HISTORY OF THE WAR
Date 6 JUN 1918

Army Form C. 2118

WAR DIARY
or
INTELLIGENCE SUMMARY
(Erase heading not required.)   Sheet 1.

Instructions regarding War Diaries and Intelligence Summaries are contained in F.S. Regs., Part II and the Staff Manual respectively. Title Pages will be prepared in manuscript.

Place	Date	Hour	Summary of Events and Information	Remarks and references to Appendices
SAINS	1st.		Very quiet night. Only six patients received and these were evacuated to NAMPS. At 11 a.m. I visited BOVES and saw the A.D.M.S. and was informed that the Division would probably be relieved tonight. At 7-0 p.m. received orders to move Unit via ST.FAUCHIEN, PONT-des-METS to BRIQUEMESNIL. At 8-15 p.m. marched out with Unit less Major QUINN and party, and Major ROGERSON. Sent QrMr on in advance to pick up heavy transport at CREUSE and find billets.	J. M.2.
	2nd		After an hours march received message to say our destination was changed to NAMPS. Sent car on to warn advance party and made for NAMPS. Arrived at 4-0 a.m. Found advance party and transport had arrived and billets arranged in the chateau, part of which was already occupied by personnel of 61 C.C.S. Major ROGERSON and party had also arrived from BOVES before main body. Major QUINN and party arrived about 11 a.m.	J.M.2.
NAMPS	3rd		No remarks.	J.M.2.
	4th		Heavy rain during night. At 9-0 a.m. received orders to be ready to move to new area to-day. At 11-30 a.m. D.A.D.M.S. called with orders to move with whole Unit to HORNOY. At 2-0 p.m. sent Major ROGERSON with billetting party on in advance. Marched off at 2-0 p.m. At 2-15 p.m. received a message from A.D.M.S. that all units were to stand fast until tomorrow. Returned to billets and sent Ford Car to recall advance party.	J.M.2.
	5th		No remarks.	J.M.2.
	6th		Orders received to find billets at CAMPSART. Sent Major QUINN with billetting party. Received orders to march to CAMPSART tomorrow morning.	J.M.2.
	7th		Moved off at 9-0 a.m. Sent transport via QUEVAUVILLERS and FRICAMPS- took personnel by second class road to THEUILLOY where we picked up transport and halted for dinner at 1-0 p.m. At 2-30 p.m. moved off from THEUILLOY and arrived at CAMPSART at 5-0 p.m.	J.M.2.
CAMPSART	8th		Under orders from A.D.M.S. detailed Major QUINN to visit Regt'l M.O's to instruct them in their duties and in checking medical and surgical equipment and submitting indents.	J.M.2.
	9th		Received orders to move tomorrow to INVAL via FRESNOY, and ANDAINVILLE, OISEMONT, FRUCOURT, and LIMEUX. Sent Major QUINN with billetting party to find billets. Arranged hot baths for the men.	J.M.2.

1875. Wt. W593/826 1,000,000 4/15 J.B.C.& A. A.D.S.S./Forms/C.2118.

Army Form C. 2118

WAR DIARY
or
INTELLIGENCE SUMMARY
(Erase heading not required.) Sheet 2.

Instructions regarding War Diaries and Intelligence Summaries are contained in F. S. Regs., Part II. and the Staff Manual respectively. Title Pages will be prepared in manuscript.

Place	Date	Hour	Summary of Events and Information	Remarks and references to Appendices
CAMPSART	9th		A.D.M.S. called at 1-0 p.m. and wished horsed ambulances sent with Brigade tomorrow to pick up stragglers and men falling out on the march. Received Brigade Order re marching out. Received message from Major QUINN - billets found at BOENCOURT and not at INVAL.	Ap.2.
	10th		Marched out at 9-30 a.m. Left Major ROGERSON with Ambulance Cars behind to evacuate Brigade sick. Arrived at BOENCOURT at 4-45 p.m. Leaving again tomorrow for FEUQUIERES via BEHEN and TOURES.	Ap.2.
BOENCOURT HARCELAINES	11th		Marched out at 10-0 a.m. Sent Major ROGERSON with billetting party on in advance. Received message that billets had been found in HARCELAINES. Arrived there at 1-30 p.m. Capt. H.F.W. ADAMS, R.A.M.C. transferred to Medical Charge of 20th M.G.Battalion and struck off the strength. T3/024062 Dvr DEEBANKS A. A.S.C.(H.T) attached Unit evacuated sick and struck off the strength.	Ap.2.
	12th		No remarks.	Ap.2.
	13th		A.D.M.S., 20th Division S.24 dated 13-4-18 received.	Ap.2.
	14th		T/343529 Staff Sergt.Major GOLTON S.R., A.S.C.(H.T) transferred to 160 Coy. A.S.C. and struck off the strength.	Ap.2.
			T/20982 T/S.S.M. RICE O.M., A.S.C.(H.T) transferred to Unit from 160 Coy. A.S.C. and taken on the strength.	Ap.2.
	15th		A.D.M.S., 20th Division S.26 and S.27 dated 15-4-18 received.	Ap.2.
	16th		T2/294254 Dvr. SEAL H., A.S.C.(H.T) joined Unit and taken on the strength.	Ap.2.
			60 Infantry Brigade B.O.6 and B.O.7 and 1916/1 dated 16-4-18 received.	
			A.D.M.S. 20th Division S.31 and S.33 dated 16-4-18 received.	
			Unit to be prepared to move with Division to First Army area from 17th instant.	Ap.2.

Army Form C. 2118

WAR DIARY
or
INTELLIGENCE SUMMARY
(Erase heading not required.)

Sheet 3.

Instructions regarding War Diaries and Intelligence Summaries are contained in F.S. Regs., Part II. and the Staff Manual respectively. Title Pages will be prepared in manuscript.

Place	Date	Hour	Summary of Events and Information	Remarks and references to Appendices
HARCELAINES	17th		Sent Major QUINN on in advance with billetting party to report to D.A.A.G. 20th Division at TINQUES to find billets.	Au.2.
			355967 Pte. REILY J., R.A.M.C. } evacuated sick and struck off the strength. 85961 Pte. HUNT H.R., " }	Au.2.
			M/350453 Pte. TAYLOR D.W., A.S.C.(M.T) } joined Unit and taken on the strength. M2/117759 " RUSSELL A.H. }	
			At 4-0 p.m. received orders from A.D.M.S. that transport of Unit was to be ready to move at 6-30 p.m., and that personnel would proceed by rail following day at a time to be notified later.	
			At 7-0 p.m. received orders from A.D.M.S. for transport to proceed by road to EAUCOURT forthwith, and report to Transport Officer of 61st Infantry Brigade for orders as to subsequent moves. Transport will proceed via AUXI-les-CHAPELLES to new area by road probably arriving on evening of 20th.	
			At 9-0 p.m. received orders from A.D.M.S. that personnel of Unit was to be at WOINCOURT at 5-30 a.m. on 18th instant to entrain for new area. At 10-30 p.m. received orders from A.D.M.S. cancelling previous order and ordering personnel of Unit to be at EU at 8-0 a.m. on 18th instant to entrain.	Au.2.
EU	18th		Unit marched out at 3-45 a.m. and proceeded by road to EU arriving about 7-30 a.m. Unit entrained but did not leave EU until 12 noon; Unit detrained at TINQUES at 9-45 p.m. Met Major QUINN who informed me that Unit was to be billetted in huts in ESTREE-CAUCHIE Unit marched off from TINQUES at 10-30 p.m. and arrived in billets at 1-0 a.m. on 19th.	Au.2. Au.2.
ESTREE CAUCHIE	19th		No remarks	
	20th		Transport of Unit arrived at 4-45 p.m.	

Army Form C. 2118

WAR DIARY
or
INTELLIGENCE SUMMARY

(Erase heading not required.)

Sheet 4.

Place	Date	Hour	Summary of Events and Information	Remarks and references to Appendices
ESTREE CAUCHIE	21st		A.D.M.S., 20th Division S.40 and S.41 dated 21-4-18 received.	Jew 2.
	22nd		21966 Pte. SHEARD J.A. R.A.M.C. struck off the strength in accordance with G.R.O.3765.	Jew 2.
	23rd		A.D.M.S., 20th Division S.42 and S.43 dated 22-4-18 received.	Jew 2.
	24th		251863 Pte. SHAW J., R.A.M.C. Dur.L.I. attached Unit evacuated sick and struck off the strength.	Jew 2
			37694 Sergt. WORFOLK R., R.A.M.C. transferred to Unit from Directorate of D.G.M.S. 2nd Echelon and taken on the strength.	Jew 2
			A.D.M.S., 20th Division S.45 dated 24-4-18 received.	Jew 2
	25th		No remarks.	
	26th		2882 Pte. McDONALD R., R.A.M.C. evacuated sick and struck off the strength.	Jew 2
	27th		No remarks.	Jew 2
	28th		A.D.M.S., 20th Division S.64 dated 28-4-18 received.	Jew 2
	29th		26392 Pte. EMMETT A.G. R.A.M.C. evacuated sick and struck off the strength.	Jew 2
			A.D.M.S., 20th Division S.63 and S.64 dated 29-4-18 received.	
			60 Infantry Brigade 1369/01 dated 29-4-18 received.	

Army Form C. 2118

WAR DIARY
or
INTELLIGENCE SUMMARY

(Erase heading not required.)

Sheet 5.

Place	Date	Hour	Summary of Events and Information	Remarks and references to Appendices

ESTREE CAUCHIE			Systematic training of Unit has been carried out since the beginning of the month whilst the Division has been in reserve.
			
			HONOURS and REWARDS.- Awarded during month
			
			T/Capt. J.P.JONES M.C., R.A.M.C., BAR to Military Cross.
			
			31862 Pte. O'NEILL P.J., R.A.M.C. ⎫
			53884 Pte. APLIN A.C. " ⎪
			M.2/105298 Pte. BURGESS G.H., A.S.C.(M.T) ⎬ Military Medal
			M.2/104031 Pte. KAVANAGH G.C. " ⎪
			M.2/227050 Pte. THORLBY H. " ⎭
			
			Strength of Unit at end of April 1918.-
			
			    Officers 7
			    O.R., R.A.M.C. 176
			    O.R., A.S.C.(H.T) 26
			    O.R., A.S.C.(M.T) 13
			    O.R., Category "B" 9
			                 TOTAL 231
				✓M.

F. M_____
Lieut.Col.,
O.C.61 Field Amb.

Confidential

No 32
140/283

War Diary
of
61st Field Ambulance

May 1918.

Army Form C. 2118

WAR DIARY
or
INTELLIGENCE SUMMARY
(Erase heading not required.) Sheet 1.

Instructions regarding War Diaries and Intelligence Summaries are contained in F.S. Regs, Part II. and the Staff Manual respectively. Title Pages will be prepared in manuscript.

Place	Date	Hour	Summary of Events and Information	Remarks and references to Appendices
ESTREE CAUCHIE	1st		A.D.M.S. 20th Division S.71 dated 1-5-18 received.	
			Unit moves by road to ABLAIN ST.NAZAIRE, moving off at 4-30 p.m. and arriving at 7-0 p.m.	
			A.D.M.S. 20th Division S.76 dated 1-5-18 received.	
			A.D.M.S. 20th Division 0.0.2 dated 1-5-18 received.	
			M.2/076767 Pte. WEIGHT A.F., A.S.C.(M.T) joined Unit and taken on the strength.	
ABLAIN ST. NAZAIRE.	2nd		60 Infantry Brigade O.0.10 dated 2-5-18 received.	
			A.D.M.S. 20th Division S.75 dated 2-5-18 received.	
			Advanced Dressing Station at PAULINES (S.4.a.2.8. Sheet 36c.) taken over from 9th Canadian Field Ambulance. Field Ambulance Bearers proceed to line with 60 Infantry Brigade and relieve bearers of 9th Canadian Field Ambulance in three Regimental Aid Posts and one Relay Post.	
			Orders received from A.D.M.S. 20th Division that Unit is to open a Divisional Main Dressing Station at ABLAIN ST.NAZAIRE (X.10a.8.8. Sheet 36b.). Arrangements made and Field Ambulance prepared to receive sick and wounded by 6-0 p.m.	
	3rd		A.D.M.S. 20th Division S.82 dated 3-5-18 received.	
			1/Lieut. A.R.PEARCE, M.R.C., U.S.A. joined Unit and taken on the strength.	
	4th		437291 Pte. TURNER A., R.A.M.C. evacuated sick and struck off the strength.	
	5th		A.D.M.S. 20th Division S.95 and M.20/1903 dated 5-5-18 received.	
			40460 Pte. ARCHBOLD J.H., (Category "B") evacuated sick and struck off the strength.	
			6598 Pte. HALSEY A., R.A.M.C. joined Unit and taken on the strength.	

Army Form C. 2118

WAR DIARY
or
INTELLIGENCE SUMMARY
(Erase heading not required.)

Sheet 2.

Instructions regarding War Diaries and Intelligence Summaries are contained in F.S. Regs., Part II. and the Staff Manual respectively. Title Pages will be prepared in manuscript.

Place	Date	Hour	Summary of Events and Information	Remarks and references to Appendices
ABLAIN ST. NAZAIRE	6th		A.D.M.S. 20th Division M.20/1921 dated 6-5-18 received.	App.2.
	7th		A.D.M.S. 20th Division S.101 dated 7-5-18 received.	App.2.
			60 Infantry Brigade O.O.11 dated 7-5-18 received.	
			102748 Pte. NEEDHAM L., R.A.M.C. evacuated sick and struck off the strength.	
	8th		T/326698 Dvr. GrEAVES F., A.S.C.(H.T) Category "B") joined Unit and taken on the strength.	App.2.
			T3/024053 " KING E.J., " " ")	
	9th		A.D.M.S. 20th Division S.110 dated 9-5-18 received.	App.2.
			81138 Pte. CHARLTON G.E., R.A.M.C. evacuated sick and struck off the strength.	
			D.D.M.S., XVIII Corps orders heavy transport of Field Ambulance to be moved back to a rear Echelon. Heavy Transport sent back at 3-0 p.m. to camp near CHATEAU de la HAIE.	
	10th		A.D.M.S. 20th Division M.20/2000 dated 10-5-18 received.	App.2.
	11th		A.D.M.S. 20th Division S.120 dated 11-5-18 received.	App.2.
	12th		A.D.M.S. 20th Division S.116 dated 12-5-18 received.	App.2.
			251863 Pte. SHAW J., Dur.L.I.(Category "B") rejoined Unit and taken on the strength.	
	13th		60 Infantry Brigade O.O.12 dated 13-5-18 received.	App.2.
			67977 Pte. MONTAGUE F., R.A.M.C.) joined Unit and taken on the strength.	
			58133 " PURNELL F.C. ")	
			T.1/4618 Dvr. LEE D., A.S.C.(H.T) Category "B") joined Unit and taken on the strength.	
			T.3/023970 " THOROGOOD M. -do-	

Army Form C. 2118

WAR DIARY
or
INTELLIGENCE SUMMARY
(Erase heading not required.)

Sheet 3.

Instructions regarding War Diaries and Intelligence Summaries are contained in F. S. Regs., Part II. and the Staff Manual respectively. Title Pages will be prepared in manuscript.

Place	Date	Hour	Summary of Events and Information	Remarks and references to Appendices
ABLAIN ST. NAZAIRE	13th		T.3/024053 Dvr. KING E.J., A.S.C.(H.T) Category "B" transferred to 160 Coy. A.S.C. and struck off the strength.	App 2.
	14th		A.D.M.S. 20th Division. M.20/3017 and S.112 dated 14-5-18 received.	App 2.
			32898 Pte. WILLIAMS W., R.A.M.C. joined Unit and taken on the strength.	App 2.
	15th		A.D.M.S. 20th Division M.20/3039 and M.20/3052 dated 15-5-18 received.	App 2.
	16th		60 Infantry Brigade 1567/0.12 dated 16-5-18 received.	App 2.
	17th		A.D.M.S. 20th Division M.20/3077 dated 17-5-18 received.	App 2.
			56036 Pte. WHITEHOUSE H., R.A.M.C.) 51753 " WARE W. ") 42200 " WATTS F. ") joined Unit and taken on the strength. 3758 " WEAKE R. ") 64030 " WHITE A. ")	
			90530 Pte. McKENZIE M., R.A.M.C. struck off the strength in accordance with G.R.O. 3765	App 2.
	18th		M.2/105298 Pte. BURGESS G.H., A.S.C.(M.T) wounded.	
			21965 Pte. SELLERS E., R.A.M.C. transferred to 132 Field Ambulance and struck off the strength.	App 2.
			10517 Pte. HEYS W., R.A.M.C.) joined Unit and taken on the strength. 120431 " HOWSON J.L. ")	
	19th		60 Infantry Brigade 1589/0.2, 1624/0.12 and 0.0.13 dated 19-5-18 received.	App 2.
			A.D.M.S. 20th Division S.143 dated 19-5-18 received.	

Army Form C. 2118

WAR DIARY
or
INTELLIGENCE SUMMARY
(Erase heading not required.) Sheet 4.

Place	Date	Hour	Summary of Events and Information	Remarks and references to Appendices
ABLAIN ST. NAZAIRE	20th		A.D.M.S. 20th Division M.20/3165 dated 20-5-18 received.	App2.
	21st		59 Infantry Brigade Z.1960 dated 20-5-18 received.	App2.
			A.D.M.S. 20th Division S.145, S.147, and S.150 dated 21-5-18 received.	App2.
			405337 Pte. SHAW D., R.A.M.C. transferred to ENGLAND as candidate for temporary commission and struck off the strength.	
	22nd		59 Infantry Brigade O.O. 112 and 113 dated 22-5-18 received.	App2.
			A.D.M.S. 20th Division S.152 and S.153 dated 22-5-18 received.	App2.
	23rd		60 Infantry Brigade G.20 dated 23-5-18 received.	App2.
			A.D.M.S. 20th Division S.155 dated 23-5-18 received.	App2.
	24th		A.D.M.S. 20th Division S.158, S.159, M.20/3232 dated 24-5-18 received.	App2.
	25th		No remarks.	App2.
	26th		A.D.M.S. 20th Division S.168 dated 26-5-18 received.	App2.
	27th		60 Infantry Brigade O.O.14 dated 27-5-18 received.	App2.
	28th		A.D.M.S. M.20/3350 dated 28-5-18 received.	App2.
	29th		100732 Pte. NICHOLSON R., R.A.M.C. joined Unit from 60 Field Ambulance and taken on the strength.	App2.
	30th		No remarks.	App2.

Army Form C. 2118

WAR DIARY
or
INTELLIGENCE SUMMARY
(Erase heading not required.)

Sheet 5.

Place	Date	Hour	Summary of Events and Information	Remarks and references to Appendices
ABLAIN ST. NAZAIRE.			D.M.S. First Army visited Unit on 20th and inspected the Main Dressing Station.	App.
			During the month a reserve Advanced Dressing Station has been established at GIVENCHY, in case of a retirement necessitating the evacuation of the A.D.S. at FAULINES.	
			Strength of Unit at end of May :-	
			Officers 8	
			O.R., R.A.M.C. 182	
			O.R., A.S.C.(H.T) 26	
			O.R., A.S.C.(M.T) 13	
			O.R., Category "B" 11	
			240	
			J. McQueen	
			Lieut.Col.;	
			O.C. 61 Field Ambulance.	

War Diary

61st Field Ambulance

June 1918.

Army Form C. 2118.

WAR DIARY
or
INTELLIGENCE SUMMARY.

Sheet 1.

(Erase heading not required.)

Instructions regarding War Diaries and Intelligence Summaries are contained in F. S. Regs., Part II. and the Staff Manual respectively. Title pages will be prepared in manuscript.

Place	Date	Hour	Summary of Events and Information	Remarks and references to Appendices
ABLAIN ST. NAZAIRE.	30th		A. D. M. S. 20th Div. S.179 dated 30-5-18 received.	
	31st		A.D.M.S., 20th Div. S.182 and S.186 dated 31-5-18 received.	
	1st		A.D.M.S., 20th Division M.20/3486 dated 1-6-18 received.	
	2nd		A.D.M.S., 20th Division M.20/3501 and M.20/3526 dated 2-6-18 received.	
	3rd		A.D.M.S. 20th Division M.20/3526 and S.198 dated 3-6-18 received.	
	4th		No remarks.	
	5th		A.D.M.S., 20th Division M.20/3529 and S.202 dated 5-6-18 received.	
	6th		61st Infantry Brigade O.O.9 dated 6-6-18 received.	
	7th		A.D.M.S., 20th Division M.20/3622 and S.210 dated 7-6-18 received.	
	8th		A.D.M.S., 20th Division M.20/3646 dated 8-6-18 received.	
	9th		60th Infantry Brigade B.O.17 dated 9-6-18 received.	
	10th		6299 Pte. Phillips R.T., R.A.M.C. evacuated sick and struck off the strength.	
	11th		T.3/024163 Sergt. Walsh L.C.M., A.S.C.(H.T.) transferred to ENGLAND for a course of instruction with a view to employment with R.A.F. (Auth: A.G., G.H.Q., No.2150/135 (0) dated 6-6-18.) and struck off the strength.	
	12th		A.D.M.S., 20th Division S.225 dated 12-6-18 received.	
	13th		No remarks.	

Army Form C. 2118.

WAR DIARY
or
INTELLIGENCE SUMMARY. Sheet 2.
(Erase heading not required.)

Instructions regarding War Diaries and Intelligence Summaries are contained in F.S. Regs., Part II. and the Staff Manual respectively. Title pages will be prepared in manuscript.

Place	Date	Hour	Summary of Events and Information	Remarks and references to Appendices
ABLAIN ST. NAZAIRE.	14th		No remarks.	App.2
	15th		60th Infantry Brigade O.O.18 dated 15-6-18 received.	App.2
	A.D.M.S.		A.D.M.S., 20th Division S.231 dated 15-6-18 received.	App.2
	16th		A.D.M.S., 20th Division S.233 dated 16-6-18 received.	App.2
			62005 Pte. Beesley W., R.A.M.C. evacuated sick and struck off the strength.	App.2
	17th		82230 Pte. Alcock A.A., R.A.M.C. } joined unit and taken on the strength. 46869 " Taylor G., "	App.2
	18th		64256 Pte. Goodwin E.G., R.A.M.C. evacuated sick and struck off the strength.	App.2
	19th		A.D.M.S., 20th Division S.237 dated 19-6-18 received.	App.2
	20th		No remarks.	
	21st		A.D.M.S., 20th Division S.239 dated 21-6-18 received.	App.2
			59th Infantry Brigade O.O.122 dated 21-6-18 received.	App.2
			62005 Pte. Beesley W., R.A.M.C. rejoined Unit from C.C.S. and taken on the strength.	
			1/Lieut. A.R.Pearce, M.O.R.C., U.S.A. attached to 1/2 Lowland Field Ambulance for duty under instructions from A.D.M.S., 20th Division.	
	22nd		A.D.M.S., 20th Division S.243 dated 22-6-18 received.	
			59th Infantry Brigade P.652 dated 22-6-18 received.	

Army Form C. 2118.

WAR DIARY
or
INTELLIGENCE SUMMARY.

(Erase heading not required.) Sheet 3.

Instructions regarding War Diaries and Intelligence Summaries are contained in F.S. Regs., Part II. and the Staff Manual respectively. Title pages will be prepared in manuscript.

Place	Date	Hour	Summary of Events and Information	Remarks and references to Appendices
ABLAIN ST. NAZAIRE.	22nd		Captain C.M.Stallard, R.A.M.C. takes over temporary medical charge of 7th SOM.L.I.	
	23rd		45774 Cpl.HUNTER J., R.A.M.C., evacuated sick and struck off the strength.	
			(signed) Lieut.Col.	
	24th		Major G.J.ROGERSON M.C., R.A.M.C., took over command of Unit vice Lieut.Col.F.McLENNAN R.A.M.C., to 3rd. Division as Acting A.D.M.S.	
	25th		59th. Inf.Bde. O.O.123 dated 25th. received. Captain C.M.STALLARD R.A.M.C., rejoins Unit from 7th. SOM.L.I.	
	26th		251863 Pte.SHAW J., DUR.L.I.,(Cat"B") transferred to 160Coy. A.S.C., and struck off the strength.	
	27th		No remarks.	
	28th		No remarks.	
	29th		1/Lieut.A.R.PEARCE M.O.R.C.,U.S.A., rejoins Unit from 1/2 Lowland Field Ambulance.	
	30th		No remarks.	
			Strength of Unit at end of May:- Officers 8 O.R., R.A.M.C. 181 A.S.C., H.T. 26 A.S.C., M.T. 13 Cat."B" personnel 10 Total 238	
			(signed) Major R.A.M.C., a/O.C. 61 Field Ambulance.	

Confidential

Vol 34

16/3131

61st Field Ambulance

War Diary.

61st Field Ambulance.

July 1918.

Army Form C. 2118.

WAR DIARY
or
INTELLIGENCE SUMMARY.

(Erase heading not required.) Sheet 1.

Instructions regarding War Diaries and Intelligence Summaries are contained in F. S. Regs., Part II. and the Staff Manual respectively. Title pages will be prepared in manuscript.

Place	Date	Hour	Summary of Events and Information	Remarks and references to Appendices
ABLAIN ST. NAZAIRE.	1st		A.D.M.S., 20th Division M.20/4104 dated 1-7-18 received.	
	2nd		A.D.M.S., 20th Division M.20/4135 dated 2-7-18 received.	
	3rd		No remarks.	
	4th		60 Infantry Brigade 0.0.20 dated 4-7-18 received.	
	5th		A.D.M.S., 20th Division S.265 dated 4-7-18 received.	
	5th		No remarks.	
	6th		A.D.M.S., 20th Division S.267 dated 6-7-18 received.	
	7th		No remarks.	
	8th		1/Lieut. H.P.METZGER, M.O.R.C., U.S.A. joined unit and taken on the strength.	
			64256 Pte. GOODWIN E.G., R.A.M.C. rejoined Unit from O.C.S. and taken on the strength.	
	9th		No remarks.	
	10th		No remarks.	
	11th		60 Infantry Brigade G.661 dated 11-7-18 received.	
			39173 Pte. WELTON A.J., R.A.M.C. transferred to 20th Division H.Qrs. and struck off the strength.	
	12th		60 Infantry Brigade G.679 dated 12-7-18 received.	
	13th		A.D.M.S., 20th Division S.279 dated 13-7-18 received.	
			60 Infantry Brigade 0.0.21 dated 13-7-18 received.	

Army Form C. 2118.

WAR DIARY
or
INTELLIGENCE SUMMARY.
(Erase heading not required.)

Sheet 2.

Instructions regarding War Diaries and Intelligence Summaries are contained in F. S. Regs., Part II. and the Staff Manual respectively. Title pages will be prepared in manuscript.

Place	Date	Hour	Summary of Events and Information	Remarks and references to Appendices
ABLAIN ST. NAZAIRE.	14th		No remarks.	
	15th		No remarks.	
	16th		No remarks.	
	17th		No remarks.	
	18th		No remarks.	
	19th		A.D.M.S., 20th Division M.20/4527 dated 19th received.	
			54312 Pte. MITCHELL A., R.A.M.C. officially reported by War Office as a Prisoner of War in GERMANY and struck off the strength from 25-3-18. (Auth: O i/c R.A.M.C. Section G.H.Q. No. 2/229/18 dated 19-7-18.)	
			39116 Q.M.S. MITCHELL E., R.A.M.C. promoted to rank of Warrant Officer Class II from 22-6-18 (Auth: Army Order 194 of 1918).	
	20th		A.D.M.S. 20th Division S.293 dated 20-7-18 received.	
			69827 Pte. STUART N., R.A.M.C. joined Unit from 142 Field Ambulance and taken on the strength.	
	21st		59th Infantry Brigade O.O.127 dated 21-7-18 received.	
			50501 Pte. KENWARD V.J., R.A.M.C. transferred to 142 Field Ambulance and struck off the strength.	
	22nd		No remarks.	
	23rd		60 Infantry Brigade Z.1.821 and O.O.22 dated 23-7-18 received.	
	24th		59 Infantry Brigade O.O.128 dated 24-7-18 received.	

Army Form C. 2118.

WAR DIARY
or
INTELLIGENCE SUMMARY

(Erase heading not required.) Sheet 3.

Instructions regarding War Diaries and Intelligence Summaries are contained in F. S. Regs., Part II. and the Staff Manual respectively. Title pages will be prepared in manuscript.

Place	Date	Hour	Summary of Events and Information	Remarks and references to Appendices
ABLAIN ST. NAZAIRE	25th		A.D.M.S., 20th Division S.300 dated 25-7-18 received.	
	26th		No remarks.	
	27th		No remarks.	
	28th		A.D.M.S., 20th Division S.308 dated 28-7-18 received.	
	29th		60 Infantry Brigade G.903 dated 29-7-18 received.	
	30th		No remarks.	
	31st		60 Infantry Brigade G.957 dated 31-7-18 received.	
			GENERAL REMARKS :- Very quiet during whole of month - no offensive or defensive action. General improvements carried out to Field Ambulance posts in forward area, and to Main Dressing Station.	
			Strength of Unit at end of July 1918 :-	
			Officers 8	
			O.R., R.A.M.C. 180	
			O.R., ASC(H.T) 26	
			O.R., ASC(M.T) 13	
			O.R., Cat. "B" 10	
			237	

Major, R.A.M.C.
a/O.C. 61 Field Ambulance.

Confidential

Vol 35
140/3204.

War Diary
of
61 Field Ambulance
August, 1918.

Army Form C. 2118.

WAR DIARY
or
INTELLIGENCE SUMMARY.

(Erase heading not required.) Sheet 1.

Instructions regarding War Diaries and Intelligence Summaries are contained in F.S. Regs., Part II. and the Staff Manual respectively. Title pages will be prepared in manuscript.

Place	Date	Hour	Summary of Events and Information	Remarks and references to Appendices
ABLAIN ST. NAZAIRE.	1st		387 Pte. (a/Sergt) BAILEY F., R.A.M.C. transferred to Office of D.D.M.S. VIII Corps for duty and struck off the strength from 1-8-18. (Auth: D.D.M.S. VIII Corps 103/205 dated 31-7-18).	JPQ
			Capt. C. LODGE PATCH, M.C., R.A.M.C. joined Unit and taken on the strength (Auth: A.D.M.S. 20th Div'n. N.259/18 dated 1-8-18.)	JPQ
	2nd		No remarks.	JPQ
	3rd		No remarks.	JPQ
	4th		53884 Pte. APLIN A.C., M.M., R.A.M.C. transferred to No. 16 Squadron R.A.F. and struck off the strength from 17-7-18.	JPQ
			60th Infantry Brigade G.60 and G.62 dated 4-8-18 received.	JPQ
	5th		A.D.M.S., 20th Division S.323, S.324 and M.20/4971 dated 5-8-18 received.	JPQ
	6th		No remarks.	JPQ
	7th		A.D.M.S., 20th Division S.326 dayed 7-8-18 received.	JPQ
			39116 Q.M.S. MITCHELL E., R.A.M.C. promoted to rank of Temporary Sergeant-Major, with seniority from 16-3-18. (Auth: Supplement to Combined R.A.M.Corps Order No. 2. d/1-6-18.	JPQ
			56001 Pte. BUSSON W.H.P., R.A.M.C. promoted to rank of Corporal with seniority from 16-3-18. (Auth: Combined R.A.M.Corps Order No. 1 dated 1-6-18.)	
	8th		A.D.M.S., 20th Division S.328 dated 8-8-18 received.	JPQ
			56036 Pte. WHITEHOUSE H., R.A.M.C. evacuated sick and struck off the strength.	
			21906 Pte. SHEARD J., R.A.M.C. rejoined unit from hospital and taken on the strength.	JPQ

Army Form C. 2118.

WAR DIARY
or
INTELLIGENCE SUMMARY.

(Erase heading not required.)

Sheet 2.

Place	Date	Hour	Summary of Events and Information	Remarks and references to Appendices
ABLAIN ST. NAZAIRE.	9th		421330 Pte. STOKES B., R.A.M.C. transferred to ENGLAND as candidate for commission in R.A.F. and struck off the strength. (Auth: A.G. G.H.Q. 2148/526(o) dated 31-7-18.	JPQ
	10th		37944 Pte. (a/Corpl) NORMAN C.H., R.A.M.C. transferred to ENGLAND for course of instruction with a view to transfer to R.A.F. and struck off the strength. (Auth: A.G. G.H.Q. No. 2150/148/(o) dated 5-8-18.	JPQ
			90329 Pte. McKENZIE K., R.A.M.C. evacuated sick and struck off the strength from 9-8-18.	JPQ
	11th		60th Infantry Brigade B.O.25 dated 11-8-18 received.	JPQ
	12th		59th Infantry Brigade G.C.106 dated 12-8-18 received.	JPQ
	13th		No remarks.	
	14th		A.D.M.S. 20th Division S.339 dated 14-8-18 received.	
			60th Infantry Brigade B.O.26 dated 14-8-18 received.	
			1/Lieut. H.P.METZGER, M.O.R.C., U.S.A. relieved 1/Lieut. GARDNER, M.O.R.C., U.S.A. in medical charge of 12 R.B. Lieut. METZGER struck off the strength: Lieut GARDNER taken on the strength.	JPQ
	15th		A.D.M.S. 20th Division S.345 dated 15-8-18 received.	JPQ
	16th		A.D.M.S. 20th Division S.345 dated 16-8-18 received.	
			Major C.J.ROGERSON, M.C., R.A.M.C. proceeded on one months leave to U.K. under A.C.I.2327 (Auth: VIII Corps No. A.1/1571/950 dated 14-8-18.	
			Major J.P.QUINN, M.C., R.A.M.C. assumed command of the Unit vice Major C.J.ROGERSON, M.C. RAMC on leave.	JPQ

Army Form C. 2118.

WAR DIARY
or
INTELLIGENCE SUMMARY.

(Erase heading not required.) Sheet 3.

Place	Date	Hour	Summary of Events and Information	Remarks and references to Appendices
ABLAIN ST. NAZAIRE.	17th		No remarks.	JPQ
	18th		59th Infantry Brigade O.O.132 dated 18-8-18 received.	JPQ
			45774 Pte. (a/Corpl) HUNTER J., R.A.M.C. joined unit and taken on the strength.	
	19th		60th Infantry Brigade B.O.27 dated 19-8-18 received.	JPQ
			305003 Q.M.S. DUNCAN W.M., R.A.M.C. joined unit and is taken on the strength. (Auth: Officer i/c R.A.M.C. Section No. 59/66/29/18 dated 14-8-18.	
	20th		60th Infantry Brigade G.299 dated 20-8-18 received.	
			A.D.M.S. 20th Division. No.s S.354, S.356 and M.20/5272 dated 20-8-18 received.	JPQ
			59th Infantry Brigade G.C. 333 dated 20-8-18 received.	
	21st		59th Infantry Brigade G.C.332/54, G.C.343 & G.358 dated 21-8-18 received.	
			60th Infantry Brigade O.O.28 (G.314) dated 20-8-18 received.	
			A.D.M.S. 20th Division S.357 dated 21-8-18 received.	
			81488 Pte. (a/L/Cpl. without pay) CARRINGTON W.G., R.A.M.C. appointed Acting L/Cpl with pay. (Auth: A.D.M.S. 20th Division M.20/5295)	JPQ
	22nd		A.D.M.S. 20th Division S.359 dated 22-8-18 received.	JPQ
			59th Infantry Brigade G.C.380 dated 22-8-18. received.	
	23rd		30232 Sergt-Major DESMOND T., R.A.M.C. evacuated sick and struck off the strength.	JPQ
			39116 T/Sergt-Major MITCHELL E., R.A.M.C. assumed duties of Sergt-Major of the Unit.	

Army Form C. 2118.

WAR DIARY
or
INTELLIGENCE SUMMARY.

(Erase heading not required.)

Sheet 4.

Place	Date	Hour	Summary of Events and Information	Remarks and references to Appendices
ABLAIN ST. NAZAIRE.	24th		59th Infantry Brigade No. G.C. 401 dated 24-8-18 received.	SPQ
	25th		21966 Pte. SHEARD J.A., R.A.M.C. evacuated sick and struck off the strength. A.D.M.S. 20th Division S.364 and M.20/5354 dated 25-8-18 received. 41872 Cpl. (a/Sergt) RAWLINS E.H.P., R.A.M.C. transferred to H.Q. 3rd Division for duty as Chief Clerk to A.D.M.S., and struck off the strength. (Auth: D.G.M.S. B.A. inF. No. D.G. 84/186 dated 21-8-18).	SPQ
	26th		A.D.M.S. 20th Division S.365 and M.20/5400 dated 26-8-18 received. 59th Infantry Brigade O.O.133 dated 26-8-18 received. A.D.M.S. 20th Division S.366 dated 26-8-18 received.	SPQ
	27th		A.D.M.S. 20th Division M.20/5414 and R.A.M.C. O.O.No.3 dated 27-8-18 received. 60th Infantry Brigade No. 50 dated 27-8-18 received. 59th Infantry Brigade O.O.134 dated 27-8-18 received. VIII Corps Commander inspected Divisional Main Dressing Station (Field ambulance H.Qrs) and Advanced Dressing Station (Fosse 6) and expressed himself satisfied with all he saw.	
	28th		A.D.M.S. 20th Division M.20/5444 dated 29-8-18 received.	SPQ
	29th		A.D.M.S. 20th Division S.372 dated 29-8-18 received. 60th Infantry Brigade G.499 dated 29-8-18 received.	SPQ

Army Form C. 2118.

WAR DIARY
or
INTELLIGENCE SUMMARY

(Erase heading not required.)   Sheet 5.

Instructions regarding War Diaries and Intelligence Summaries are contained in F. S. Regs., Part II. and the Staff Manual respectively. Title pages will be prepared in manuscript.

Place	Date	Hour	Summary of Events and Information	Remarks and references to Appendices
ABLAIN ST. NAZAIRE.	30th		A.D.M.S. 20th Division S.376 dated 30-8-18 received. 59th Infantry Brigade G.C.492 dated 30-8-13 received.	JPQ
	31st		No remarks.	JPQ
			GENERAL REMARKS :- Very quiet during the month. Improvements carried out to Main Dressing Station and Advanced Posts in the forward area. Two Regimental Aid Posts constructed.	
			Strength of Unit on 31-8-18.-	
			Officers 9 O.R., R.A.M.C. 174 O.R., A.S.C.(H.T) 26 O.R., A.S.C.(M.T) 13 O.R., Category "B" 10 ——— 232 ===	

J P Quinn
Major, R.A.M.C.
a/O.C. 61 Field Ambulance.

War Diary

61st Field Ambulance

September 1918

Army Form C. 2118.

WAR DIARY
or
INTELLIGENCE SUMMARY.
(Erase heading not required.)

Sheet 1.

Instructions regarding War Diaries and Intelligence Summaries are contained in F. S. Regs., Part II. and the Staff Manual respectively. Title pages will be prepared in manuscript.

Place	Date	Hour	Summary of Events and Information	Remarks and references to Appendices
ABLAIN ST. NAZAIRE.	1st		M.2/103895 a/Sergt. BROMBY G.W., A.S.C.(MT) joined Unit and taken on strength from 31-8-18.	
			A.D.M.S. 20th Division S.379 and 5531 dated 1-9-18 received.	
	2nd		59th Infantry Brigade O.O.135 dated 1-9-18 received.	
	3rd		59th Infantry Brigade O.O.136 dated 2-9-18 received.	
	4th		A.D.M.S. 20th Division M.20/5565 dated 3-9-18 received.	
			A.D.M.S. 20th Division S.388 dated 4-9-18 received.	
			59th Infantry Brigade O.O.157 dated 4-9-18 received.	
	5th		A.D.M.S. 20th Division S.390 dated 5-9-18 received.	
	6th		A.D.M.S. 20th Division M.20/5648 dated 6-9-18 received.	
	7th		A.D.M.S. 20th Division S.395 and S.396 dated 7-9-18 received.	
			5548 Pte. ADAMS J. R.A.M.C. ⎞	
			91722 " BAILEY E.C. " ⎟	
			61386 " BIRTWHISTLE J. " ⎟ joined unit and are taken on	
			4733202 " HINDBY N. " ⎟ the strength 7-9-18.	
			3882264 " ILDERTON H. " ⎟	
			12135 " MOORE J. " ⎟	
			423116 " ROBINSON A.F. " ⎟	
			515141 " STARKEY " ⎠	
	8th		A.D.M.S. 20th Division S.400 dated 8-9-18 received.	
	9th		A.D.M.S. 20th Division M.20/5715 dated 9-9-18 received.	

Army Form C. 2118.

WAR DIARY
or
INTELLIGENCE SUMMARY.

(Erase heading not required.) Sheet 2.

Instructions regarding War Diaries and Intelligence Summaries are contained in F. S. Regs., Part II. and the Staff Manual respectively. Title pages will be prepared in manuscript.

Place	Date	Hour	Summary of Events and Information	Remarks and references to Appendices
ABLAIN ST. NAZAIRE	10th		No remarks.	
	11th		T.S./998 Sergt. Watson H.J., A.S.C.(HT) joined Unit and taken on the strength.	
			A.D.M.S. 20th Division M.20/5774 and S.402 dated 11-9-18 received.	
			60th Infantry Brigade G.649 and G.687 dated 11-9-18 received.	
			59th Infantry Brigade G.C.621 dated 11-9-18 received.	
	12th		91722 Pte. Bailey E.C., R.A.M.C. evacuated sick and struck off the strength.	
			59th Infantry Brigade O.O.138 dated 12-9-18 received.	
	13th		D.M.2/117759 Pte. RUSSELL A.H., A.S.C.(MT) transferred to 62nd Fd.Amb. and struck off the strength.	
			A.D.M.S. 20th Division S.410 dated 13-9-18 received.	
			59th Infantry Brigade G.906 dated 13-9-18 received.	
	14th		59th Infantry Brigade O.O.139 dated 14-9-18 received.	
	15th		No remarks.	
	16th		Lieut.Colonel F.McLENNAN, R.A.M.C. appointed A.D.M.S. 3rd Division and is struck off the strength from 24-8-18. (Auth: A.G. Appts/3741 dated 10-9-18).	
			59th Infantry Brigade G.C.689/54 dated 16-9-18 received.	

Army Form C. 2118.

WAR DIARY
or
INTELLIGENCE SUMMARY

(Erase heading not required.) Sheet 3.

Place	Date	Hour	Summary of Events and Information	Remarks and references to Appendices
ABLAIN ST. NAZAIRE.	17th		24246 Pte. LEE A., R.A.M.C. struck off the strength from 17-9-18 in accordance with G.R.O. 3765.	
			60th Infantry Brigade G.626 dated 17-9-18 received.	
			A.D.M.S. 20th Division S.419 dated 17-9-18 received.	
			17-9-18.	
			Major, R.A.M.C. a/O.C. 61 Field Ambulance.	

Army Form C. 2118.

WAR DIARY
or
INTELLIGENCE SUMMARY.

(Erase heading not required.)

Sheet 4.

Instructions regarding War Diaries and Intelligence Summaries are contained in F. S. Regs., Part II. and the Staff Manual respectively. Title pages will be prepared in manuscript.

Place	Date	Hour	Summary of Events and Information	Remarks and references to Appendices
ABLAIN ST. NAZAIRE.	17th		Major C.J. ROGERSON, M.C., R.A.M.C. re-assumed command of the Unit.	
	18th		1/Lieut. M.M. GARDNER, M.O.R.C., U.S.A. proceeded to join A.E.F. for duty and struck off the strength (Auth: D.G.M.S. 10/52 dated 9-9-18.)	
	19th		A.D.M.S. 20th Division M.20/5943 dated 18-9-18 received.	
			59th Infantry Brigade G.C. 729 dated 19-9-18 received.	
			64256 Pte. Goodwin E.G., R.A.M.C. struck off the strength from 19-9-18 in accordance with G.R.O. 3765.	
			54311 Pte. Williams R.E., R.A.M.C. killed in action 19-9-18.	
			31137 Pte. Hornby J., R.A.M.C. wounded and at duty 19-9-18.	
	20th		A.D.M.S. 20th Division M.20/6000 dated 20-9-18 received.	
	21st		T./20982 S.S.M. Rice O.M., A.S.C.(H.T) evacuated sick and struck off the strength.	
	22nd		A.D.M.S. 20th Division S.429 dated 22-9-18 received.	
			59th Infantry Brigade O.O. 140 dated 22-9-18 received.	
	23rd		A.D.M.S. 20th Division S.431 dated 23-9-18 received.	
	24th		30175 Pte. Boxall W.J., R.A.M.C. held to serve under the Military Service Act from 24-8-18 on completion of engagement (Auth: O. i/c R.A.M.C. Records dated 19-9-18).	
	25th		A.D.M.S. 20th Division S.436 and M.20/6100 dated 25-9-18 received.	

Army Form C. 2118.

WAR DIARY
or
INTELLIGENCE SUMMARY.

(Erase heading not required.) Sheet 5.

Instructions regarding War Diaries and Intelligence Summaries are contained in F.S. Regs., Part II. and the Staff Manual respectively. Title pages will be prepared in manuscript.

Place	Date	Hour	Summary of Events and Information	Remarks and references to Appendices
ABLAIN ST. NAZAIRE.	26th		A.D.M.S. 20th Division M.20/6117 dated 26-9-18 received.	
	27th		59 Infantry Brigade O.O.141 dated 26-9-18 received.	
			59 Infantry Brigade O.O.142 dated 27-9-18 received.	
	28th		Major J.P.QUINN, M.C., R.A.M.C. granted leave to U.K. from 28-9-18 to 12-10-18. (Auth: A.D.M.S. 20th Division M.20/6097 dated 25-9-18).	
			A.D.M.S. 20th Division S.448 dated 28-9-18 received.	
	29th		A.D.M.S. 20th Division S.453 dated 29-9-18 received.	
	30th		No remarks.	
			Strength of Unit on 30-9-18 :-	
			Officers 7	
			O.R., R.A.M.C. 178	
			O.R., A.S.C.(H.T) 26	
			O.R., A.S.C.(M.T) 13	
			O.R., Category "B" 10	
			234	

Major, R.A.M.C.
O.C. 61 Field Ambulance.

Confidential

Vol 37

140/3324

War Diary
61st Field Ambulance.
October 1918.

COMMITTEE FOR THE WAR
MEDICAL HISTORY OF THE
4 DEC 1918
Date

19
Oct. 1918

Army Form C. 2118.

WAR DIARY
or
INTELLIGENCE SUMMARY.
(Erase heading not required.) Sheet 1.

Instructions regarding War Diaries and Intelligence Summaries are contained in F. S. Regs., Part II. and the Staff Manual respectively. Title pages will be prepared in manuscript.

Place	Date	Hour	Summary of Events and Information	Remarks and references to Appendices
ABLAIN ST. NAZAIRE.	29th		60th Infantry Brigade No. G.37 dated 29-9-18 received.	
	30th		A.D.M.S. 20th Division S.460 dated 30-9-18 received.	
			T/Qr.Mr. & Lieut. G.Drummond, R.A.M.C. to be Captain as from 16-9-18. (Auth: W.O.Letter 106437/1 dated 28-9-18. London Gazette dated 30-9-18).	
	1st		59th Infantry Brigade G.C.890 dated 1-10-18 received.	
			59th Infantry Brigade G.C.889 and O.O.143 dated 1-10-18 received.	
			A.D.M.S. 20th Division O.O.4 and O.O.5 dated 1-10-18 received.	
	2nd		A.D.M.S. 20th Division S.467 dated 2-10-18 received.	
			59th Infantry Brigade O.O.144 and Amd.1 dated 2-10-18 received.	
			39624 Pte. Greenland F.G., R.A.M.C. evacuated sick and struck off the strength 2-10-18.	
	3rd		M.D.S. moved forward from ABLAIN ST.NAZAIRE to FOSSE 6 (PAULINS). A.D.S. moved forward from FOSSE 6 to LA COULOTTE. Right R.A.P. established at F.3.a.3.6. Sheet 44A.(Junction of BALSAM and CYRIL Trenches.	
			A.D.M.S. 20th Division M.20/6301 dated 3-10-18 received.	
	4th		A.D.M.S. 20th Division M.20/6320 and O.O.6 dated 4-10-18 received.	
	5th		59th Infantry Brigade O.O.145 dated 5-10-18 received.	
			A.D.M.S. 20th Division M.20/6344/5 dated 5-10-18 received.	
			24246 Pte. Lee A., M.M., R.A.M.C. rejoined unit from hospital and taken on the strength.	

Army Form C. 2118.

WAR DIARY
or
INTELLIGENCE SUMMARY.

(Erase heading not required.)

Sheet 2.

Instructions regarding War Diaries and Intelligence Summaries are contained in F.S. Regs., Part II. and the Staff Manual respectively. Title pages will be prepared in manuscript.

Place	Date	Hour	Summary of Events and Information	Remarks and references to Appendices
ABLAIN ST. NAZAIRE.	6th		No remarks.	
	7th		Unit relieved by 38th Field Ambulance.	
HOUVELIN			Unit moves to and takes over billets at HOUVELIN.	
	8th		A.D.M.S. 20th Division M.20/6385 dated 7-10-18 received.	
	9th		T.2/294254 Dvr. Seal H., A.S.C.(H.T) transferred to 62 Fd.Amb. and struck off the strength.	
	10th		No remarks.	
	11th		No remarks.	
	12th		One tent sub-division reports at VIII Corps Rest Station for duty.	
	13th		A.D.M.S. 20th Division S.492 dated 13-10-18 received.	
	14th		No remarks.	
	15th		No remarks.	
	16th		No remarks.	
	17th		1 N.C.O. and 18 Other Ranks report at VIII Corps Rest Station for duty.	
			50426 Pte. Henson G., M.M., R.A.M.C. evacuated sick and struck off the strength.	
	18th		No remarks.	

Army Form C. 2118.

WAR DIARY
or
INTELLIGENCE SUMMARY. Sheet 3.
(Erase heading not required.)

Place	Date	Hour	Summary of Events and Information	Remarks and references to Appendices
HOUVELIN	19th		155192 Pte. Clarkson D., R.A.M.C. ⎫ 155181 " Clayton G.D., " ⎬ Joined Unit and taken on the strength. 155068 " Carruth J., " ⎭	
	20th		No remarks.	
	21st		No remarks.	
	22nd		Tent sub-division rejoins Unit from VIII Corps Rest station.	
	23rd		357261 Sergt. Renshaw W., R.A.M.C. joins Unit and is taken on the strength. Tent sub-division with three ambulance cars under command of Major Quinn, M.C., R.A.M.C. proceed to Ecole Normale, DOUAI, to treat civilian sick and wounded from country evacuated by the enemy.	
	24th		50426 Pte. Henson G., M.M., R.A.M.C. rejoins Unit from hospital and is taken on the strength.	
	25th		No remarks.	
	26th		7688 Pte. Garland R., R.A.M.C. evacuated sick and struck off the strength.	
	27th		No remarks.	
	28th		No remarks.	
	29th		No remarks.	
	30th		A.D.M.S. 20th Division S.504 dated 29-10-18 received. 60th Infantry Brigade G.297 dated 29-10-18 received. A.D.M.S. 20th Division M.20/6787 dated 30-10-18 received.	

Army Form C. 2118.

WAR DIARY
or
INTELLIGENCE SUMMARY.
(Erase heading not required.) Sheet 4.

Instructions regarding War Diaries and Intelligence Summaries are contained in F. S. Regs., Part II. and the Staff Manual respectively. Title pages will be prepared in manuscript.

Place	Date	Hour	Summary of Events and Information	Remarks and references to Appendices
HOUVELIN	30th	(cont)	A.D.M.S. 20th Division R.45 and S.506 dated 30-10-18 received.	
			Strength of Unit on 30-10-18.-	
			Officers 7	
			O.R., R.A.M.C. 180	
			O.R., ASC(H.T) 25	
			O.R., ASC(MT) 12	
			O.R., Cat. "B" 10	
			234	

                                           Major, R.A.M.C.
                                     O.C. 61 Field Ambulance.

Confidential
96/38
149/3401.

War Diary
of
61st Field Ambulance
November, 1918.

Army Form C. 2118.

WAR DIARY
or
INTELLIGENCE SUMMARY.
(Erase heading not required.) Sheet 1

Place	Date	Hour	Summary of Events and Information	Remarks and references to Appendices
HOUVELIN	31st		Unit complete with Transport marched to TINQUES. Entrained at TINQUES at 1300 hours with 60th Infantry Brigade. Detrained at FREMICOURT and proceeded by Bus to CAMBRAI.	
CAMBRAI	1st		No remarks.	
	2nd		A.D.M.S. 20th Division S.512 dated 2-11-18 received. 60th Infantry Brigade G.320, A.357 and B.M.57 dated 2-11-18 received.	
	3rd		60th Infantry Brigade B.M.58, B.O.45, F.B.227 and B.M.62 dated 3-11-18 received. Unit complete with Transport proceeds with 60th Infantry Brigade by road to RIEUX.	
RIEUX	4th		60th Infantry Brigade B.O.46 dated 4-11-18 received. A.D.M.S. 20th Division M.20/6897 and S.515 dated 4-11-18 received. Unit complete with Transport proceeds with 60th Infantry Brigade by road to VENDEGIES-SUR-ECAILLON.	

Major, R.A.M.C.
O.C. 61 Field Ambulance.

Army Form C. 2118.

WAR DIARY
or
INTELLIGENCE SUMMARY.   Sheet 2.
(Erase heading not required.)

Instructions regarding War Diaries and Intelligence Summaries are contained in F. S. Regs., Part II. and the Staff Manual respectively. Title pages will be prepared in manuscript.

Place	Date	Hour	Summary of Events and Information	Remarks and references to Appendices
VENDEGIES-SUR-ECAILLON (Q.14.d. Sheet 51 1/40,000)	5th		Capt. (a/Major) M.WHITE, R.A.M.C. joins the Unit and assumes Command. (Auth: D.G.M.S. B.A. in F. No. D.G./32/73 dated 25-10-18).	
			21966 Pte. Sheard J.A., R.A.M.C. joins the Unit and is taken on the strength.	
			60th Infantry Brigade S.C.88, B.M.75, B.O.47 and S.C.97 dated 5-11-18 received.	
			Capt. C.L.Patch, M.C., R.A.M.C. and two O.Ranks proceeds to 20th Divisional Reception Camp for temporary duty.	
	6th		Unit, complete with transport, proceeds with 60th Infantry Brigade by road to SEPMERIES (K.36.c.8.2. Sheet 51a 1/40,000)	
			60th Infantry Brigade G.340, B.M.84 dated 6-11-18 received.	
SEPMERIES	7th		Unit, complete with transport, proceeds with 60th Infantry Brigade by road to JENLAIN (L.17.b.2.8. Sheet 51a 1/40,000)	
			60th Infantry Brigade F.B.6, F.B.9, B.O.48, S.C.113 and B.M.93 dated 7-11-18 received.	
			A.D.M.S. 20th Division S.519 dated 7-11-18 received.	
JENLAIN	8th		Unit, complete with transport, proceeds with 60th Infantry Brigade by road to ST.WAAST (H.22.a.8.2. Sheet 51 1/40,000)	
			60th Infantry Brigade B.O.49, S.C.114 and B.M.100 dated 8-11-18 received.	
			2 O.Ranks (Clerks) attached to XVII Corps Main Dressing Station (WARGNIES-LE-PETIT) for temporary duty.	

Army Form C. 2118.

WAR DIARY
of
INTELLIGENCE SUMMARY.
(Erase heading not required.)   Sheet 3.

Place	Date	Hour	Summary of Events and Information	Remarks and references to Appendices
ST. WAAST	9th		Unit complete with transport, proceeds with 60th Infantry Brigade by road to FEIGNIES (J.29.a.1.5. Sheet 51 1/40,000)	
FEIGNIES	10th		60th Infantry Brigade B.O.50 and B.M.101 dated 9-11-18 received.	
			A.D.M.S. 20th Division S.524 dated 9-11-18 received.	
			60th Infantry Brigade B.O.51 dated 10-11-18 received.	
			A.D.M.S. 20th Division M.20/6998 dated 10-11-18 received.	
			1 N.C.O. and 8 O.Ranks attached to 12th R.B. in left sector of divisional front and Regt'l Aid Post established at K.13.a.3.7. Sheet 51 1/40,000.	
			1 N.C.O. and 8 O.Ranks attached to 12th K.R.R.C. in the right sector of the divisional front and Regt'l Aid Post established at K.21.b.8.3.	
			Car Post established at K.14.d.6.9. with 2 N.C.Os and 8 O.Ranks and 2 Cars.	
			Regt'l Aid Post for left sector (12th R.B) moved up later to K.9.a.0.6. Sheet 51.	
	11th		60th Infantry Brigade B.M.114 dated 11-11-18 received.	
			60th Infantry Brigade wire "Hostilities will cease at 1100 hours" received at 0900 hours.	
	12th		Personnel rejoin Unit from Regt'l Aid Posts and Car Post.	
	13th		A.D.M.S. 20th Division Disposition Report No. 8 dated 13-11-18 received.	
	14th		60th Infantry Brigade B.O.52 dated 14-11-18 received.	
	15th		1/Lieut. A.R.Pearce, M.O.R.C., U.S.A. proceeds to 20th Div'l Ammunition Column for temporary duty during the absence on leave of the Medical Officer in charge.	

Lieut.Col., R.A.M.C.
O.C. 61 Field Ambulance.

Army Form C. 2118.

WAR DIARY
or
INTELLIGENCE SUMMARY.

Sheet 4.

(Erase heading not required.)

Instructions regarding War Diaries and Intelligence Summaries are contained in F. S. Regs., Part II. and the Staff Manual respectively. Title pages will be prepared in manuscript.

Place	Date	Hour	Summary of Events and Information	Remarks and references to Appendices
FEIGNIES	16th		Major C.J.Rogerson, M.C., R.A.M.C. assumes command of the Unit during the absence of Lieut.Col. M. White, R.A.M.C. on leave.	
			61st Infantry Brigade A.295/31 dated 16-11-18 received.	
	17th		TS/998 a/Sergt. Watson H.J., A.S.C.(H.T) promoted Sergeant with effect from 11-6-18 (Auth: Officer 1/c A.S.C. Section G.H.Q. 3rd Echelon No. P.50/18110 dated 9-11-18.)	
			One Section complete with transport proceeds to BAVAI under orders of D.D.M.S. XVII Corps to establish a Corps Sick Collecting Station.	
			M./350458 Pte. Taylor D.W., A.S.C.(M.T) struck off the strength in accordance with G.R.O.3765.	
			11873 Pte. Byrne W., R.A.M.C. and 115192 Pte. Clarkson D., R.A.M.C. evacuated sick and struck off the strength.	
			M.2/103895 Corpl (a/Sgt) Bromby G.W., A.S.C.(M.T) promoted Sergt. with effect from 7-1-17 (Auth: Officer 1/c A.S.C. Section G.H.Q. 3rd Echelon No. P.50/18109 dated 9-11-18).	
			M.2/116652 Pte. (a/Cpl) McHale J., R.S.C.(M.T) promoted Corporal with effect from 7-4-17 (Auth: Officer 1/c A.S.C. Section G.H.Q. 3rd Echelon No. P.50/18108 dated 15-11-18).	
			45912 Pte. Squire R., R.A.M.C. admitted to Military Hospital, SUNDERLAND on 7-11-18 whilst on leave from FRANCE and struck off the strength from that date. (Auth: Officer 1/c R.A.M.C. Section G.H.Q. 3rd Echelon No. 28/805 dated 17-11-18).	
	18th		One Officer and five Other Ranks R.A.M.C. proceed to BINCHE with three ambulance cars to establish a Repatriated Prisoners' Aid Post.	
	19th		No remarks.	

Army Form C. 2118.

WAR DIARY
or
INTELLIGENCE SUMMARY.

(Erase heading not required.) Sheet 5.

Instructions regarding War Diaries and Intelligence Summaries are contained in F.S. Regs., Part II. and the Staff Manual respectively. Title pages will be prepared in manuscript.

Place	Date	Hour	Summary of Events and Information	Remarks and references to Appendices
FEIGNIES	20th		No remarks.	
	21st		No remarks.	
	22nd		Detachment rejoins from Repatriated Prisoners' Aid Post. About 2,500 Allied Repatriated Prisoners of War and a number of repatriated civilians, fed and evacuated. M.1/07141 Pte. Dunk F., A.S.C.(M.T) joins the Unit and is taken on the strength. A.D.M.S. 20th Division M.20/7147 dated 22-11-18 received. 61st Infantry Brigade O.O. 49 and Q.332/23 dated 22-11-18 received. 60th Infantry Brigade Order No. 63 dated 22-11-18 received.	
	23rd		Unit complete with transport, less one section complete with transport, moves with 61st Infantry Brigade by road LA FLAMENGRIE. Detached Section complete with transport moves with 60th Infantry Brigade by road from BAVAI to BLY.	
LA FLAMENGRIE	24th		61st Infantry Brigade Order No. 50 and Nos. Q.343/23 and S.C.620 received. Unit complete with transport, less one section, moves with 61st Infantry Brigade by road to PREUX AU SART. Detached section moves with 60th Infantry Brigade by road to VENDEGIES SUR ECAILLON.	
PREUX AU SART	25th		61st Infantry Brigade Order No. 51 dated 25-11-18 received. Unit complete with transport, less one section, moves with 61st Infantry Brigade by road to VENDEGIES SUR ECAILLON.	

Army Form C. 2118.

WAR DIARY
or
INTELLIGENCE SUMMARY.
(Erase heading not required.) Sheet 6.

Place	Date	Hour	Summary of Events and Information	Remarks and references to Appendices
VENDEGIES	25th		Detached Section proceeds with 60th Infantry Brigade by road to AVESNES-LEZ-AUBERT.	
	26th		61st Infantry Brigade 0.52 dated 26-11-18 and Q.353/23 dated 26-11-18 received.	
			70052 Pte. Stagg G.F., R.A.M.C. evacuated sick 26-11-18 and struck off the strength.	
			M.1/07141 Pte. Dunk F., A.S.C.(M.T) joined Unit 22-11-18 and taken on the strength.	
			34812 Pte. Griffiths T., R.A.M.C. continued in the Service under the Military Service Act as from 31-8-18 on completion of engagement. (Auth: Office i/c R.A.M.C. Records T.218/119 dated 14-11-18).	
			34762 Pte. Evans D.L., R.A.M.C. joined Unit 26-11-18 and is taken on the strength.	
	27th		Unit complete with transport, less one section, proceeds with 61st Infantry Brigade by road to CAGNONCLES.	
CAGNONCLES	28th		61st Infantry Brigade G./656/16 dated 28-11-18 received.	
			Detached section moves with 60th Infantry Brigade to CAMBRAI.	
			155181 Pte. Clayton, R.A.M.C. evacuated sick 25-11-18 and struck off the strength.	
			72368 Pte. Goold J.H., R.A.M.C. evacuated sick 28-11-18 and struck off the strength.	
	29th		61st Infantry Brigade O.O.53 dated 29-11-18 received.	
			Strength of Unit on 29-11-18 :- Officers 8 O.R., R.A.M.C. 175 O.R., ASC(H.T) 25 O.R., ASC(M.T) 13 O.R., Cat"B" 10 ——— 231	

Major, R.A.M.C.
a/O.C. 61 Field Ambulance.

Confidential

Dec 1916

Original

WR 39
1405451

61st
FIELD
AMBULANCE.
No............
Date............

War Diary.

61st Field Ambulance.

December 1918.

COMMITTEE FOR THE
MEDICAL HISTORY OF THE WAR
6 MAR 1919
Date

Army Form C. 2118.

WAR DIARY
or
INTELLIGENCE SUMMARY.
(Erase heading not required.) Sheet 1.

Instructions regarding War Diaries and Intelligence Summaries are contained in F. S. Regs., Part II. and the Staff Manual respectively. Title pages will be prepared in manuscript.

Place	Date 1918	Hour	Summary of Events and Information	Remarks and references to Appendices
CAGNONCLES	NOV. 30th		Unit, less one Section, moves with 60th Infantry Brigade by road to CAMBRAI. Transport moves under Brigade arrangements, en route for MARIEUX, (sheet 11 LENS. 5 F. 4.3.) via FAVREUIL.	
CAMBRAI.	DEC. 1.		Detached Section moves by 'bus to MARIEUX. 61st Infantry Brigade 0054 dated 1-12-18 received.	
	2nd		Unit less one Section moves by 'bus to MARIEUX.	
MARIEUX.	3rd		A.D.M.S., 20th Division Disposition Report No.12 20th Division dated 3-12-18 received.	
	4th		Capt. C.J.L. PATCH, M.C., R.A.M.C. rejoined from temporary duty with 20th Division Reception Camp, and is attached to 11th Bn. Rifle Brigade for temporary duty, as Medical Officer in charge.	
	5th		No remarks.	
	6th		No remarks.	
	7th		No remarks.	
	8th		1/Lieut. A.R. PEARCE, U.S.M.C., rejoins from temporary duty with 20th Division Ammunition Col., and is attached to 12th Bn. Rifle Brigade for temporary duty as Medical Officer in charge.	
	9th		No remarks.	
	10th		Capt.(a/Lt.Col) M.WHITE, R.A.M.C., awarded MILITARY CROSS. (IX Corps No.H.R/664 dated 22-11-18)	

Major R.A.M.C.,
a/O.C. 61st Field Ambulance.

Army Form C. 2118.

WAR DIARY
or
INTELLIGENCE SUMMARY.
(Erase heading not required.)

Instructions regarding War Diaries and Intelligence Summaries are contained in F. S. Regs., Part II. and the Staff Manual respectively. Title pages will be prepared in manuscript.

Place	Date 1918	Hour	Summary of Events and Information	Remarks and references to Appendices
MARIEUX.	Dec. 11th		Captain (Acting Lieut.Colonel) M.WHITE, M.C., R.A.M.C., re-assumed command of Unit on return from leave to U.K.	
	12th		No Remarks.	
	13th		No.120431 Pte. HOWSON J.L., R.A.M.C., despatched to England for demobilization and struck off the strength. (Authority: A.D.M.S., No.D.1. dated 12-12-18.	
	14th		No remarks.	
	15th		No remarks.	
	16th		No remarks.	
	17th		No remarks.	
	18th		No remarks.	
	19th		No remarks.	
	20th		D.D.M.S. XVII Corps inspects the Unit, and was satisfied with all arrangements.	
	21st		No.M/412591 Pte. CRABTREE J. A.S.C.,M.T., joined Unit and is taken on the strength.	
			The u/m. men proceeded to England for transfer to Class "W" of the Reserve whilst employed as Coal Miners:	
			No. 82230 Pte. Alcock AA. R.A.M.C. No. 53896 Pte. Muir. T. R.A.M.C.	
			" 31935 " Evans A. " " 341333 " McCabe O. "	
			" 10517 " Heys W. " " 2616 " Martin B.J. "	
			" 53541 " Hunter R.B. " " 100732 " Nicholson R. "	
			" 388264 " Ilderton H. " " 35688 " Randall W. "	
			" 101736 " Sproston W. " " 38989 " Whiteford A. "	
			" 64030 " White G. " " 36027 " Wilson R. "	
				Lieut.Col., O.C., 61st Field Amb.

Army Form C. 2118.

WAR DIARY
or
INTELLIGENCE SUMMARY.

(Erase heading not required.)

Instructions regarding War Diaries and Intelligence Summaries are contained in F.S. Regs., Part II. and the Staff Manual respectively. Title pages will be prepared in manuscript.

Place	Date 1918.	Hour	Summary of Events and Information	Remarks and references to Appendices
MARIEUX	DEC. 22nd		No remarks.	
	23rd.		No remarks.	
	24th.		No remarks.	
	25th.		No remarks.	
	26th.		Captain (Acting Major) J.P. QUINN, M.C., R.A.M.C., appointed D.A.D.M.S., 52nd Division, and struck off the strength. (Authority: AG/8034(O) dated 17-12-18).	
	27th.		No remarks.	
	28th.		No remarks.	
	29th.		No. M1/07141 Pte. DUNK F. A.S.C., M.T., admitted to Hospital and struck off the strength.	
			Captain J.P. JONES, M.C., R.A.M.C., proceeds to take over temporary Medical Charge of 92nd Brigade, R.F.A., during the absence on leave of Medical Officer in charge. (Authority: A.D.M.S., 20th Division No.M20/7512 dated 16-12-18.	
	30th.		No remarks.	
	31st.		Captain H.F.W. ADAMS, R.A.M.C., joined Unit and is taken on the strength.	
			Strength of Unit on 31-12-18: Officers 6 O.R's. R.A.M.C. 160 O.R's. A.S.C., H.T. 25 O.R's. A.S.C., M.T. 13 O.R's. Cat. "B" 10 214	

Lieut. Col.,
O.C., 61st Field Ambulance.

Confidential

WO 40
140/3496

20 DIV Box 1635

War Diary

61st Field Ambulance

January 1919.

16
Jan 1919.

COMMITTEE FOR THE
MEDICAL HISTORY OF THE WAR
11 MAR 1919
Date

Army Form C. 2118.

WAR DIARY

INTELLIGENCE SUMMARY

Sheet No. 1.

(Erase heading not required.)

Instructions regarding War Diaries and Intelligence Summaries are contained in F. S. Regs., Part II. and the Staff Manual respectively. Title pages will be prepared in manuscript.

Place	Date	Hour	Summary of Events and Information	Remarks and references to Appendices
MARIEUX.	1918. Dec.25th.		No.770364 Dvr.Payne R., R.F.A., despatched to England for transfer to Class "W" of the Reserve whilst employed as a coal-miner, and struck off the strength.	
	31st.		The u/m men proceeded to England for transfer to Class "W" of the Reserve whilst employed as coal-miners, and struck off the strength. 30948 Pte.Bagshaw B.T., R.A.M.C. 89123 " Robinson I., "	
	1919. Jan. 1st.		No remarks.	
	2nd.		Lieut. D.C.Bowie, R.A.M.C., joined Unit and taken on the strength.	
	3rd.		No remarks.	
	4th.		No remarks.	
	5th.		The u/m N.C.O. and men despatched to England for Demobilization, and struck off the strength. 31953 Cpl.Williamson J.R., R.A.M.C. 34762 Pte.Evans D.L., " 78492 " Owen W.L., " 40861 " Smith S., " 48971 " Williams J.R., "	
	6th.		No remarks.	
	7th.		No remarks.	
	8th.		No remarks.	
	9th.		No remarks.	
	10th.		No remarks.	

W.White
Lieut.Col.,
O.C.61 Field Ambulance.

Army Form C. 2118.

WAR DIARY
or
INTELLIGENCE SUMMARY.

Sheet No.1.

(Erase heading not required.)

Instructions regarding War Diaries and Intelligence Summaries are contained in F.S. Regs., Part II. and the Staff Manual respectively. Title pages will be prepared in manuscript.

Place	Date	Hour	Summary of Events and Information	Remarks and references to Appendices
MARIEUX. (Somme).	1918. Dec.28th.		No.33974 Pte.Nixon J.W., R.A.M.C., demobilized whilst on leave to U.K., and struck off the strength.	
	1919. Jan.10th.		No.36043 Pte.Pugh A., R.A.M.C., demobilized whilst on leave to U.K., and struck off the strength.	
	15th.		No.T5/023910 Dvr.Berry A.V., R.A.S.C, H.T., demobilized whilst on leave to U.K., and struck off the strength.	
	16th.		No.37686 Pte.Sayward J., R.A.M.C., demobilized whilst on leave to U.K., and struck off the strength.	
	18th.		No.305003 Q.M.S.Duncan W.M., R.A.M.C., demobilized whilst on leave to U.K., and struck off the strength.	
	23rd.		No.37968 Pte.Pepler H.W., R.A.M.C., demobilized whilst on leave to U.K., and struck off the strength.	
	28th.		No.35848 Pte.Wallace T., R.A.M.C., demobilized whilst on leave to U.K., and struck off the strength.	
	31st.		No.M2/268067 Pte.Chapelow H.W., R.A.S.C., M.T., transferred to 20th.Div.M.T. Coy., and struck off the strength. No.47212 Sgt.(a/S/Sgt.) Tesseyman W.F., R.A.M.C., promoted S/Sgt. with effect from 19-9-17. No.39262 Cpl.(A/Sgt.) Williams I., " Sgt. " 1-9-16. No.40581 Cpl.(a/Sgt.) Harrison F., " Sgt. " 25-12-16. No.31417 Pte.(a/Sgt.) Marsh T., " Sgt. " 31-1-17. No.35918 Cpl. (a/Sgt.) Radburn G., " Sgt. " 6-7-17. No.53902 Pte.(a/Sgt.) Quy G., " Sgt. " 14-9-17. No.36045 Pte.(a/Cpl.) Nelson D., " Cpl. " 1-9-16. No.45774 Pte.(a/Cpl.) Hunter J., " Cpl. " 31-1-17. No.50410 Pte.(a/Cpl.) Genever D., " Cpl. " 7-4-17. No.55958 Pte.(L/Sgt.)Palmer C.J., " Cpl. " 6-7-17.	

Army Form C. 2118

WAR DIARY
or
~~INTELLIGENCE SUMMARY~~

Sheet No. 2.

(Erase heading not required.)

Instructions regarding War Diaries and Intelligence Summaries are contained in F.S. Regs., Part II. and the Staff Manual respectively. Title Pages will be prepared in manuscript.

Place	Date	Hour	Summary of Events and Information	Remarks and references to Appendices
MARIEUX.	1919. Jan.11th.		Major C.J.Rogerson, M.C., R.A.M.C., proceeded to No.36 Cas.Cl.Stn. for duty, and struck off the strength. (Auth: D.G.M.S., No.DG/6/593 dated 5-1-19).	
	12th.		The u/m men despatched to England for Demobilization, and struck off the strength. 30289 Pte.Joslin A., R.A.M.C. 15998 " Page V.W., " 538287 " Tracey H.J., " 42200 " Watts F.C., " 3758 " Weake R.E., "	
	13th.		No remarks.	
	14th.		No.64188 Pte.Wells J., R.A.M.C., despatched to England for Demobilization, and struck off the strength.	
	15th.		No remarks.	
	16th.		No remarks.	
	17th.		Lieut. D.C.Bowie, R.A.M.C., proceeded to 6th.Bn.,K.Shrop.L.I., for temporary duty as Medical Officer. 1/Lieut. A.R.Fearce, M.O.R.C., U.S.A., rejoined Unit from temporary medical charge of 6th. Bn., K.Shrop.L.I.	
	18th.		The u/m W.O. and men despatched to England for Demobilization, and struck off the strength. 39116 S.M.Mitchell E., R.A.M.C. 50426 Pte.Henson G., R.A.M.C. 421317 Pte.Abbott J., " 37937 " Nash E.S.E., " 74353 " Boycott A., " 36030 " Walters W., " 1380 " Cross F., " 51753 " Ware W., " 30894 " Eaton E., " T2/11074 Dvr.Luff F.L., R.A.S.C., H.T.	
	19th.		No remarks.	

Lieut.Col.,
O.C.61st.Field Ambulance.

Army Form C. 2118

WAR DIARY

~~INTELLIGENCE SUMMARY~~

Sheet No. 3.

(Erase heading not required.)

Instructions regarding War Diaries and Intelligence Summaries are contained in F. S. Regs., Part II. and the Staff Manual respectively. Title Pages will be prepared in manuscript.

Place	Date	Hour	Summary of Events and Information	Remarks and references to Appendices
MARIEUX.	1919 Jan. 20th.		Capt. C.M.Stallard, R.A.M.C., proceeded to 12th.Bn., K.L'pool.Regt., for temporary duty as Medical Officer. Capt. H.F.W.Adams, R.A.M.C., rejoined Unit from temporary medical charge of 12th.Bn., K.L'pool.Rgt. No.37687 Pte.Sanders S., R.A.M.C., passed through Oswestry Dispersal Station for Demobilization, whilst on leave to U.K., and struck off the strength.	
	21st.		No remarks.	
	22nd.		No remarks.	
	23rd.		No remarks.	
	24th.		No remarks.	
	25th.		No remarks.	
	26th.		No remarks.	
	27th.		No remarks.	
	28th.		No remarks.	
	29th.		No remarks.	
	30th.		The u/m N.C.O. and men proceeded for duty under administration of A.D.M.S., ABBEVILLE, and struck off the strength. (Auth: D.D.M.S., XVII Corps No.25/138 dated 27-1-19). 40704 Cpl.Jones T.L., R.A.M.C. 24236 Pte.Hodson E.G., " 24246 " Lee A., " 67977 " Montague F.A., " 423116 " Robinson A.F., " 515141 " Starkey E.A., " 69827 " Stuart N., " O.C.61st.Field Ambulance. Lieut.Col.,	

Army Form C. 2118

WAR DIARY
or
~~INTELLIGENCE SUMMARY~~
(Erase heading not required.)

Sheet No. 4.

Instructions regarding War Diaries and Intelligence Summaries are contained in F. S. Regs., Part II. and the Staff Manual respectively. Title Pages will be prepared in manuscript.

Place	Date	Hour	Summary of Events and Information	Remarks and references to Appendices
MARIEUX.	1919. Jan.31st.		No remarks. Strength of Unit on 31-1-19:- Officers 7 " O.R's., R.A.M.C., 130 " " RASC.HT., 24 " " RASC.MT., 13 " " Cat."B"., 9 Total. 183	

M White
Lieut.Col., R.A.M.C.,
O.C. 61st. Field Ambulance.

Original
984/
140/939

War Diary
of
61st Field Ambulance

February, 1919.

Army Form C. 2118.

WAR DIARY
or
INTELLIGENCE SUMMARY.

Sheet No. 2.

(Erase heading not required.)

Instructions regarding War Diaries and Intelligence Summaries are contained in F. S. Regs., Part II. and the Staff Manual respectively. Title pages will be prepared in manuscript.

Place	Date	Hour	Summary of Events and Information	Remarks and references to Appendices
MARIEUX. (Somme).	1919. Feb. 1st.		No.9093 Dvr.Stibbs J., R.F.A., despatched to England for Demobilization, and struck off the strength.	
	2nd.		No remarks.	
	3rd.		No remarks.	
	4th.		No remarks.	
	5th.		No remarks.	
	6th.		No remarks.	
	7th.		No.TS/7308 S/Smith.Sloan P., R.A.S.C., H.T., despatched to England for Demobilization, and struck off the strength.	
	8th.		No remarks.	
	9th.		No.38983 Pte.Wedekind E., R.A.M.C., demobilized whilst on leave to U.K., and struck off the strength.	
	10th.		No.30970 Pte.Hetherington, E., R.A.M.C., evacuated sick and struck off the strength.	
	11th.		No remarks.	
	12th.		No remarks.	
	13th.		No.39382 Sgt.Williams I., R.A.M.C., embarked for U.K. for Demobilization, and struck off the strength.	
	14th.		No.35756 S/Sgt.Cash P., R.A.M.C., embarked for U.K. for Demobilization, and struck off the strength.	

Army Form C. 2118.

WAR DIARY
or
INTELLIGENCE SUMMARY.

Sheet No. 3.

(Erase heading not required.)

Instructions regarding War Diaries and Intelligence Summaries are contained in F.S. Regs., Part II. and the Staff Manual respectively. Title pages will be prepared in manuscript.

Place	Date	Hour	Summary of Events and Information	Remarks and references to Appendices
MARIEUX. (Somme).	1919. Feb.15th.		No remarks.	
	16th.		No remarks.	
	17th.		Capt.H.F.W.Adams, R.A.M.C., transferred to VI Corps School, and struck off the strength.	
	18th.		No.47212 S/Sgt.Tesseyman W.F., R.A.M.C., and No.31985 Pte.Leighton C., R.A.M.C., embarked for U.K. for demobilization and struck off the strength.	
	19th.		No.64256 Pte.Goodwin E.G., R.A.M.C., joined Unit and taken on the strength.	
	20th.		No remarks.	
	21st.		No remarks.	
	22nd.		No remarks.	
	23rd.		No remarks.	
	24th.		No remarks.	
	25th.		No remarks.	
	26th.		No remarks.	
	27th.		No remarks.	
	28th.		No remarks.	

Effective Strength of Unit on 28-2-19.

```
Officers, R.A.M.C.,            5
Officers, U.S.M.C.,            1
O.R's., R.A.M.C.,            120
O.R's., R.A.S.C., H.T.,       22
O.R's., R.A.S.C., M.T.,       12
O.R's., Category "B",          8
                Total.      168
```

Confidential — Nov 3, 1919
Oct 28, 1918 – Nov 3, 1919

19

War Diary

of

No. 61 Field Ambulance

March 1919

Maj C+z
No/3557

17 JUL 1919

61st
FIELD
AMBULANCE.

To:..........
Date:..........

Army Form C. 2118.

WAR DIARY
or
INTELLIGENCE SUMMARY.

Sheet 1.

(Erase heading not required.)

Instructions regarding War Diaries and Intelligence Summaries are contained in F. S. Regs., Part II. and the Staff Manual respectively. Title pages will be prepared in manuscript.

Place	Date	Hour	Summary of Events and Information	Remarks and references to Appendices
MARIEUX. (Somme).	1918. Dec.22nd.		No.M.2/180836 Pte.Freeman H.J., R.A.S.C., M.T., passed through Dispersal Station whilst on leave to U.K., and struck off the strength.	
	1919. Jan. 2nd.		No.M.2/101863 Pte. Wellcome W., R.A.S.C., M.T., passed through Dispersal Station whilst on leave to U.K., and struck off the strength.	
	8th.		No.T.S./998 Sgt.Watson H.J., R.A.S.C.,H.T., passed through Dispersal Station whilst on leave to U.K., and struck off the strength.	
	10th.		Capt.J.P.Jones, M.C., R.A.M.C., appointed Acting-Major from 10-1-19. (Auth: F.M.C.-in-C., G.H.Q.)	
	Feb.13th.		No.38098 L/Cpl.Peace W., R.A.M.C., and No.21966 Pte.Sheard J.A., R.A.M.C., embarked for U.K. for Demobilization, and struck off the strength.	
	20th.		No.39468 a/Cpl.Ramsden C., R.A.M.C., and No.30162 Pte.Lilley W.E., R.A.M.C., embarked for U.K. for Demobilization, and struck off the strength.	
	24th.		The u/m N.C.O's. and men embarked for U.K. for Demobilization, and are struck off the strength. No.40581 Sgt.Harrison F., R.A.M.C. No.31234 " Gee H.G., " No.36056 " Thornhill A.L., " No.39176 L/Cpl.Wright F.M., " No.41868 Pte.Robson P., " No.37684 " Snook C., "	
	25th.		No.36031 Pte.Smith T.C.B., R.A.M.C., embarked for U.K. for Demobilization, and struck off the strength.	
	Mar. 1st.		No remarks.	
	2nd.		No remarks.	

Lieut.Col.,
O.C.61st.Field Ambulance.

Army Form C. 2118.

WAR DIARY
or
INTELLIGENCE SUMMARY.

Sheet 2.

(Erase heading not required.)

Instructions regarding War Diaries and Intelligence Summaries are contained in F.S. Regs., Part II. and the Staff Manual respectively. Title pages will be prepared in manuscript.

Place	Date	Hour	Summary of Events and Information	Remarks and references to Appendices
MARIEUX. (Somme).	1919. Mar. 3rd.		No.50410 Cpl.Genever D., R.A.M.C., embarked for U.K. for Demobilization, and struck off the strength.	
	4th.		The u/m N.C.O's. and men embarked for U.K. for Demobilization, and are struck off the strength. No.31417 Sgt.Marsh T., R.A.M.C. No.35958 L/Sgt.Palmer C.J., " No.36045 Cpl.Nelson D., " No.32789 L/Cpl.Moss A., " No.40420 Pte.Bell G.B., " No.30175 " Boxall W.J., " No.31142 " Hankinson R., " No.36054 " Neal H., " No.31862 " O'Neill P.J., " No.35837 " Orton T.E., " No.37583 " Radley F.H., " No.36346 Pte.Schofield W., R.A.M.C., appointed Lance-Corporal with Pay from 14-2-19. (Auth:A.D.M.S., 20th.Division No.M.20/825 dated 4-3-19).	
	5th.		No remarks.	
	6th.		No.M.1/06288 Pte.Goble W., R.A.S.C., M.T., transferred to 20th.Div.M.T.Coy., and struck off the strength. No.463 Pte.Fisher F.C., R.A.M.C., evacuated sick and struck off the strength.	
	7th.		No remarks.	
	8th.		No remarks.	
	9th.		No remarks.	
	10th.		No.112939 Pte.Palmer G.H., R.A.M.C., transferred to No.6 Stationary Hospital and struck off the strength. No.114972 Pte.Byway J.G., R.A.M.C., transferred from No.6 Stationary Hospital and taken on the strength.	

Army Form C. 2118.

WAR DIARY
or
INTELLIGENCE SUMMARY.

Sheet 3.

(Erase heading not required.)

Instructions regarding War Diaries and Intelligence Summaries are contained in F. S. Regs., Part II. and the Staff Manual respectively. Title pages will be prepared in manuscript.

Place	Date	Hour	Summary of Events and Information	Remarks and references to Appendices
MARIEUX (Somme).	1919. Mar.11th.		No remarks.	
	12th.		No remarks.	
	13th.		No.M.2/076767 Pte.Weight A.F., R.A.S.C., M.T., transferred to 20th.Div.M.T.Coy., and struck off the strength. No.34481 Cpl.Sutherland G.W.G.; R.A.M.C., appointed Acting-Sergeant with Pay from 4-1-19. No.39775 L/Cpl.Holman H.R., " " " 1-1-19. No.33202 L/Cpl.Adcock W.E., " " Corporal " 11-1-19. (Auth: O. i/c R.A.M.C.Section No.59/2064/19 dated 13-3-19).	
	14th.		No remarks.	
	15th.		No.T./20564 Acting-S.S.M.Perkins H.C., R.A.S.C., H.T., joined Unit and taken on the strength.	
	16th.		No remarks.	
	17th.		No remarks.	
	18th.		No.461261 Pte.Blackman H.B., R.A.M.C.; and No.30735 Pte.Knight A.R., R.A.M.C., appointed Lance-Corporals with pay. (Auth: A.D.M.S., 20th.Division No.M.20/1000 dated 18-3-19).	
	19th.		No remarks.	
	20th.		No remarks.	
	21st.		No remarks.	
	22nd.		No remarks.	

Lieut.Col.,
O.C.61st.Field Ambulance.

Army Form C. 2118.

WAR DIARY or INTELLIGENCE SUMMARY.

(Erase heading not required.)

Sheet 4.

Place	Date	Hour	Summary of Events and Information	Remarks and references to Appendices
MARIEUX. (Somme).	1919. Mar.23rd.		No.473202 Pte.Hindby N.A., R.A.M.C., transferred to M.M.P., and struck off the strength. (Auth: W.O.Telegram No.23/Endn./72(A.G.1.) dated 4-3-19).	
	24th.		No remarks.	
	25th.		No remarks.	
	26th.		No remarks.	
	27th.		Lieut.D.G.Bowie, R.A.M.C., withdrawn from Medical Charge of 60th.Inf.Bde., and transferred to administration of D.M.S., Second Army, and struck off the strength. Capt.A.R.Pearce, M.O.R.C., U.S.A., assumed Medical Charge of 60th.Inf.Bde.	
	28th.		No remarks.	
	29th.		Acting-Major J.P.Jones, M.C., R.A.M.C., and Capt.C.M.Stallard, M.C., R.A.M.C., transferred to administration of D.D.M.S., DOULLENS Area, and struck off the strength. Acting-Major J.P.Jones, M.C., R.A.M.C., reverts to his permanent rank of Captain. (Auth: A.G's. wire No.596).	
	30th.		Capt.A.R.Pearce, M.O.R.C., U.S.A., with-drawn from Medical Charge of 60th.Inf.Bde., and despatched to No.1 Replacement Depot, U.S.A., ST.AIGNAN, France, and struck off the strength.	

	31st.		No remarks. Effective Strength of Unit on 31-3-19.
			
			    Officers, R.A.M.C., 2
			    O.R's., R.A.M.C., 81
			    " R.A.S.C., H.T., 23
			    " R.A.S.C., M.T., 8
			    " Category "B", 8
			                Total. 122	

Lieut.Col.,
O.C.61st.Field Ambulance.

WD 44
Nettles apl
Ind/3000

27 JUL 1948

War Diary
of
6i. Sikh Pioneers
April 1919

April 1919

Compendium

Army Form C. 2118.

WAR DIARY
or
INTELLIGENCE SUMMARY.

Sheet No. 3

(Erase heading not required.)

Instructions regarding War Diaries and Intelligence Summaries are contained in F. S. Regs., Part II. and the Staff Manual respectively. Title pages will be prepared in manuscript.

Place	Date 1919	Hour	Summary of Events and Information	Remarks and references to Appendices
MARIEUX (SOMME)	Apr 5		No remarks	
	6		No remarks	
	7		No remarks	
	8		No 60478 Pte Sipeman J. R.A.M.C.) Transferred No. 36 C.C.S. acute meningitis	
			322473	
	9		702/6 Pte Townsend W. - Admitted sick to Divisional Sanitation Section meningitis	— do —
			57109 - Stevens Sgt.	— do —
	10		No remarks	
	11		No remarks	
	12		No remarks	
	13		No remarks	
	14		No remarks	
	15		No remarks	
	16		No remarks	
	17		No remarks	
	18		No remarks	
	19		No remarks	

W.W.White
Lt.Col.
O.C. b' Gam.

Army Form C. 2118.

WAR DIARY
or
INTELLIGENCE SUMMARY.

(Erase heading not required.)

Place	Date 1918	Hour	Summary of Events and Information	Remarks and references to Appendices
MARIEUX (SOMME.)	Sept 20		No.T/389/07 Pte Baynes C.W. Rgtc., 4T, Transferred to 61 Div. Train, returned to strength.	
	21		No movement.	
	22		No movement.	
	23		No movement.	
	24		No. 90488 Pte Armytage R, Ronne. Transferred from No. 18 C.C.S, taken on strength	
			No. 10/801 Pte Carey R. }	
			No. 366325 " Cox S.E. } Transferred to No.13 A.C.S, returned to strength.	
			No. 101830 " Green J.R. }	
			No. 491398 " Punch P. }	
			No. 78410 " Todd T.W. }	
	25		No movement.	
	26		No movement.	
	27		No movement.	
	28		No. 47820 Pte Lansdowne R.J., K.O. Scot. L.I., Transferred to 61 Div. Train, struck off strength.	

W. Smith
Capt.
O.C. 91 D. Train.

Army Form C. 2118.

WAR DIARY
or
INTELLIGENCE SUMMARY.
(Erase heading not required.)

Sheet No. 5.

Instructions regarding War Diaries and Intelligence Summaries are contained in F. S. Regs., Part II. and the Staff Manual respectively. Title pages will be prepared in manuscript.

Place	Date 1919	Hour	Summary of Events and Information	Remarks and references to Appendices
MARIEUX (SOMME)	Apr 29		Nonmonko.	Meads Views
	30		Nonmonko.	
			Approximate strength of unit on 30.4.19.	
			Officers & nurses — 2	
			O.R.s — 48	
			A.A.S.C. Att. — 21	
			A.A.S.C. M.T. — 9	
			Lucy's "B" — 7	
			Total — 87	

W/White
Lieut. Col.
O.C. 5 ??

D. D. & L., London, E.C.
(A500) Wt. W1771/M2191 750,000 5/17 Sch. 52 Forms/C2118/14

98 44
Ceased

War Diary

for the Month of May, 1919

61st Field Ambulance

Not
Confidential

WAR DIARY
or
INTELLIGENCE SUMMARY

(Erase heading not required.)

Army Form C. 2118.

Instructions regarding War Diaries and Intelligence Summaries are contained in F.S. Regs., Part II. and the Staff Manual respectively. Title pages will be prepared in manuscript.

Place	Date	Hour	Summary of Events and Information	Remarks and references to Appendices
Marieux. May.	1st. 2nd.		No.M2/105298.Pte.Burgess H.H.transferred to 19th.Div.M.T.Coy,& struck off the strength. Capt.(a/Lt.Col.)M.White,M.B.R.A.M.C.relinquishes the rank of Lt.Col.&reverts to the permanent rank of Captain.(Auth.D.A.G.H.Q.B.E.F.& F.letter No.C.R.8938 (Mob).dated 2/5/19)	
	3rd. 4th.		No remarks No.37683 Pte.Spellor A.A.R.A.M.C.dispatched to Calais Dispersal Station for Demobilisation in France and struck off the strength.	
	5th. 6th.		No.38984 Pte.Wood H. R.A.M.C. transferred to 36 C.C.S.and struck off the strength. The u/m W.O.N.C.O's and men transferred to 160th.Coy,R.A.S.C.(H.T.)and struck off the strength.	

T/20564 S.S.M.Perkins H.C.	R.A.S.C.(H.T.)	T3/023993 Dvr.Stone E.G. R.A.SC(H.T.)
T/S.R/305 Sgt.Grantham W.	"	T/36349 Dvr.Shoebottom A. "
T3/024059 Cpl.McGuire H.	"	T3/024056 Dvr.Taylor G.C. "
T3/024022 Dvr.Bellis J.	"	T3/023970 Dvr.Thoroggod M "
T3/024069 Dvr.Dale W.E.	"	T3/024052 Dvr.Whitten H.A. "
T3/024104 Dvr.Epps E.C.	"	T2/016280 Dvr.Whittaker H.H. "
T4/143695 Dvr.Gray C.	"	T2/016311 Dvr.Webber T.J.P. "
T4/326698 Dvr.Greaves F.	"	21/528 Pte.Brown W. D.L.I
T3/025168 Dvr.Jones A.	"	42196 Pte.Dolphin E. "
T1/4618 Dvr.Lee D.	"	201478 Pte.Longstaffe A.V. "
T3/023976 Dvr.Martin E.A.	"	32653 Pte.Sleep W.J. "
T3/027135 Dvr.Marshall C.R.	"	(Auth.20th.Div.Packet No.A451/157 dated 2/5/19
T4/093955 Dvr.Mahoney W.	"	
T4/036571 Dvr.Pickard W.H.	"	
T/38756 Dvr.Prattent S.	"	
T2/015982 Dvr.Rogers W.	"	
T2/015983 Dvr.Robinson A.J.	"	

W.White
Capt, R.A.M.C.
O.C.61st.Field Ambulance.

Army Form C. 2118.

WAR DIARY
or
INTELLIGENCE SUMMARY.
(Erase heading not required.)

Instructions regarding War Diaries and Intelligence Summaries are contained in F. S. Regs., Part II. and the Staff Manual respectively. Title pages will be prepared in manuscript.

Place	Date	Hour	Summary of Events and Information	Remarks and references to Appendices
Marieux.	May 7th.		No remarks	
	8th.		No remarks	
	9th.		No remarks	
	10th.		The u/m N.C.O. and men dispatched to U.K. for Demobilisation and struck off the strength	
			35836 Sgt. Newson C. R.AM.C.	
			62005 Pte. Beesley W. "	
			100868 Pte. Craven W.R. "	
			31137 Pte. Hornby J. "	
			352058 Pte. Littlewood A. "	
			34315 Pte. Meade W. "	
			34556 Pte. Miller E.B. "	
			50618 Pte. Norris G.H. "	
			46869 Pte. Taylor G. "	
			34468 Pte. Smith T.H. "	
	11th.		No remarks	
	12th.		No remarks	
	13th.		S.M.O.20th.Div.Packet wire No.D.446 received,"61st.Field Ambulance Cadre will entrain at Longeau on 25th.inst."	
	14th.		No remarks	
	15th.		Temporary Hospital at Marieux Wood closed for the Admission of Sick	
			The u/m N.C.O. and men dispatched to U.K. for Demobilisation and struck off the strength	
			357261 Sgt. Renshaw W R.A.M.C.	
			155068 Pte. Carruth J. "	
			29170 Pte. Newbold F.H. "	
	16th.		No remarks	
	17th.		No remarks	
	18th.		No remarks	
	19th.		No.3 Area - Train Forecast - No 4 received, entraining station Longeau, destination Portsmouth 61st. Field Ambulance Cadre Serial No C.149 received, time of entraining 10-00 hours, time of departure 15-14 hours	

O.C.61st.Field Ambulance Cadre
Capt.R.A.M.C.

Army Form C. 2118.

WAR DIARY
or
INTELLIGENCE SUMMARY

(Erase heading not required.)

Instructions regarding War Diaries and Intelligence Summaries are contained in F. S. Regs., Part II. and the Staff Manual respectively. Title Pages will be prepared in manuscript.

Place	Date	Hour	Summary of Events and Information	Remarks and references to Appendices
Marieux	May 20th. 21st.		No remarks 20th.Div.Packet No.Q.535 received "The Cadre of the 61st.Field Ambulance will proceed by lorry to Longeau,on the 23rd.and 24th.inst.,prior to entraining on the 25th.inst.	
	22		No Remarks	
	23		No Remarks	
	24		Capt. M. White. M.C. handed over Command of the unit to Capt. & Q.M.G. Drummond. R.A.M.C.	

M. White
Capt.
O.C. 3 Ambce

Army Form C. 2118.

WAR DIARY
INTELLIGENCE SUMMARY
(Erase heading not required.)

Instructions regarding War Diaries and Intelligence Summaries are contained in F. S. Regs., Part II. and the Staff Manual respectively. Title pages will be prepared in manuscript.

Place	Date	Hour	Summary of Events and Information	Remarks and references to Appendices
MARIEUX. May	24th.		Instructions received from 20th. Div. Packet that 61st. Field Ambulance Cadre will not proceed to England, but will be disbanded in France. All previous orders cancelled.	
	25th.		No remarks.	
	26th.		No remarks.	
	27th.		No remarks.	
	28th.		No remarks.	
	29th.		No remarks.	
	30th.		No remarks.	
	31st.		No remarks.	

Capt, R.A.M.C.,
O.C. 61st. Field Ambulance.Cadre.

160/3785

13 AUG 1919

Cpt. F. A.

June 1919

Army Form C. 2118.

WAR DIARY
OF
INTELLIGENCE SUMMARY
(Erase heading not required.)

Instructions regarding War Diaries and Intelligence Summaries are contained in F. S. Regs., Part II. and the Staff Manual respectively. Title pages will be prepared in manuscript.

61ST FIELD AMBULANCE

Place	Date	Hour	Summary of Events and Information	Remarks and references to Appendices
MARIEUX	June 1		No Remarks	
	2		No Remarks	
	3		Orders received from A.D.M.S. No 3 Area, stating 61st/3rd Ambulance would break up forthwith and preserve its identity. All wagons and equipment of 61st/3rd Amb. will be handed in to S.C.S. CANDAS, and medical equipment to No 34 A.D.M Stores, POULAINVILLE. The personnel will be posted 1/3 41 Stationary Hospital, POULAINVILLE.	
	4		No Remarks	
	5		No Remarks	
	6		Movement order received by 61st Inf Bde. No D.Q 356, stating Horses will be sent to remove wagons to CANDAS and lorries to convey personnel and equipment to their destination.	
	7		Orders received from L.m.O Doullens Area all 91st men and men enumerated on the Beaufiline Roll referred to in Chap. 4. Section 2. para II of Army Demobilization instructions France, will proceed forthwith to Circulation Camp CANDAS for Demobilization. The Quartermaster and remaining personnel to proceed to 41 Stationary Hospital, POULAINVILLE for duty.	
	8		No Remarks	
	9		Equipment and stores satisfactorily handed in to Ordnance. Personnel disposed of, and units disbanded.	

G. Drummond Capt.
O/C 61st Field Amb

www.ingramcontent.com/pod-product-compliance
Lightning Source LLC
Chambersburg PA
CBHW080923230426
43668CB00014B/2187